The Best
AMERICAN
ESSAYS
1997

GUEST EDITORS OF
THE BEST AMERICAN ESSAYS

The Best AMERICAN ESSAYS 1997

Edited and with an Introduction
by IAN FRAZIER

ROBERT ATWAN
Series Editor

HOUGHTON MIFFLIN COMPANY
BOSTON • NEW YORK 1997

ISSN 0888-3742
ISBN 0-395-85694-9
ISBN 0-395-85695-7 (PBK.)

Printed in the United States of America
QUM 10 9 8 7 6 5 4 3 2 1

"Notes on My Mother" by Hilton Als. First published in *The New Yorker.* Copyright © 1996 by Hilton Als. Reprinted by permission of Farrar, Straus & Giroux, Inc., from *The Women.*

"The Fourth State of Matter" by Jo Ann Beard. First published in *The New Yorker.* Copyright © 1996 by Jo Ann Beard. Reprinted by permission of Sterling Lord Literistic, Inc.

"First Tell Me What Kind of Reader You Are" by Roy Blount, Jr. First published in *The Oxford American.* Copyright © 1996 by Roy Blount, Jr. Reprinted by permission of the author.

"Labyrinthine" by Bernard Cooper. First published in *The Paris Review.* Copyright © 1996 by Bernard Cooper. Reprinted by permission of International Creative Management, Inc.

"Legends of the Fall" by Louis de Bernières. First published in *Harper's Magazine.* Copyright © 1996 by Louis de Bernières. Reprinted by permission of the author.

"Who Shot Johnny?" by Debra Dickerson. First published in *The New Republic.* Copyright © 1996 by Debra Dickerson. Reprinted by permission of the author.

"In the Face" by Richard Ford. First published in *The New Yorker.* Subsequently published in *The Fights,* photographed by Charles Hoff (Chronicle Books, 1996). Copyright © 1996 by Richard Ford. Reprinted by permission of International Creative Management, Inc.

"Rat Patrol: A Saga" by Frank Gannon. First published in *Harper's Magazine.* Copyright © 1996 by Frank Gannon. Reprinted by permission of Frank Gannon.

"Northeast Direct" by Dagoberto Gilb. First published in *The Threepenny Review.* Copyright © 1996 by Dagoberto Gilb. Reprinted by permission of the author.

"We Are Still Only Human" by Verlyn Klinkenborg. First published in *The New*

Contents

Foreword

A CENTURY or so ago, the essay occupied a prominent place in literary circles. It fell into the class of writing that critics called "polite letters." The essayists, for the most part gentlemen, addressed the literate world in an urbane, congenial, comfortable style. They almost always possessed three names — James Russell Lowell, Oliver Wendell Holmes, Thomas Wentworth Higginson — and more often than not they lived in New England. In this era, when "coming out" referred only to a young woman's debut, the typical essay was proper, genteel, and Anglophilic. Though it atrophied around the 1930s, the polite essay retained for many years an insidious power over America's college students, who were often forced to imitate its polished civility in that shadow genre known as the freshman theme. The goal of English teachers, Kurt Vonnegut recalls, was to get you "to write like cultivated Englishmen of a century or more ago."

Today the essay is flourishing again, though it no longer can be characterized by its homogeneity. In fact, its diversity may be its most noticeable characteristic. In light of the essay's transformations, today's poetry and fiction appear stagnant: the essay is now our most dynamic literary form. We see narrative essays that seem indistinguishable from short stories, mosaic essays that read like prose poems. We have literary criticism with an autobiographical spin, journalism attuned to drama and metaphor, reflection with a heavy dose of information. Some essayists write polemic that sounds like poetry. Physicists, mathematicians, and philosophers are finding that complex ideas and a memorable prose style are not irreconcilable. Even law review articles have turned literary. In other words, today's essay is incredibly difficult to nail down.

For the past twelve years, this series has been showcasing the essay's astonishing variety. This is done in two ways: by screening essays from an enormous range of periodicals and by inviting a distinguished American writer to serve each year as the guest editor.

To ensure diversity, the series welcomes all types of journals and magazines; this year, for instance, we feature writing from some of our leading national periodicals *(The Atlantic Monthly, Harper's Magazine, The New Yorker)*, from a number of outstanding literary reviews and quarterlies published throughout the nation *(The Paris Review, The Threepenny Review)*, from some very popular men's and women's magazines *(Allure, Sports Afield)*, and magazines with a strong regional flavor *(The Oxford American,* published in Mississippi by the best-selling novelist John Grisham). Not all selections, however, come from prestigious or well-established periodicals. Few readers will be familiar with *Under the Sun,* a brand-new literary journal edited by Michael O'Rourke and published by Tennessee Technological University: "Thank you," O'Rourke wrote upon being notified of the selection, "for looking past the fact that we still had a ways to go, cosmetically, in that first issue, and just reading what we printed." A glance at the list of Notable Essays in the back of the volume will quickly display the spectrum of periodicals annually consulted: it runs from *A. Magazine,* the "Inside Asia America" bimonthly, to Howard Junker's splendid San Francisco literary quarterly, *ZYZZYVA.*

But the commitment to diversity goes beyond the enormous range of periodicals. Each collection of *The Best American Essays* is shaped and informed by a unique literary perspective: Gay Talese showed how New Journalism had transformed the conventional essay; Annie Dillard viewed the contemporary essay as a literary form that rivals the best fiction and poetry; Justin Kaplan concentrated on the essay's role in interpreting public issues and events; Susan Sontag emphasized the essay's long-standing ties to criticism and intellectual controversy; Joyce Carol Oates featured the essay as an influential vehicle for multicultural voices; and Jamaica Kincaid made us aware of how brilliantly (and ironically) the essay can transgress familiar boundaries. This year, Ian Frazier's collection introduces a major strain of the essay that most previous volumes had surprisingly underplayed: humor.

Ian Frazier's selections also reacquaint us with the literature of politeness — not the old-boy kind, but one intimately in touch with the pressures and contradictions of our time. "I was brought up to be polite," Roy Blount, Jr., informs us before he lets off some comic steam. Verlyn Klinkenborg writes that he has learned to depend on his politeness "and to hate it, because it so often feels like a hand clutching my windpipe," a sentiment Natalie Kusz understood when confronted with the "incomprehensible politeness of America's Midwest." In Debra Dickerson's short, intense essay, we see polite behavior backfiring into inexplicable violence; Hilton Als introduces us to his enigmatic mother, who "was always polite, even at the end." And at Fidel Castro's palace in Havana with Muhammad Ali, Gay Talese records one of the most amusing stretches of "polite conversation" I have ever read.

If the contemporary essay itself is tough to nail down, so too is this collection. With selections ranging from the hilarious to the terrifying, it manages to combine storytelling and speculation, reminiscence and obsession, nostalgia and invective. Ian Frazier's brightly eclectic edition serves as the perfect introduction to the extraordinary diversity of the new American essay.

The Best American Essays features a selection of the year's outstanding essays, essays of literary achievement that show an awareness of craft and a forcefulness of thought. Hundreds of essays are gathered annually from a wide variety of national and regional publications. These essays are then screened and approximately one hundred are turned over to a distinguished guest editor, who may add a few personal discoveries and who makes the final selections.

To qualify for selection, the essays must be works of respectable literary quality, intended as fully developed, independent essays on subjects of general interest (not specialized scholarship), originally written in English (or translated by the author) for publication in an American periodical during the calendar year. Periodicals that want to make sure their contributors will be considered each year should include the series on their complimentary subscription list (Robert Atwan, Series Editor, *The Best American Essays*, P.O. Box 220, Readville, MA 02137-9998).

For this year's volume I want to thank Richard Poirier, who introduced me to the pleasures of American literature — especially Emerson's essays — in his graduate seminars and in his brilliant books of criticism. For decades his has been one of the most intelligent, sensible, and eloquent voices in our critical literature. On a more practical level, I am again grateful to Matthew Howard, who graciously helped out with a score of details, many of them at the last minute. I am indebted as always to the indispensable support I receive from the Houghton Mifflin staff — in particular from my editor, Janet Silver, her assistant, Sandra Riley, and my manuscript editor, Larry Cooper.

It was an enormous pleasure to work with Ian Frazier, whose keen sense of humor, acute observations, and unwavering commitment to community have helped make him one of America's favorite writers. These qualities — plus his dedication to the art and craft of prose — can be felt throughout this remarkable collection.

R. A.

Introduction

LIKE OTHER ACTIVITIES I enjoy, writing essays is something I would rather do than talk about. But here I'm doing both, so I guess it's O.K. I had planned to begin this introduction by trying the reader with the small amount I know about the history of the essay form. I recently learned, however, that for decades now I have been mispronouncing the name "Montaigne." Though the correct pronunciation has since been explained to me, I am still rather hazy on it. It's not like "champagne" — or not like the way I pronounce "champagne." This discovery has chastened me, and caused me to shelve the whole history-of-the-essay opening, due to lack of qualifications. I will add that I am glad to have worked Montaigne in so early, and gotten him out of the way.

An essay is a person talking. Whether the subject matter the person chooses is too informational or made-up or theoretical or otherwise non-essayistic for the work to be considered an essay is a question I set aside. I'm more interested in the talking part — in the voice unspooling in the essay's present time. Wandering is acceptable in an essay, and as I look in a dictionary my eye wanders from the entry for "essay," the noun, to the entry just above, which defines it as a verb. There, its first meaning is "To put to a test." Evidently, the word was around for a long time as a verb before it acquired its additional meaning as a noun; the verb still overshadows its offspring. I think it's good to regard "the essay" as a verblike noun — not so much an object as an action disguised as one.

If kids still write essays in school the way people my age used to, they meet the essay first as pure object. In school, it is (or was) a written paper of a certain length, on an assigned subject, with specified margins and neatness, due on the teacher's desk at a certain date. From about fourth grade on, I wrote many essays. "An essay a week" was a philosophy lots of grammar school teachers subscribed to back then. Recently I came across an essay of mine I'd saved from the fifth grade. It's called "If I Had Three Wishes." My first wish, as I described it, was for lots of fishing equipment, my second was for a canoe in which to go fishing, and my third was for a cabin in the woods somewhere near good fishing. I have more or less gotten those wishes, writing occasional essays about fishing all the while. Even in its present state as childhood artifact, "If I Had Three Wishes" retains its purposeful object-ness: the three-ring-binder paper with regular lines and space at the top for student's name, teacher's name, and date; the slow, newly learned script, in blue ballpoint, almost without mistakes; and the circled good grade in the teacher's hand.

But it was in school, too, that I first saw writing as something alive. In this case the writing was not an essay, but Truman Capote's *In Cold Blood*, a work of reporting, and the object it leaped from was an issue of *The New Yorker*. I was a freshman in high school and had never given the writing in magazines much thought before. One day our English teacher, Mr. Waring, walked into class reading an issue of *The New Yorker* that he had just picked up at his mailbox down the hall. Mr. Waring was old and he did as he pleased. He sat at his desk and continued to read, and we watched him read. After a while he looked up and announced that instead of doing what we'd planned for that session he would read this article aloud to us. And he read us *In Cold Blood* from the magazine where it first appeared, seeing it for the first time himself as he read it out loud to us. When I tell this story — I tell it often — I generally exaggerate and say he read the whole book to us, all four installments, week after week. Most likely he didn't. I like that version, though, because the story is sort of a creation myth for me.

When I went home that evening, my father was reading the same piece. Lots of people in our town read it and talked about it. People talked about it at lunch at school. My father could not wait for the issue with the next installment, so early the next week he went to a newsstand up in Cleveland and bought it rather than trusting the magazine to come as usual in the mail. We bought the book when it came out. The book's cover, its title accented with the long, stylized drop of blood, could be seen on copies lying face-down and open on couches and nightstands all over town. *In Cold Blood* colored that year, 1965, and for me colored especially the rainy fall season in which it appeared in the magazine. The color was a sixties-style, Diane-Arbus-y, documentarian black and white, and it lasted for years. After college I wrote for *The New Yorker* myself, then left New York and traveled around on the Great Plains, and eventually came across the house in Holcomb, Kansas, where the murders in *In Cold Blood* had taken place. Back in New York, I met with William Shawn, then editor of *The New Yorker,* who had worked with Capote from the beginning on the book and had edited it for the magazine. I told Mr. Shawn that I had just seen the *In Cold Blood* house, and Shawn shook his head ruefully. He said he had been very disappointed in how that piece had turned out. He said he had wanted it to be about the reaction of that small Kansas town to the murders; he had not, he said, wanted it to be (he paused with distaste) about the *killers.*

Presumably Truman Capote was disappointed in the book as well. After it was published he began to say that it was a sort of novel. Anyone who witnessed the sea change its publication caused knows that it was certainly something; but the something wasn't a novel. Capote may have wished that this, his major book, would be in a form familiar from masterpieces of the past. Having a great book to his credit was fine, but he'd rather have a great novel. Writers are like that. They ask not simply for inspiration, but for inspiration of a specific kind. Then inspiration comes, and it's not what they wanted — it's inspiration for a better way to mow the yard, maybe, or for a funny comment to make if they should ever happen to host the Academy Awards. If the inspiration is at least literary, no matter the form, that's blessing enough. Perhaps the hope was for an epic poem, or a terza rima, or a novel better than *Madame Bovary,* and what arrives instead is an off-brand, hard-to-categorize paragraph or two leading toward a vague destination somewhere down the page. You, the writer, can suppress this un-asked-for inspiration like an impure thought, or you can say "why not?" and go with it. Acting on the second impulse may produce unpublishable white elephants, or *sui generis* classics that people will try unsuccessfully to copy forever. Most often, what it produces is essays.

That's what I mean about the essay as an action. Beneath the object — the physical piece of writing with its unpredictable content — is the action that produced it. The action, it seems to me, is easier to characterize. The difference is like that between a golf ball in the air and the swing of the golfer that propelled it: the flight of a struck ball varies, but the swing tends always to be the same. An essay is a golf swing, an angler's cast, a tennis serve. For example, say an experience happens to you, one that seems to have literary potential. You wait for it to grow in your mind into a short story or even just an episode of *Friends,* but somehow it doesn't. Then a further experience, or an odd chance, or something a friend says, or something in the newspaper chimes with the first experience, and suddenly you understand you can write about it, and you do. You quit longing for form and write what's there, with whatever serviceable prose comes to hand, for no better reason than the fun and release of saying. That sequence — that combination of patience with sudden impatience, that eventual yielding to the simple desire to tell — identifies the essay.

And what are you left with? A letter to the editor, perhaps, or a letter to a friend, or an E-mail sent to fifty addresses at a click. (E-mail, by the way, makes for the sloppiest essays, the speed of the technology catching nascent thoughts before they're real thoughts at all.) Or maybe it's just a long entry in your journal, or a rebuttal to something your spouse said, or a self-justifying explanation composed in full detail in your head during a traffic jam. Part of the essay's appeal is that it's a people's art. Sooner or later, everybody tries one, even if it's only a hypothetical discourse telling off the boss. The shadow of the essay can be seen under the TV announcer's ninety seconds of commentary, the hard-to-follow handwritten photocopied flyer outlining the supposed dangers of Ritalin, and the transcribed speeches of Indians at treaty gatherings two hundred years ago. An essay is its own form, but all kinds of other forms can contain essays. The next question is one of intent: Did you write it hoping, consciously or not, that it would see print? In certain good circumstances, what you're left with is a piece of some hundreds or thousands of words that a magazine will buy and publish, like the essays in this book.

One of my favorite essayists is Martin Luther King, Jr. An essay by him was above all an action — from the anger and sense of injustice that impelled it, through the disciplined prose with which it meant to tear injustice down. I like his essays, too, for their language. King showed that American writing was a lot more than the laconic, Hemingwayesque flat-affect prose some of us had assumed it was. King could use a word like "interposition" or "nettlesome" or "commensurate" or "prodigious" and make it worth every penny. Another pleasure is to see him demolish then-prevailing arguments which we know by hindsight stayed demolished after he was done. One casualty was the argument that black people should give social justice time, that progress would come if only they would wait. "For years now I have heard the word 'Wait!'" he wrote. "It rings in the ear of every Negro with a piercing familiarity. This 'Wait' has almost always meant 'Never.'"

Of course when I reread him I always return to the "I Have a Dream" speech, his greatest hit. In it, phrases and whole sentences from his philosophical and political essays reappear, but set to an oratorical beat. Sometimes I also watch it on a video that I have of him giving it. If an essay is a golf swing, then we must admit that usually its outcome is like that of a golf swing at a crowded driving range: the swing is made, the missile goes out into the world, and it comes to rest ignored in a numberless throng of its fellows. But sometimes, rarely, it hits something out there — as if the golf ball at the driving range struck another ball which struck another which struck another and so on, until the whole range, the cars in the parking lot and the rental booths and the soft-drink machines and the neighboring trees and buildings, all resounded with a multiplicity of ricochets. In the video of King's speech, you can see an effect like that happen before your eyes. What he has to say is so simple: I have a dream that white people and black people can live together in peace. But the purity of his swing — its sweetness and the manifest fact that his whole life and a people's history are in it — causes every syllable he speaks to hit bone. You can see the reaction growing in the crowd as they listen. They would leap to their feet if they weren't standing already. Instead, they seem to shiver, they vibrate back and forth, their eyebrows rise, a cheer builds in them before they know they're cheering. The world is a little different after each sentence than it was before, and by the end of the speech, in the space of its fifteen minutes, the world has changed. I watch the video every so often to remind myself that the swing we work on when we write has the power to do such a thing.

* * *

Since the first *Best American Essays* appeared, in 1986, its editors have had more and more essays to choose from every year. Lots more people are writing them, short and long, on all kinds of subjects, for magazines that pay and for magazines that really don't. Maybe this is because the world has gotten more overwhelming and we want to make sense of it fast, and the essay is a handy tool for the job. Maybe we've reached a retrospective point, in our lives or in our culture, and the essay provides a way to tell the narratives and speculate on them at the same time. The witnessing of history can't help but bring with it an urge to say what it means; maybe that urge has struck a lot of us at once. Unavoidably, with time we know more about the people we love. True character is revealed, unguessed enormities come out in the wash. For some reason, the essay is especially apt at describing the accumulation of consequences that is a family. Writing about the family is one common thread among the essays collected here.

The essays this series considers are ones published in America. America is itself only an idea, and it has always depended on people thinking about what it meant, defining and redefining it. Essays have had a great bearing upon it. Centuries of thinking and writing about subjects like man's relationship to God or how people should best be governed converged at its beginnings. Sometimes an essayist's effect has been as immediate as Thomas Paine's, whose pamphlet *Common Sense,* reprinted by the hundreds of thousands, inflamed people to revolution. More often, the essayist in America has viewed his or her country more obliquely, telling what it feels like to be an individual in this would-be democracy, and measuring its sickness or health in what one person can see. Recently I read a writer from another country saying that Americans seem so hopeful and optimistic about their country, and that they write so wistfully about what it could be. Well, we are, and we do. Despite plentiful evidence to the contrary, many of us think it could be a glorious place. What I sense under the upsurge of essay-writing today, partly, is this persistent hopefulness about America. It's as if we believe that by taking stock, looking around, describing what we see, explaining what we'd like to see, we can get it right somehow. Certainly the idea of America needs a great volume of surrounding ideas to keep it afloat; maybe the writers of essays are just working harder to replenish the supply.

I think the essays in this collection are great. I liked many essays that I did not choose, but I liked these best. To say what moved me about various specific ones would not be to tell you much of use to you. Also, I would have the summarizer's problem of praising a few at the risk of seeming to dispraise those I leave out. Some of these essays I loved because they're funny and unexpected and effortless and they made me laugh out loud. In some, what's funny about them coincides exactly with what's sad. Anger drives others, marshals the words and makes the sentences stand in line. Some I liked because the author lays out an argument that I agree with completely but could not explain so well myself. Some are about suffering, in voices made incidentally beautiful by it. A few are by authors I've admired for years, and these reminded me why. Others that floored me are by authors I've never read before. In a few the force at work is curiosity, immediately engaged and allowed to go where it leads. Some do sleight-of-hand structural moves to which my hat is off, as they veer from one narrative into a long involved other and then back with hardly a jar. In some, not much happens at all, to excellent effect. As a group, what they share is strong intention elegantly followed through. The reader finishes each in a heightened and lively frame of mind, to a sound of loud internal applause.

IAN FRAZIER

The Best
AMERICAN
ESSAYS
1997

HILTON ALS

Notes on My Mother

FROM THE NEW YORKER

UNTIL THE END, my mother never discussed her way of being.
She avoided explaining the impetus behind her emigration from
Barbados to New York. She avoided explaining that she had not
been motivated by the same desire for opportunity that drove most
female immigrants but instead had followed a man whom she had
known in Barbados as her first and only husband's closest friend
— a man who eventually became my father. She was silent about
the fact that she had left her husband, by whom she had two
daughters, after he returned to Barbados from the Second World
War addicted to morphine, and that, having been married once,
she refused to marry again. She was also silent about the fact that
my father, who had grown up relatively rich in Barbados, had emigrated to America with his two sisters and his mother — women
with whom he continued to live, throughout my childhood, in a
brownstone in Brooklyn. My mother never discussed how she
would visit my father in his room there, at night, and afterward
sneak back to her own home and her six children, four of them
produced by her union with my father: two girls and two boys. She
never explained the bond that they shared, a bond so deep and
mysterious that we children felt forever excluded from their love,
and forever diminished by it.

My mother also never told me whether she recognized or understood where my fascination with her would take me, a boy of
seven, and eight, and ten: to a dark crawl space behind her closet,
where I put on her hosiery one leg at a time, my heart racing, and,
over the hose, my jeans and sneakers, so that I could have her,

what I so admired and coveted, near me, always. As a Negress —
for that was what she called herself — my mother was powerful in
her silence, and for years she silently watched me, her first son,
try to emulate her forbearance. She avoided discussing what that
forbearance was worth.

For years before and after her death, I tried to absorb my mother
by referring to myself as a Negress, and by living the prescribed
life of an auntie man, which is what Barbadians call a faggot. I
socialized myself as an auntie man long before I committed my
first act as one. I had four older sisters, and I also wore their clothes
when they were not home; the clothes relieved some of the pressure I felt at being different from them. My mother responded to
the Negress inside me with pride and anger: pride because I identified with women like herself; anger because I identified with
women at all. When I was five or six years old, we were sitting on
a bench in the subway station near our building, and seated not
far from us was a woman my mother knew from the neighborhood
with her teenage son. My mother did not speak to this woman,
because she did not approve of the woman's son, who, like me,
was a Negress. Unlike me, he dressed the part. He was wearing
black shoes with princess heels, flesh-colored hose through which
dark hairs sprouted, a lemon-yellow shift with grease stains on it,
a purple head scarf, and bangles. He carried a strapless purse,
from which he removed a compact and lipstick, so that he could
dress his face, too. As my mother looked at that boy, she brushed
my eyes closed with the back of her hand, and she hissed the words
"auntie man." I've never known whether she was referring to both
of us.

   Did my mother call herself a Negress as a way of wryly reconcil-
ing herself to that most hated of English colonial words, which
fixed her as a servant in the eyes of Britain and of God? I don't
think so; she was not especially interested in Britain or in history.
My mother was capricious in her views about most things, including race. As a West Indian who lived among other West Indians,
she did not feel "difference"; in her community, she was in the
majority. She dropped her West Indian accent a few years after she
became a United States citizen, in the early 1950s. She didn't like
people who capitalized on being exotic. She didn't like accents in

general. She lived in America and wanted to sound like an American, which she did, unless she was angry. She was capable of giving a nod toward the history of "injustice," but only if it suited her mood. I think my mother took some pleasure in the embarrassment that white and black Americans alike felt when she called herself a Negress, since their image of her, she thought, was largely sentimental, heavy with suffering. When my mother laughed in the face of their deeply presumptuous view of her, one of her front teeth flashed gold.

My mother's lack of interest in politics freed her mind for other things, like her endless ill health, which she treated as though it were a protracted form of suicide. She first became sick when my father fell in love with someone else and her thirty-year love affair with him ended. The difference between my mother and my father's new girlfriend was this: the new woman consented to live with my father while my mother had not. (After my mother refused to marry him, in the early fifties, my father never asked her again.) When my mother became ill with one thing and another, I was eight; by the time she died, I was twenty-eight. I was so lonely knowing her; she was so busy dying.

My mother was always polite, even at the end. For a long time, she imposed her will by not telling anyone what was really wrong; this kept everyone poised and at her service. She would not speak of the facts that contributed to her dying. She was quietly determined, functional, and content in her depression; she would not have forfeited her sickness for anything, since it had taken her so many years to admit to her need for attention, and being ill was one way of getting it. When diabetes cost her one of her legs, she said politely, "Oh, I'm dying now." When they removed a lymph node in her neck as a test for something, she said politely, "Oh, I'm really dying now." When her kidneys failed and a machine functioned in their place, she was still polite. She said, "Well, I'm dying." When she lost the vision in one eye, when, eventually, she could not breathe without effort, when her blood pressure was abnormally high and her teeth were bad and she could not urinate or take sugar in her tea or eat pork or remember a conversation, she remembered these two things: that she was polite and that she was dying.

One of my aunts told me that my mother encountered my father's girlfriend once, on the street, and took a good look at her. She saw a certain resemblance between herself and this woman: they were both homely but spirited, like Doris Day. It was clear to my mother that, like her, this woman would be capable of withstanding my father's tantrums, his compulsive childishness, and his compulsive lying. I think the resemblance my mother saw between herself and my father's new girlfriend shattered any claim to originality that she had. In the end, I think my mother's long and public illness was the only thing she experienced as an accomplishment, as something separate from her roles as mother, lover, Negress. And it was.

Certain facts about my mother's religious, cultural, culinary, sexual, and literary interests: She attended Sunday services at St. George's Episcopal Church, a Gothic structure in the Bedford-Stuyvesant section of Brooklyn, surrounded by brownstones, vacant lots, and children. The congregation was largely West Indian, and was judgmental of my mother because she had chosen not to marry my father, while she did choose to have his children. Many of the women in that congregation had had children out of wedlock as well, but they judged my mother just the same, because she wasn't bitter about not being married. At St. George's, my mother sometimes sang, in her sweet, reedy voice, "I Surrender All," her favorite hymn.

My mother wanted to be different from her own mother, who had always been a bitter woman, but she avoided contradicting my grandmother when she said things like "Don't play in the sun. You are black enough" — which is what my grandmother said to me once. My mother attempted to separate herself from her parents and siblings by being "nice," which they weren't. An early memory of this: my mother's family sitting in a chartered bus as it rained outside during a family picnic; my mother, alone, in the rain, cleaning up the mess as my great-aunt said, "Marie is one of God's own," and my heart breaking as the bus rocked with derisive laughter.

She loved the foods of her country: *sous*, blood pudding, coconut bread, *cou-cou*. She enjoyed her own mother most when her mother prepared those foods for her on special occasions: birthdays, Christmas, wakes. She herself was a mediocre cook who pretended to be better at it than she was by preparing elaborate meals from French cookbooks. I learned to cook in reaction to the meals she prepared.

She was in love with my father until she died; they spoke every day on the telephone. They amused and angered each other. She called him Cyp, which was short for Cyprian, his given name. When he said her name, Marie, he said it in a thick Bajan accent, so that the *a* was very flat. In his mouth, her name sounded like this: *Ma*-ree.

My mother was bright and had a high school education, but she saw clearly that her passport to the world was restricted. Over the years, in Brooklyn, she worked as a housekeeper, as a hairdresser in a beauty salon, and as a teacher's assistant in a nursery school. My mother told one story about being a servant among the Jews when she was a young woman and new to America. With other women her age, she would go to the Flatbush section of Brooklyn and wait on a particular street corner for people — mostly Jews — to drive by in their big cars, from which they would look out to see which of the women seemed healthy and clean enough to do day work in their homes. "We called ourselves Daily Woikers," my mother said in a Yiddish-American accent, laughing. She called the hair salon where she worked "the shop." It was frequented by Negresses. I went there after school. At the shop, my mother wore a white smock. She straightened hair and rubbed bergamot into women's scalps. She listened to women talk all day. After a while, their problems became pretty general to her. People complained, no matter what; she learned that for some people complaining was a way of being. After a while, she didn't respond to her customers' problems; she knew that they didn't really want a solution. The more my mother heard, the more impersonal she became in her support and encouragement of everyone. She addressed most of those women as "honey," because, after a while, she couldn't remember their names.

We lived for many years in a two-story brownstone with a narrow stairway in Flatbush. The Schwartzes, the elderly Jewish couple who owned the building, lived below us. Sometimes my brother and I would watch television with the Schwartzes. I marveled at the orderliness of Mr. and Mrs. Schwartz's home, the strange smells, and the candles that they burned on Friday nights. I loved them. I wanted to be a Jew. I told Mrs. Schwartz that I wanted to be a Jew, but how? One day when I was with my mother, Mrs. Schwartz stopped her on that narrow stairway to tell her that I wanted to be a Jew. I was ten. My mother looked at me. She told Mrs. Schwartz that I wanted to be a *writer.* Shortly afterward, Mrs. Schwartz gave me a gift. It was a typewriter that had belonged to her son, the Doctor.

My mother was not ambitious for her children, but she was supportive of their ambitions. After I decided to be a writer, my mother gave me writing tablets at Christmas; she also gave me books to read that she bought at the Liberation Bookshop, on Nostrand Avenue in Bedford-Stuyvesant. The books were almost always novels or collections of poems, and were almost always written by women. She gave me Alice Childress's *A Hero Ain't Nothin' But a Sandwich* and *Maud Martha* by Gwendolyn Brooks and *A Tree Grows in Brooklyn* by Betty Smith. I felt just like the heroine, Francie, who dreams of being a writer and longs to see the world but can't imagine how she's ever going to get out of Brooklyn to do so.

My mother spent many hours alone with me, in the dark, in her bedroom, listening to me lie. Somehow, she knew that most writers became writers after having spent their childhood lying. Or perhaps she didn't know that at all. But she was extremely tolerant of my lies. And she was not impatient with my pretensions. When, at thirteen or fourteen, I began wearing a silk ascot to school, and took to writing by the light of a kerosene lamp like my then hero, Horace Greeley, the famous nineteenth-century journalist, she didn't say a word.

My mother loved *Crime and Punishment.* She read it over and over again while locked in the bathroom. Her second-favorite novel was Paule Marshall's *Brown Girl, Brownstones,* the story, in part, of a Brooklyn girl named Selina who is of Bajan descent. My mother passed this book on to me, and I read it eleven times. I was eleven years old. I read the author's biography on the book flap and looked her name up in the Manhattan telephone directory. When Paule Marshall answered the telephone, I told her, in a rush, how much my mother loved her novel, and that we did not live very far from where Selina had grown up. Paule Marshall was surprised and pleased; she made her son pick up the extension and listen in. Later, when I told my mother what I had done, she looked at me in amazement. She knew that I had telephoned Paule Marshall for both of us.

My brother and I didn't like Barbados. In the summers we were sent there, with packages of clothes and food as gifts, but we preferred to imagine the island through my mother's memories of it. In 1979, when I was seventeen, I read a story by a writer from the West Indies. In the story, "Wingless" by Jamaica Kincaid, I read this description of the Caribbean Sea and its surroundings: "The sea, the shimmering pink-colored sand, the swimmers with hats, two people walking arm in arm, talking in each other's faces, dots of water landing on noses, the sea spray on ankles, on overdeveloped calves, the blue, the green, the black, so deep, so smooth, a great and swift undercurrent, glassy, the white wavelets." This story changed everything for me. After reading it, I read it aloud to my mother, and when I finished she said, "Exactly."

As a pubescent Negress, I spent a great deal of time in thrall to the sister who was eleven years older than I was; she continued to live at home for years after our other sisters had left. She was the only college student I knew. She created a world in her bedroom that resonated with style and intellectual possibility. She was beautiful: she had long legs and a long neck and shoulder-length black hair that she wore in a chignon. She wore straight skirts and cardigans and flats. She had many lovers, which later prompted one of our other sisters to say, "She's so nasty. Like a dog." In her room, we danced to Dionne Warwick singing "Don't Make Me Over" as my sister began getting dressed for the evening. When she asked for my advice on what to wear, I knew she was pleased with me. Sometimes, in a sudden fit of pique, she would demand to know what I was anyway, hanging around a girl's bedroom.

As I grew up, it became increasingly clear that one of the reasons for my sister's occasional sharp annoyance with me was this: she wanted to be able to see herself in contrast to me. All the women in my family wanted me to become a black male for the same reason: they wanted to define themselves against me. I tried to please them, because I adored them. I thought that being an auntie man was a fair compromise, but it wasn't.

When I was thirteen, I went to a party given by one of my

mother's relatives. I didn't know why my mother did not attend the party until I returned home and told her about it. We were standing in the kitchen, and I told her how I had met a man there who had asked after her. I described him: bald head, a square figure, deep dark skin. I met him on the stoop of the house where the party was. I remembered everything about the meeting, and spoke of it excitedly. I didn't tell my mother about the man's charm, and my attraction to his charm. Nor did I describe the orange sun setting behind his large brown head; rubbing my moist hands against the stoop's bumpy concrete; admiring his graceful saunter as he walked away. My mother's face became hard when I mentioned his first name, Eldred. She would not look at me when she said, "That was the man I was married to. That was my husband." The air was still between us; it became a wall. I knew I was a Negress because of the jealousy I felt at her having rejected someone I wanted. I glanced at my mother; her face, her body, told me that she had been where I wanted to be long before I began imagining it. We stood in the kitchen for quite some time. I saw myself in my mother's eyes: a teenage girl, insecure, jealous, and vengeful.

Like my sister, I grew up to lie with first one man and then another, or, more accurately, to bend over one man and then another in parked cars that lined the piers on the West Side Highway. Until the end, I avoided recounting these facts to my mother. I avoided explaining the impetus that propelled me to leave her home in Brooklyn for the piers on the West Side Highway. I avoided explaining that I had been motivated by the same desire and romantic greed that had propelled her to move from Barbados to New York. I avoided explaining that when I sat in parked cars with one man and then another, I felt closer to her experience of the world than I ever did in her actual presence. I avoided mentioning that the men I seduced were almost always white, and that, with my mouth tentatively poised over another man's mouth, I sometimes thought, I am not my mother; this is *my* story. I sometimes fantasized, If she knew I was performing this act, this gesture, she would perhaps die, releasing me to live fully in the moment. I never told her how I met other Negresses like myself, the boy children of women who had emigrated to New York from islands like Jamaica, Cuba, Antigua, Anguilla, Barbados, Barbuda. And we never men-

tioned to one another how, when we left those cars and bars in
our soiled bluejeans, and after the long subway ride home to
Brooklyn or Queens or the Bronx, we were met at the kitchen door
by our mirror image — Mom, a Negress, who rarely recounted
anything at all about her life.

My mother died in Barbados, our ancestral home. Before she left
New York for the last time, I did not visit her; this was only one of
many leave-takings, and we could not bear to say goodbye. Neither
did she say goodbye to her sister, who was to return to Barbados
later, after my mother's death. "I knew she wouldn't come back to
New York. I knew she would die here," my aunt told me when I
went there to see where my mother had died. My visit meant
nothing to my aunt. She is unsentimental — a family trait. She said
several things when I went to visit her in her ugly house surrounded by coconut trees on a pitiful plot of land. She said, "Your
mother was so angry at the end." She asked, "When did you know
you were going to be an auntie man?" She asked, "When will you
write a story about me?" And I did not ask myself, "Am I not a
Negress, too? Will I ever be capable of writing a story about any
of us?" In that ugly house in Barbados as the trade winds blew, my
aunt was telling me that I would.

JO ANN BEARD

The Fourth State of Matter

FROM THE NEW YORKER

THE COLLIE WAKES ME UP about three times a night, summoning me from a great distance as I row my boat through a dim, complicated dream. She's on the shoreline, barking. Wake up. She's staring at me with her head slightly tipped to the side, long nose, gazing eyes, toenails clenched to get a purchase on the wood floor. We used to call her the face of love.

She totters on her broomstick legs into the hallway and over the doorsill into the kitchen, makes a sharp left at the refrigerator — careful, almost went down — then a straightaway to the door. I sleep on my feet in the cold of the doorway, waiting. Here she comes. Lift her down the two steps. She pees and then stands, Lassie in a ratty coat, gazing out at the yard.

In the porch light the trees shiver, the squirrels turn over in their sleep. The Milky Way is a long smear on the sky, like something erased on a blackboard. Over the neighbor's house, Mars flashes white, then red, then white again. Jupiter is hidden among the anonymous blinks and glitterings. It has a moon with sulfur-spewing volcanoes and a beautiful name: Io. I learned it at work, from the group of men who surround me there. Space physicists, guys who spend days on end with their heads poked through the fabric of the sky, listening to the sounds of the universe. Guys whose own lives are ticking like alarm clocks getting ready to go off, although none of us are aware of it yet.

The dog turns and looks, waits to be carried up the two steps. Inside the house she drops like a shoe onto her blanket, a thud, an adjustment. I've climbed back under my covers already but her leg's stuck underneath her, we can't get comfortable. I fix the leg, she rolls over and sleeps. Two hours later I wake up and she's gazing at me in the darkness. The face of love. She wants to go out again. I give her a boost, balance her on her legs. Right on time: 3:40 A.M.

There are squirrels living in the spare bedroom upstairs. Three dogs also live in this house, but they were invited. I keep the door of the spare bedroom shut at all times, because of the squirrels and because that's where the vanished husband's belongings are stored. Two of the dogs — the smart little brown mutt and the Labrador — spend hours sitting patiently outside the door, waiting for it to be opened so they can dismantle the squirrels. The collie can no longer make it up the stairs, so she lies at the bottom and snores or stares in an interested manner at the furniture around her.

I can take almost anything at this point. For instance, that my vanished husband is neither here nor there; he's reduced himself to a troubled voice on the telephone three or four times a day.

Or that the dog at the bottom of the stairs keeps having mild strokes, which cause her to tilt her head inquisitively and also to fall over. She drinks prodigious amounts of water and pees great volumes onto the folded blankets where she sleeps. Each time this happens I stand her up, dry her off, put fresh blankets underneath her, carry the peed-on blankets down to the basement, stuff them into the washer and then into the dryer. By the time I bring them back upstairs they are needed again. The first few times this happened, I found the dog trying to stand up, gazing with frantic concern at her own rear. I praised her and patted her head and gave her treats until she settled down. Now I know whenever it happens, because I hear her tail thumping against the floor in anticipation of reward. In retraining her I've somehow retrained myself, bustling cheerfully down to the basement, arms drenched in urine, the task of doing load after load of laundry strangely satisfying. She is Pavlov and I am her dog.

I'm fine about the vanished husband's boxes stored in the spare bedroom. For now, the boxes and the phone calls convince me that things could turn around at any moment. The boxes are filled with thirteen years of his pack-ratness: statistics textbooks that still harbor an air of desperation; smarmy suit coats from the Goodwill; various old Halloween masks and one giant black papier-mâché thing he made that was supposed to be Elvis's hair but didn't turn out. A collection of ancient Rolling Stones T-shirts. You know he's turning over a new leaf when he leaves the Rolling Stones behind.

What I can't take is the squirrels. They come alive at night, throwing terrific parties in the spare bedroom, making thumps and crashes. Occasionally a high-pitched squeal is heard amid bumps and the sound of scrabbling toenails. I've begun sleeping downstairs, on the blue vinyl dog couch, the sheets slipping off, my skin stuck to the cushions. This is an affront to the two younger dogs, who know the couch belongs to them; as soon as I settle in, they creep up and find their places between my knees and elbows.

I'm on the couch because the dog on the blanket gets worried at night. During the day she sleeps the catnappy sleep of the elderly, but when it gets dark her eyes open and she is agitated, trying to stand whenever I leave the room, settling down only when I'm next to her. We are in this together, the dying game, and I read for hours in the evening with one foot on her back, getting up only to open a new can of beer or take blankets to the basement. At some point I stretch out on the vinyl couch and close my eyes, one hand hanging down, touching her side. By morning the dog arm has become a nerveless club that doesn't come around until noon. My friends think I'm nuts.

One night, for hours, the dog won't lie down. I call my office pal, Mary, and wake her up. *"I'm weary,"* I say, in italics.

Mary listens, sympathetic, on the other end. "Oh my God," she finally says. *"What* are you going to do?"

I calm down immediately. "Exactly what I'm doing," I tell her. The dog finally parks herself with a thump on the stack of damp blankets. She sets her nose down and tips her eyes up to watch me. We all sleep then, for a bit, while the squirrels sort through the boxes overhead and the dog on the blanket keeps nervous watch.

I've called in tired to work. It's midmorning and I'm shuffling around in my long underwear, smoking cigarettes and drinking coffee. The whole house is bathed in sunlight and the faint odor of used diapers. The dogs are being mild-mannered and charming; I nudge the collie with my foot.

"Wake up and smell zee bacons," I say. She lifts her nose groggily and falls back asleep. I get ready for the office.

"I'm leaving and I'm never coming back," I say while putting on my coat. I use my mother's aggrieved, underappreciated tone. The little brown dog transfers her gaze from me to the table, the last place she remembers seeing toast. The Labrador, who understands English, begins howling miserably. She wins the toast sweepstakes and is chewing loudly when I leave, the little dog barking ferociously at her.

At the office, there are three blinks on the answering machine, the first from a scientist who speaks very slowly, like a kindergarten teacher, asking about reprints. "What am I, the village idiot?" I ask the room, taking down his number in large backward characters. The second and third blinks are from my husband, the across-town apartment dweller.

The first of his calls makes my heart lurch in a hopeful way. "I have to talk to you right *now*," he says grimly. "Where *are* you? I can never find you."

"Try calling your own house," I say to the machine. In his second message he has composed himself.

"I'm *fine* now," he says firmly. "Disregard previous message and don't call me back, please; I have meetings." Click, dial tone, rewind.

My leaping heart settles back into its hole in my chest. I say "Damn it" out loud, just as Chris strides into the office.

"What?" he asks defensively. He tries to think if he's done anything wrong recently. He checks the table for work; things are in good shape. A graduate student, Gang Lu, stops by to drop off some reports. Chris and I have a genial relationship these days, reading the paper together in the mornings, congratulating ourselves on each issue of the journal. It's a space-physics monthly, and he's the editor and I'm the managing editor. I know nothing about the science part; my job is to shepherd the manuscripts through the review process and create a journal out of the acceptable ones.

Christoph Goertz. He's hip in a professorial, cardigan/jeans kind of way. He's tall and lanky and white-haired, forty-seven years old, with an elegant trace of accent from his native Germany. He has a great dog, a giant black outlaw named Mica, who runs through the streets of Iowa City at night inspecting garbage cans.

She's big and friendly but a bad judge of character, and frequently runs right into the arms of the dogcatcher. Chris is always bailing her out.

"They don't understand dogs," he says.

I spend more time with Chris than I ever did with my husband. The morning I told him I was being dumped he was genuinely perplexed. "He's leaving *you?*" he asked.

Chris was drinking coffee, sitting at his table in front of the blackboard. Behind his head was a chalk drawing of a hip, professorial man holding a coffee cup. It was a collaborative effort; I had drawn the man and Chris framed him, using blue chalk and a straightedge. The two-dimensional man and the three-dimensional man stared at me intently.

"He's leaving *you?*" And for an instant I saw myself from their vantage point across the room — Jo Ann — and a small bubble of self-esteem percolated up from my depths. Chris shrugged. "You'll do fine," he said.

During my current turmoils I've come to think of work as my own kind of Zen practice, the constant barrage of paper hypnotic and soothing. Chris lets me work an eccentric schedule; in return I update his publications list for him and listen to stories about outer space.

Besides being an editor and a teacher, he's the head of a theoretical-plasma-physics team made up of graduate students and research scientists. He travels all over the world telling people about the magnetospheres of various planets, and when he comes back he brings me presents — a small bronze box from Africa with an alligator embossed on the top, a big piece of amber from Poland with the wings of flies preserved inside it, and, once, a set of delicate, horrifying bracelets made from the hide of an elephant.

Currently he is obsessed with the dust in the plasma of Saturn's rings. Plasma is the fourth state of matter. You've got your solid, your liquid, your gas, and then your plasma. In outer space there's the plasmasphere and the plasmapause. I avoid the math when I can and put a layperson's spin on these things.

"Plasma is blood," I told him.

"Exactly," he agreed, removing the comics page and handing it to me.

This is the kind of conversation we mostly have around the office, but today he's caught me at a weak moment, tucking my heart back inside my chest. I decide to be cavalier.

"I wish my *dog* was out tearing up the town and my *husband* was home sleeping on a blanket," I say.

Chris is neutral about my marriage problems, but he thinks the dog thing has gone far enough. "Why are you letting this go on?" he asks solemnly.

"I'm not *letting* it, that's why," I tell him. There are stacks of manuscripts everywhere, and he has all the pens over on his side of the room. "It just *is*, is all. Throw me a pen." He does, I miss it, stoop to pick it up, and when I straighten up again I might be crying.

"You have control over this," he explains in his professor voice. "You can decide how long she suffers."

This makes my heart pound. Absolutely not, I cannot do it. And then I weaken and say what I really want: for her to go to sleep and not wake up, just slip out of her skin and into the other world.

"Exactly," he says.

I have an ex–beauty queen coming over to get rid of the squirrels for me. She has long red hair and a smile that can stop trucks. I've seen her wrestle goats, scare off a giant snake, and express a dog's anal glands, all in one afternoon. I told her on the phone that a family of squirrels is living in the upstairs of my house.

"They're making a monkey out of me," I said.

So Caroline climbs into her car and drives across half the state, pulls up in front of my house, and gets out carrying zucchini, cigarettes, and a pair of big leather gloves. I'm sitting outside with my old dog, who lurches to her feet, staggers three steps, sits down, and falls over. Caroline starts crying.

"Don't try to give me zucchini," I say.

We sit companionably on the front stoop for a while, staring at the dog and smoking cigarettes. One time I went to Caroline's house and she was nursing a dead cat that was still breathing. At some point that afternoon, I saw her spoon baby food into its mouth, and as soon as she turned away the whole puréed mess plopped back out. A day later she took it to the vet and had it euthanized. I remind her of this.

"You'll do it when you do it," she says firmly.

I pick the collie up like a fifty-pound bag of sticks and feathers, stagger inside, place her on the damp blankets, and put the two other nutcases in the back yard. From upstairs comes a crash and a shriek. Caroline stares up at the ceiling.

"It's like having the Wallendas stay at your house," I say cheerfully. All of a sudden I feel fond of the squirrels and fond of Caroline and fond of myself for heroically calling her to help me. The phone rings four times. It's the husband, and his voice over the answering machine sounds frantic. He pleads with whoever Jo Ann is to pick up the phone.

"Please? I think I might be freaking out," he says. "Am I ruining my life here, or what? Am I making a *mistake?* Jo?" He breathes raggedly and sniffs into the receiver for a moment, then hangs up with a muffled clatter.

Caroline stares at the machine as if it's a copperhead.

"Holy fuckoly," she says, shaking her head. "You're *living* with this crap?"

"He wants me to reassure him that he's strong enough to leave me," I tell her. "Else he won't have fun on his bike ride. And guess what? I'm too tired to." But now I can see him in his dank little apartment, wringing his hands and staring out the windows. In his rickety dresser is the new package of condoms he accidentally showed me last week.

Caroline lights another cigarette. The dog pees and thumps her tail.

I need to call him back because he's suffering.

"You call him back and I'm forced to kill you," Caroline says. She exhales smoke and points to the phone. "That is evil shit."

I tend to agree. It's blanket time. I roll the collie off onto the floor and put the fresh blankets down, roll her back. Caroline has put on the leather gloves, which go all the way to her elbows. She's staring at the ceiling with determination.

The plan is that I'm supposed to separate one squirrel from the herd and get it in a corner. Caroline will take it from there. But when I'm in the room with her and the squirrels are running around, all I can do is scream. I'm not afraid of them, but my screaming button is on and the only way to turn it off is to leave the room.

"How are you doing?" I ask from the other side of the door. I can hear Caroline crashing around and swearing. The door opens and she falls out into the hall with a gray squirrel stuck to her glove. She clatters down the stairs and out the front door, and returns looking triumphant.

The collie appears at the foot of the stairs with her head cocked and her ears up. For an instant she looks like a puppy, then her feet start to slide. I run down and catch her and carry her upstairs so she can watch the show. The squirrels careen around the room, tearing the ancient wallpaper off the walls. The last one is a baby, so we keep it for a few minutes, looking at its little feet and its little tail. We show it to the collie, who stands up immediately and tries to get it.

Caroline patches the hole where they got in, cutting the wood with a power saw down in the basement. She comes up wearing a tool belt and lugging a ladder. I've seen a scrapbook of photos of her wearing evening gowns with a banner across her chest and a crown on her head. Curled hair, lipstick. She climbs down and puts the tools away. We eat nachos.

"I only make food that's boiled or melted these days," I tell her.

"I know," she replies.

The phone rings again, but whoever it is hangs up.

"Is it him?" she asks.

"Nope."

Caroline gestures toward the sleeping collie and remarks that it seems like just two days ago that she was a puppy.

"She was never a puppy," I tell her. "She's always been older than me."

When they say goodbye, Caroline holds the collie's long nose in one hand and kisses her on the forehead; the collie stares back at her gravely. Caroline is crying when she leaves, a combination of squirrel adrenaline and sadness. I cry, too, although I don't feel particularly bad about anything. I hand her the zucchini through the window and she pulls away from the curb.

The house is starting to get dark in that early-evening twilit way. I turn on lights and go upstairs. The black dog comes with me and circles the squirrel room, snorting loudly, nose to floor. There is a spot of turmoil in an open box — they made a nest in some disco shirts from the seventies. I suspect that's where the baby one slept. The mean landlady has evicted them.

Downstairs, I turn the lights back off and let evening have its way with me. Waves of pre-nighttime nervousness are coming from the collie's blanket. I sit next to her in the dimness, touching her ears, and listen for feet at the top of the stairs.

They're speaking in physics, so I'm left out of the conversation. Chris apologetically erases one of the pictures I've drawn on the blackboard and replaces it with a curving blue arrow surrounded by radiating chalk waves of green.

"If it's plasma, make it in red," I suggest. We're all smoking semi-illegally in the journal office with the door closed and the window open. We're having a plasma party.

"We aren't discussing *plasma*," Bob Smith says condescendingly. A stocky, short-tempered man, he's smoking a horrendously smelly pipe. The longer he stays in here, the more it feels as if I'm breathing small daggers in through my nose. He and I don't get along; each of us thinks the other needs to be taken down a peg. Once we had a hissing match in the hallway which ended with him suggesting that I could be fired, which drove me to tell him that he was *already* fired, and both of us stomped into our offices and slammed our doors.

"I had to fire Bob," I tell Chris later.

"I heard," he says. Bob is his best friend. They spend at least half of each day standing in front of blackboards, writing equations and arguing about outer space. Then they write theoretical papers about what they come up with. They're actually quite a big deal in the space-physics community, but around here they're just two guys who keep erasing my pictures.

Someone knocks on the door and we put our cigarettes out. Bob hides his pipe in the palm of his hand and opens the door.

It's Gang Lu, the doctoral student. Everyone lights up again. Gang Lu stands stiffly talking to Chris, while Bob holds a match to his pipe and puffs fiercely; nose daggers waft up and out, right in my direction. I give him a sugary smile and he gives me one back. Unimaginable, really, that less than two months from now one of his colleagues from abroad, a woman with delicate, birdlike features, will appear at the door to my office and identify herself as a friend of Bob's. When she asks, I take her down the hall to the room with the long table and then to his empty office. I do this without saying anything, because there's nothing to say, and she takes it all in with small, serious nods until the moment she sees his blackboard covered with scribbles and arrows and equations. At that point her face loosens and she starts to cry in long ragged sobs. An hour later, I go back and the office is empty. When I erase the blackboard finally, I can see where she laid her hands carefully, where the numbers are ghostly and blurred.

Bob blows his smoke discreetly in my direction and waits for Chris to finish talking to Gang Lu, who is answering questions in a monotone — yes or no or I don't know. Another Chinese student, Linhua Shan, lets himself in after knocking lightly. He nods and smiles at me and then stands at a respectful distance, waiting to ask Chris a question.

It's like a physics conference in here. I wish they'd all leave so I can make my usual midafternoon spate of personal calls. I begin thumbing through papers in a businesslike way.

Bob pokes at his pipe with a paper clip. Linhua Shan yawns hugely and then looks embarrassed. Chris erases what he put on the blackboard and tries unsuccessfully to redraw my pecking parakeet. "I don't know how it goes," he says to me.

Gang Lu looks around the room with expressionless eyes. He's sick of physics and sick of the buffoons who practice it. The tall glacial German, Chris, who tells him what to do; the crass idiot Bob, who talks to him as if he is a dog; the student Shan, whose ideas about plasma physics are treated with reverence and praised at every meeting. The woman who puts her feet on the desk and dismisses him with her eyes. Gang Lu no longer spends his evenings in the computer lab down the hall, running simulations and thinking about magnetic forces and invisible particles; he now spends them at the firing range, learning to hit a moving target with the gun he purchased last spring. He pictures himself holding the gun with both hands, arms straight out and steady; Clint Eastwood, only smarter.

He stares at each person in turn, trying to gauge how much respect each of them has for him. One by one. Behind black-rimmed glasses, he counts with his eyes. In each case the verdict is clear: not enough.

The collie fell down the basement stairs. I don't know if she was disoriented and was looking for me or what. But when I was at work she used her long nose like a lever and got the door open and tried to go down there, except her legs wouldn't do it and she fell. I found her sleeping on the concrete floor in an unnatural position, one leg still awkwardly resting on the last step. I repositioned the leg and sat down and petted her. We used to play a game called Maserati, where I'd grab her long nose like a gearshift and put her through all the gears — first second third fourth — until we were going a hundred miles an hour through town. She thought it was funny.

Friday, I'm at work, but this morning there's not much to do, and every time I turn around I see her sprawled, eyes mute, leg bent upward. We're breaking each other's heart. I draw a picture of her on the blackboard using brown chalk. I make X's where her eyes should be. Chris walks in with the morning paper and a cup of coffee. He looks around the clean office.

"Why are you here when there's no work to do?" he asks.

"I'm hiding from my life, what else?" This sounds perfectly reasonable to him. He gives me part of the paper.

His mother is visiting from Germany; she's a robust woman of eighty who is depressed and hoping to be cheered up. In the last year she has lost her one-hundred-year-old mother and her husband of sixty years. She can't be really cheered up, but she likes going to art galleries, so Chris has been driving her around the Midwest, to our best cities, showing her what kind of art Americans like to look at.

"How's your mom?" I ask him.

He shrugs and makes a flat-handed "so-so" motion.

We read, smoke, drink coffee, and yawn. I decide to go home.

"Good idea," he says.

It's November 1, 1991, the last day of the first part of my life. Before I leave, I pick up the eraser and stand in front of the collie's picture on the blackboard, thinking. I can feel Chris watching me, drinking his coffee. His long legs are crossed, his eyes are mild. He has a wife named Ulrike, a daughter named Karein, and a son named Göran. A dog named Mica. A mother named Ursula. A friend named me.

I erase the X's.

Down the hall, Linhua Shan feeds numbers into a computer and watches as a graph is formed. The computer screen is brilliant blue, and the lines appear in red and yellow and green. Four key-strokes and the green becomes purple, the blue background fades to the azure of a summer sky. The wave lines arc over it, crossing against one another. He asks the computer to print, and while it chugs along he pulls up a golf game on the screen and tees off.

One room over, at a desk, Gang Lu works on a letter to his sister in China. *The study of physics is more and more disappointing,* he tells her. *Modern physics is self-delusion,* and *All my life I have been honest and straightforward, and I have most of all detested cunning, fawning sycophants and dishonest bureaucrats who think they are always right in everything.* Delicate Chinese characters all over a page. She was a kind and gentle sister, and he thanks her for that. He's going to kill himself. *You yourself should not be too sad about it, for at least I have found a few traveling companions to accompany me to the grave.* Inside the coat on the back of his chair are a .38-caliber handgun and a .22-caliber revolver. They're heavier than they look and weigh the pockets down. *My beloved second elder sister, I take my eternal leave of you.*

The collie's eyes are almond-shaped; I draw them in with brown chalk and put a white bone next to her feet.

"That's better," Chris says kindly.

Before I leave the building I pass Gang Lu in the hallway and say hello. He has a letter in his hand and he's wearing his coat. He doesn't answer, and I don't expect him to. At the end of the hallway are the double doors leading to the rest of my life. I push them open and walk through.

Friday afternoon seminar, everyone is glazed over, listening as someone at the head of the long table explains something unexplainable. Gang Lu stands up and leaves the room abruptly, goes down one floor to see if the department chairman, Dwight, is sitting in his office. He is. The door is open. Gang Lu turns, walks back up the stairs, and enters the seminar room again. Chris Goertz is sitting near the door and takes the first bullet in the back of the head. There is a loud popping sound and then blue smoke. Linhua Shan gets the second bullet in the forehead; the lenses of his glasses shatter. More smoke and the room rings with the popping. Bob Smith tries to crawl beneath the table. Gang Lu takes two steps, holds his arms straight out, and levels the gun with both hands. Bob looks up. The third bullet in the right hand, the fourth in the chest. Smoke. Elbows and legs, people trying to get out of the way and then out of the room.

Gang Lu walks quickly down the stairs, expelling spent cartridges and loading new ones. From the doorway of Dwight's office: the fifth bullet in the head, the sixth strays, the seventh also in the head. A slumping. More smoke and ringing. Through the cloud an image comes to him — Bob Smith, hit in the chest, hit in the hand, still alive. Back up the stairs. Two scientists, young men, crouch over Bob, loosening his clothes, talking to him. From where he lies, Bob can see his best friend still sitting upright in a chair, head thrown back at an unnatural angle. Everything is broken and red. The two young scientists leave the room at gunpoint. Bob closes his eyes. The eighth and ninth bullets in his head. As Bob dies, Chris Goertz's body settles in his chair, a long sigh escapes his throat. Reload. Two more for Chris, one for Linhua Shan. Exit the building, cross two streets and the green, into the second building and up the stairs.

The administrator, Anne Cleary, is summoned from her office by the receptionist. She speaks to him for a few minutes, he produces a gun and shoots her in the face. The receptionist, a young student working as a temp, is just beginning to stand when he shoots her. He expels the spent cartridges in the stairwell, loads new ones. Reaches the top of the steps, looks around. Is disoriented suddenly. The ringing and the smoke and the dissatisfaction of not checking all the names off the list. A slamming and a running sound, the shout of police. He walks into an empty conference room, takes off his coat, folds it carefully, and puts it over the back of a chair. Checks his watch: twelve minutes since it began. Places the barrel against his right temple. Fires.

The first call comes at four o'clock. I'm reading on the bench in the kitchen, one foot on a sleeping dog's back. It's Mary, calling from work. There's been some kind of disturbance in the building, a rumor that Dwight was shot; cops are running through the halls carrying rifles. They're evacuating the building and she's coming over. Dwight, a tall, likable oddball who cut off his ponytail when they made him chair of the department. Greets everyone with a famous booming hello in the morning; studies plasma, just like

Chris and Bob. Chris lives two and a half blocks from the physics building; he'll be home by now if they've evacuated. I dial his house and his mother answers. She tells me that Chris won't be home until five, and then they're going to a play. Ulrike, her daughter-in-law, is coming back from a trip to Chicago and will join them. She wants to know why I'm looking for Chris — isn't he where I am?

No, I'm at home and I just had to ask him something. Could he please call me when he comes in.

She tells me that Chris showed her a drawing I made of him sitting at his desk behind a stack of manuscripts. She's so pleased to meet Chris's friends, and the Midwest is lovely, really, except it's very brown, isn't it?

It *is* very brown. We hang up.

The Midwest is very brown. The phone rings. It's a physicist. His wife, a friend of mine, is on the extension. Well, he's not sure, but it's possible that I should brace myself for bad news. I've already heard, I tell him — something happened to Dwight. There's a long pause, and then his wife says, "Jo Ann. It's possible that Chris was involved."

I think she means Chris shot Dwight. "No," she says gently. "Killed, too."

Mary is here. I tell them not to worry and hang up. I have two cigarettes going. Mary takes one and smokes it. She's not looking at me. I tell her about the phone call.

"They're out of it," I say. "They thought Chris was involved."

She repeats what they said: "I think you should brace yourself for bad news." Pours whiskey into a coffee cup.

For a few minutes I can't sit down, I can't stand up. I can only smoke. The phone rings. Another physicist tells me there's some bad news. He mentions Chris and Bob and I tell him I don't want to talk right now. He says O.K. but to be prepared because it's going to be on the news any minute. It's 4:45.

"Now they're trying to stir Bob into the stew," I tell Mary. She nods; she's heard this, too. I have the distinct feeling there is something going on that I can either understand or not understand. There's a choice to be made.

"I don't understand," I tell Mary.

We sit in the darkening living room, smoking and sipping our cups of whiskey. Inside my head I keep thinking, Uh-oh, over and over. I'm rattled; I can't calm down and figure this out.

"I think we should brace ourselves in case something bad has happened," I say to Mary. She nods. "Just in case. It won't hurt to be braced." I realize that I don't know what "braced" means. You hear it all the time, but that doesn't mean it makes sense. Whiskey is supposed to be bracing, but what it is is awful. I want either tea or beer, no whiskey. Mary nods again and heads into the kitchen.

Within an hour there are seven women in the dim living room, sitting. Switching back and forth between CNN and the local news reports. There is something terrifying about the quality of the light and the way voices are echoing in the room. The phone never stops ringing, ever since the story hit the national news. Physics, University of Iowa, dead people. Names not yet released. Everyone I've ever known is checking in to see if I'm still alive. California calls, New York calls, Florida calls, Ohio calls twice. My husband is having a party and all his guests call, one after another, to ask how I'm doing. Each time, fifty times, I think it might be Chris and then it isn't.

It occurs to me once that I could call his house and talk to him directly, find out exactly what happened. Fear that his mother would answer prevents me from doing it. By this time I am getting reconciled to the fact that Linhua Shan, Gang Lu, and Dwight Nicholson were killed. Also an administrator and her office assistant. The Channel 9 newswoman keeps saying there are five dead and two in critical condition. The names will be released at nine o'clock. Eventually I sacrifice all of them except Chris and Bob; *they* are the ones in critical condition, which is certainly not hopeless. At some point I go into the study to get away from the terrible dimness in the living room — all those eyes, all that calmness in the face of chaos. The collie tries to stand up, but someone stops her with a handful of Fritos.

The study is small and cold after I shut the door, but more brightly lit than the living room. I can't remember what anything means. The phone rings and I pick up the extension and listen. My friend Michael is calling from Illinois for the second time. He asks Shirley if I'm holding up O.K. Shirley says it's hard to tell. I go back into the living room.

The newswoman breaks in at nine o'clock, and of course they drag it out as long as they can. I've already figured out that if they

go in alphabetical order Chris will come first: Goertz, Lu, Nicholson, Shan, Smith. His name will come on first. She drones on, dead
University of Iowa professors, lone gunman named Gang Lu.

Gang Lu. Lone gunman. Before I have a chance to absorb that,
she says, The dead are.

Chris's picture.

Oh no, oh God. I lean against Mary's chair and then leave the
room abruptly. I have to stand in the bathroom for a while and
look at myself in the mirror. I'm still Jo Ann, white face and dark
hair. I have earrings on, tiny wrenches that hang from wires. In
the living room she's pronouncing all the other names. The two
critically wounded are the administrator and her assistant, Miya
Rodolfo-Sioson. The administrator is already dead for all practical
purposes, although they won't disconnect the machines until the
following afternoon. The student receptionist will survive but will
never again be able to move much more than her head. She was
in Gang Lu's path and he shot her and the bullet lodged in the
top of her spine and she will never dance or walk or spend a day
alone. She got to keep her head but lost her body. The final victim
is Chris's mother, who will weather it all with a dignified face and
an erect spine, then return to Germany and kill herself without
further words or fanfare.

I tell the white face in the mirror that Gang Lu did this, wrecked
everything and murdered all those people. It seems as ludicrous
as everything else. I can't get my mind to work right. I'm still op-
erating on yesterday's facts; today hasn't jelled yet. "It's a good
thing none of this happened," I say to my face. A knock on the
door, and I open it.

Julene's hesitant face. "She wanted to come visit you," she tells
me. I bring the collie in and close the door. We sit by the tub. She
lifts her long nose to my face and I take her muzzle and we move
through the gears slowly — first second third fourth — all the way
through town, until what happened has happened and we know it
has happened. We return to the living room. The second wave of
calls is starting to come in, from people who just saw the faces on
the news. Shirley screens. A knock comes on the door. Julene
settles the dog down again on her blanket. It's the husband at the
door, looking distraught. He hugs me hard, but I'm made of
cement, arms stuck in a down position.

The women immediately clear out, taking their leave, looking at the floor. Suddenly it's only me and him, sitting in our living room on a Friday night, just like always. I realize it took courage for him to come to the house when he did, facing all those women who think he's the Antichrist. The dogs are crowded against him on the couch and he's wearing a shirt I've never seen before. He's here to help me get through this. Me. He knows how awful this must be. Awful. He knows how I felt about Chris. Past tense. I have to put my hands over my face for a minute.

We sit silently in our living room. He watches the mute television screen and I watch him. The planes and ridges of his face are more familiar to me than my own. I understand that he wishes even more than I do that he still loved me. When he looks over at me, it's with an expression I've seen before. It's the way he looks at the dog on the blanket.

I get his coat and follow him out into the cold November night. There are stars and stars and stars. The sky is full of dead men, drifting in the blackness like helium balloons. My mother floats past in a hospital gown, trailing tubes. I go back inside where the heat is.

The house is empty and dim, full of dogs and cigarette butts. The collie has peed again. The television is flickering "Special Report" across the screen and I turn it off before the pictures appear. I bring blankets up, fresh and warm from the dryer.

After all the commotion the living room feels cavernous and dead. A branch scrapes against the house, and for a brief instant I feel a surge of hope. They might have come back. And I stand at the foot of the stairs staring up into the darkness, listening for the sounds of their little squirrel feet. Silence. No matter how much you miss them. They never come back once they're gone.

I wake her up three times between midnight and dawn. She doesn't usually sleep this soundly, but all the chaos and company in the house tonight have made her more tired than usual. The Lab wakes and drowsily begins licking her lower region. She stops and stares at me, trying to make out my face in the dark, then gives up and sleeps. The brown dog is flat on her back with her paws limp, wedged between me and the back of the couch.

I've propped myself so I'll be able to see when dawn starts to arrive. For now there are still planets and stars. Above the black branches of a maple is the Dog Star, Sirius, my personal favorite. The dusty rings of Saturn. Io, Jupiter's moon.

When I think I can't bear it for one more minute I reach down and nudge her gently with my dog arm. She rises slowly, faltering, and stands over me in the darkness. My peer, my colleague. In a few hours the world will resume itself, but for now we're in a pocket of silence. We're in the plasmapause, a place of equilibrium, where the forces of the earth meet the forces of the sun. I imagine it as a place of stillness, where the particles of dust stop spinning and hang motionless in deep space.

Around my neck is the stone he brought me from Poland. I hold it out. *Like this?* I ask. Shards of fly wings, suspended in amber.

Exactly, he says.

ROY BLOUNT, JR.

First Tell Me What Kind of Reader You Are

FROM THE OXFORD AMERICAN

WHEN PEOPLE of the Northeast ask what I do, I long for one of those professions that would qualify me to respond as follows:

"Before I answer that question, I am ethically obliged to inform you that as soon as I do answer, our conversation will be billable at two hundred dollars per hour or portion thereof — and the answering of the question itself shall constitute such a portion, as will what I am telling you now, retroactively."

That would dispense with a lot of the idle conversation in which I find myself bogged down, in the Northeast.

"What do you do?" people ask.

I say, "I'm a writer."

And people of the Northeast don't respond the way you'd think people would. They don't say, "I knew a writer once. He could never sit still in a boat," or "Yeah, that's about all you *look* like being, too. What do you do, make it all up, or do the medias tell you what to say?" or "Uh-huh, well I breed ostriches." I could roll with any one of those responses. One reason there are so many Southern writers is that people of the South either tell a writer things he can use, or they disapprove of him enough to keep his loins girded, or they just nod and shake their heads and leave him to it. But people of the Northeast act like being a writer is *normal*.

"Oh," they say with a certain gracious almost twinkle in their eye, "what kind?"

What am I supposed to say to that? "Living"? "Recovering"?

They'll just respond, "Oh, should I have heard of some of your books?" I don't know how to answer that question. And I'm damned if I'm going to stand there and start naming off the titles. That's *personal!* Can you imagine Flannery O'Connor standing there munching brie on a rye crisp and saying, "Well, there's *The Violent Bear It Away* . . ."

People of the Northeast don't seem to think it *is* all that personal. They seem to think that you can find out about books by having a schmooze with the writer, in the same way they might think you can find out about whiskey by chatting up someone in personnel down at the distillery.

What I want to do, when somebody asks me what kind of writer I am, is sull up for several long seconds until I am blue in the face and then, from somewhere way further back and deeper down than the bottom of my throat, I want to vouchsafe this person an utterance such that the closest thing you could compare it to would be the screech of a freshly damned soul shot through with cricket song and, intermittently, all but drowned out by the crashing of surf. But I was brought up to be polite.

I was also brought up Methodist and went to graduate school, so I can't honestly say what I want to say: "Self-taught annunciatory. I received a vision out of this corner, of this eye, at about 7:45 P.M. on January 11, 1949, and since that moment in earthly time I have been an inspired revelational writer from the crown of my hat to the soles of my shoes. And do you want to know the nature of that vision?

"The nature of that vision was a footprint in the side of an edifice, and the heel of it was cloven and the toes of it was twelve. And how could a footprint be in the side of an edifice, you wonder? Especially since I stood alone at the time, stark naked and daubed with orange clay, in a stand of tulip poplar trees some eleven miles outside of Half Dog, Alabama, way off a great ways from the closest manmade structure in any literal subannunciatory sense. That footprint could be in the side of an edifice for one reason and one reason only: because —"

But then they'd just say, "Oh, a *Southern* writer. What *are* grits?"

I don't live in the South anymore. I maintain you can't live in the South and be a deep-dyed Southern writer. If you live in the South you are just writing about folks, so far as you can tell, and it just comes out Southern. For all we know, if you moved West, you'd be a Western writer. Whereas, if you live outside the South, you are being a Southern writer either (a) on purpose or (b) because you can't help it. Which comes to the same thing in the end: you are deep-dyed.

Whether or not anybody in the South thinks you are a Southern writer is not a problem. Englishmen think of Alistair Cooke as an American. Americans think of him as English. So he's in good shape, as I see it: nobody keeps track of whether he goes to church.

One thing to be said for being in the Northeast and you being Southern is that it provokes you to keep an edge on your Southernness. Sometimes I'll bring up obscure examples of anti-Southern prejudice — "You ever think about the fact that in the book, the good witch is the Witch of the South, but when they made the movie they changed her to the Witch of the North?"

Also I make a point of taking no interest whatsoever in what passes in the North for college sports. When I was a boy in Georgia, college sports was Bobby Dodd versus Bear Bryant immemorial. Compared with that, the Harvard-Yale game is a panel discussion. When all the college sports you can follow in the local media are Nehi or Lehigh, or whatever, against Hofstra or Colgate, or somebody, why bother? You know what they call the teams at Williams College? The Ephs. Let me repeat that: the Ephs. Pronounced eefs. Do you think that anybody who is willing to be called an Eef is capable of playing any sport at a level anywhere near root-hog-or-die? Caring about college sports in the Northeast is like caring about French food in South Carolina.

A good thing about being Southern is that it often involves getting to a point where you don't know what to think. People of the Northeast act like they have never been to that point before. Certainly they think they know what to think about Southern things. Whenever such people try to prove they are down with Southern culture by professing love for, say, Garth Brooks, I look at them with a particular expression on my face and ask whether they haven't heard of the real cutting-edge genre, Faded Country — songs like "I Guess Fishin' Is Sufficient, But I'd Like a Little Love" and "I'm So Lonesome I Could Go Out and Ride Around on I-285." Or if people start telling me how deeply they respond to B.B. King, I'll say "You know they've isolated the blues gene."

I let that sink in and then I add, "Now. *What do we do with that knowledge?*"

I bring up awkward racial questions whenever possible. For some years now, drastically bad race relations have been cropping up mostly outside the South, and I want to see some Northern white people sweat. I don't accuse them of being racist, because they know they aren't *that kind of person.* What I will do is say that anybody who claims to be "colorblind" or not to have "a racist bone" in his or her body is at best *pre*-racist and has a longer way to go than the rest of us. I also spoil scintillating dinner parties by bringing up the O.J. verdict. A lot of enlightened-feeling Northern white people, who have never even suspected themselves of what we might call ethnocentric assumptions, are completely unselfconscious about blaming the whole thing on the jury.

The reason O.J. got off, people of the Northeast feel fine about asserting, is that the jury was (a) too black to have any sympathy for the victims and (b) too dumb to get out of serving on the jury.

My response to (a) is to wonder aloud whether, if we stay humble long enough, *Southern* white people will ever be qualified to get away with bald-faced color-coded mind reading. My response to (b) is that it sounds to me like the sort of assumption that enabled noncombatants to feel cozy about blaming Vietnam on American draftees.

I won't hear a word against the O.J. jury until I hear several thousand words against the L.A. cops and the prosecutors. I point to all manner of bungling on the part of these professionals, and I observe that the DNA doesn't prove anything if the specimens were planted.

"Oh," people of the Northeast say, as if they've got me now. "Was the investigation-prosecution a conspiracy, or was it incompetent? You can't have it both ways."

"The hell I can't," I counter. "Y'all never heard of an incompetent conspiracy?"

"But O.J. did it!" they say.

"Most likely. Chances are, so did some of the people who — as has not been forgotten down where *I* come from — used to get lynched."

And whatever else you think about Johnnie Cochran, whether his client was the devil or not, the son of a bitch can *preach!* Alive in his words — without *needing* impeccable high ground. I will presume to put myself in the mind of a given black juror to this extent: I believe if I were such a juror listening to Johnnie Cochran represent a black defendant, I'd be thinking, "Let's remake *To Kill a Mockingbird* with this brother here as Atticus Finch!"

I don't throw lynching at people of the Northeast lightly, but I do freely say *y'all.* The language needs a second-person plural, and *y'all* is manifestly more precise, more mannerly and friendlier than *you people* or *y'uns.* When Northerners tell me they have heard Southerners use *y'all* in the singular, I tell them *they* lack structural linguistic understanding. And when they ask me to explain grits, I look at them like an Irishman who's been asked to explain potatoes.

All too often in the Northeast, *writers themselves* seem to regard being a writer as normal. When people ask a Northeastern writer what kind he or she is, instead of expostulating, "What do you mean what *kind?* Getting-by-the-best-I-can kind! Trying-to-make-some-kind-of-semi-intelligible-sense-out-of-the-god-damn-cosmos kind! If you're interested, see if you can't find a way to read something I wrote. If I knew it by heart, I would recite the scene in *Marry and Burn* where the fire ants drive the one-legged boy insane (which I'll admit I think almost comes up to what it might have been, but it's not *simple* enough, there are too many *of*s in it, I couldn't get enough *of*s out of it to save my life!); but I don't carry it around in my head — I was trying to get it out of my head; and even if I did, reciting it wouldn't do it justice! You have to read it" — a Northeastern writer will natter away about being post-structuralist or something. And everybody's happy. Writers fitting into the social scheme of things — it don't seem right to me.

Grits is normal.

BERNARD COOPER

Labyrinthine

FROM THE PARIS REVIEW

WHEN I DISCOVERED my first maze among the pages of a coloring book, I dutifully guided the mouse in the margins toward his wedge of cheese at the center. I dragged my crayon through narrow alleys and around corners, backing out of dead ends, trying this direction instead of that. Often I had to stop and rethink my strategy, squinting until some unobstructed path became clear and I could start to move the crayon again.

I kept my sights on the small chamber in the middle of the page and knew that being lost would not be in vain; wrong turns only improved my chances, showed me that one true path toward my reward. Even when trapped in the hallways of the maze, I felt an embracing safety, as if I'd been zipped in a sleeping bag.

Reaching the cheese had about it a triumph and finality I'd never experienced after coloring a picture or connecting the dots. If only I'd known a word like "inevitable," since that's how it felt to finally slip into the innermost room. I gripped the crayon, savored the place.

The lines on the next maze in the coloring book curved and rippled like waves on water. The object of this maze was to lead a hungry dog to his bone. Mouse to cheese, dog to bone — the premise quickly ceased to matter. It was the tricky, halting travel I was after, forging a passage, finding my way.

Later that day, as I walked through our living room, a maze revealed itself to me in the mahogany coffee table. I sat on the floor, fingered the wood grain, and found a winding avenue through it. The fabric of my parents' blanket was a pattern of climbing ivy and, from one end of the bed to the other, I traced the air between the tendrils. Soon I didn't need to use a finger, mapping my path by sight. I moved through the veins of the marble heart, through the space between the paisleys on my mother's blouse. At the age of seven I changed forever, like the faithful who see Christ on the side of a barn or peering up from a corn tortilla. Everywhere I looked, a labyrinth meandered.

Soon the mazes in the coloring books, in the comic-strip section of the Sunday paper, or on the placemats of coffee shops that served "children's meals" became too easy. And so I began to make my own. I drew them on the cardboard rectangles that my father's dress shirts were folded around when they came back from the cleaner's. My frugal mother, hoarder of jelly jars and rubber bands, had saved a stack of them. She was happy to put the cardboard to use, if a bit mystified by my new obsession.

The best method was to start from the center and work outward with a sharpened pencil, creating layers of complication. I left a few gaps in every line, and after I'd gotten a feel for the architecture of the whole, I'd close off openings, reinforce walls, a slave sealing the pharaoh's tomb. My blind alleys were especially treacherous; I constructed them so that, by the time one realized he'd gotten stuck, turning back would be an exquisite ordeal.

My hobby required a twofold concentration: carefully planning a maze while allowing myself the fresh pleasure of moving through it. Alone in my bedroom, sitting at my desk, I sometimes spent the better part of an afternoon on a single maze. I worked with the patience of a redwood growing rings. Drawing myself into corners, erasing a wall if all else failed, I fooled and baffled and freed myself.

Eventually I used shelf paper, tearing off larger and larger sheets to accommodate my burgeoning ambition. Once I brought a huge maze to my mother, who was drinking a cup of coffee in the kitchen. It wafted behind me like an ostentatious cape. I draped it over the table and challenged her to try it. She hadn't looked at it for more than a second before she refused. "You've got to be kidding," she said, blotting her lips with a paper napkin. "I'm lost enough as it is." When my father returned from work that night, he hefted his briefcase into the closet, his hat wet and drooping from the rain. "Later," he said (his code word for "never") when I waved the banner of my labyrinth before him.

It was inconceivable to me that someone wouldn't want to enter a maze, wouldn't lapse into the trance it required, wouldn't sacrifice the time to find a solution. But mazes had a strange effect on my parents: they took one look at those tangled paths and seemed to wilt.

I was a late child, a "big surprise" as my mother liked to say; by the time I'd turned seven, my parents were trying to cut a swath through the forest of middle age. Their mortgage ballooned. The plumbing rusted. Old friends grew sick or moved away. The creases in their skin deepened, so complex a network of lines, my mazes paled by comparison. Father's hair receded, Mother's grayed. "When you've lived as long as we have . . . ," they'd say, which meant no surprises loomed in their future; it was repetition from here on out. The endless succession of burdens and concerns was enough to make anyone forgetful. Eggs were boiled until they turned brown, sprinklers left on till the lawn grew soggy, keys and glasses and watches misplaced. When I asked my parents about their past, they cocked their heads, stared into the distance, and often couldn't recall the details.

Thirty years later, I understand my parents' refusal. Why would anyone choose to get mired in a maze when the days encase us, loopy and confusing? Remembered events merge together or fade away. Places and dates grow dubious, a jumble of guesswork and speculation. *What's-his-name* and *thingamajig* replace the bright particular. Recollecting the past becomes as unreliable as forecasting the future; you consult yourself with a certain trepidation and take your answer with a grain of salt. The friends you turn to for confirmation are just as muddled; they furrow their brows and look at you blankly. Of course, once in a while you find the tiny, pungent details poised on your tongue like caviar. But more often than not, you settle for sloppy approximations — "I was visiting Texas or Colorado, in 1971 or '72" — and the anecdote rambles on regardless. When the face of a friend from childhood suddenly comes back to me, it's sad to think that if a certain synapse hadn't fired just then, I may never have recalled that friend again. Sometimes I'm not sure if I've overheard a story in conversation, read it in a book, or if I'm the person to whom it happened; whose adventures, besides my own, are wedged in my memory? Then there are the things I've dreamed and mistaken as fact. When you've lived as long as I have, uncertainty is virtually indistinguishable from the truth, which as far as I know is never naked, but always wearing some disguise.

Mother, Father: I'm growing middle-aged, lost in the folds and bones of my body. It gets harder to remember the days when you were here. I suppose it was inevitable that, gazing down at this piece of paper, I'd feel your weary expressions on my face. What have things been like since you've been gone? Labyrinthine. The very sound of that word sums it up — as slippery as thought, as perplexing as the truth, as long and convoluted as a life.

LOUIS DE BERNIÈRES

Legends of the Fall

FROM HARPER'S MAGAZINE

How fearful
And dizzy 'tis to cast one's eyes so low!
The crows and choughs that wing the midway air
Show scarce so gross as beetles. Half way down
Hangs one that gathers samphire, dreadful trade!
Methinks he seems no bigger than his head.
The fishermen that walk upon the beach
Appear like mice, and yond tall anchoring bark
Diminish'd to her cock, her cock a buoy
Almost too small for sight. The murmuring surge,
That on th' unnumber'd idle pebble chafes,
Cannot be heard so high. I'll look no more,
Lest my brain turn, and the deficient sight
Topple down headlong.
— *King Lear,* act 4, scene 6

LAST SPRING, in my travels around my native land, I happened upon Beachy Head, a cliff white with chalk that provides a magnificent view of the sea, a maritime panorama complete with fishing boats and two lighthouses, one of which has red and white stripes and seems to have been designed with the sensibility of a talented Victorian child. This quintessentially scenic cliff is also the most famous suicide spot in England; for centuries, people have leapt to their deaths from Beachy Head.

Although Eastbourne is the town closest to the cliff, many prospective jumpers mistakenly travel to Dover, remembering the wartime song in which it was claimed that there would be "bluebirds over the white cliffs of Dover" and believing that Beachy

Head must be one of these. (This lyric remains a most persistent irritation to ornithologists everywhere, since we do not have, and have never had, bluebirds in Britain. We do, however, have white cliffs in Dover, and white cliffs all the way along the eastern half of our southern coast. This makes us visible from France even when France is not visible to us, which is perhaps why we find the French mysterious and they find us immodest.)

The strange and inexplicable thing is that Dover residents actually drive to Beachy Head rather than make use of their own cliffs. Indeed, people who might easily have launched themselves from the ramparts of Edinburgh Castle make a point of coming down from Scotland. One young woman drove all the way from Germany, caught a ferry that she had booked in advance, drove straight to the parking lot, and jumped off. In other words, the place has attracted a stygian form of tourism, and some local people even preferred Beachy Head to Seaford Head, which is a short way off and which is undoubtedly the one that I would use. The fall from Seaford Head is more vertical, and there is a splendid golf course behind it, upon which one could play one's final melancholy round before whacking the last ball out to sea and leaping in its wake.

Beachy Head and Seaford Head are part of a chain of cliffs consisting of an undulating row of hills that has been chopped in half by the sea. A narrow road leads up to the Sisters, and a small painted sign advises, BEWARE OF THE SHEEP. These ruminants are employed to mow the verges, being cheap, thorough, and nonunionized. When I first arrived at the top of Beachy Head, I encountered two old men who were morosely, but with perverse satisfaction, contemplating the decline of Western civilization in the form of the parking lot's vandalized ticket machine. Nearby, a crafts center was being built from the burned ruins of a pub that just a year before had been the place where jumpers stopped off for their final drink. Opposite stood a small building full of rescue equipment.

Looking inland from the cliff, one sees bosky valleys dotted with diminutive houses with red-tiled roofs; the traveling shadows of clouds are cast upon hillsides coated with the brightly vulgar yellow of rapeseed. Beachy Head is divided from the other cliffs by Cuckmere Haven, a famously beautiful valley containing an otherwise unassuming river that meanders in a most classical and text-book manner. In short, one sees England's green and pleasant land, and therefore Beachy Head has become a mecca for the same kind of tourists who venture out of New York to look at the autumn leaves in Vermont. The cliff is covered with people wearing short trousers, misshapen hats, woolly socks, and sensible boots.

Most days there is a haze on the sea, and this gives rise to the curious sensation of standing at the very edge of the world, as though one has arrived in the middle of an Arthurian legend or is being reminded of some inscrutable mystic truth. On a sunny day the sea is divided into a thousand parti-colored patches, from battleship gray to Ionian blue, and on a dull day it is green and surly. In winter the waves are so ferocious that they can hurl rocks over the seawalls of nearby towns. Meanwhile, up on the cliff, you can lean your whole weight against the salty wind in perfect security, if you can stand the blur of tears.

On the days of my visit the weather was sweet. There were patches of thrift on Seaford Head that smelled of chocolate, and on Beachy Head there were spikes of indigo loosestrife interspersed with dandelions, nettles, dock, whin, cow parsley, and sea kale. Everywhere there were cheerful marguerites, butterflies, and ladybugs amid the scrapes dug by the hundreds of rabbits that emerge at dawn and in the late evening. On the edge of one cliff there was a pathetic pile of pigeon feathers, as though the bird had become depressed and jumped off, leaving its apparel behind.

Several times I went up to the edge in order to look down, and in every instance I was overwhelmed by an unconquerable nausea. Once I took a young German girl named Mona with me. She sat with her legs dangling over the side and chatted merrily about the best way to commit suicide while I lay ten feet away, white-knuckled and ill on her behalf, imploring her to remember that these cliffs were always crumbling into the sea.

"It's all right," said Mona. "It's safe." I considered the case of a young woman who had disappeared down a 100-foot crevasse that opened up before her feet. In 1813 a vicar leapt across such a crevasse in the nick of time, and then watched as a 300-by-80-foot chunk disappeared into the sea. I was vastly relieved when Mona rather charmingly decided to come away from the edge and run about in imitation of a seagull.

So, despite Mona's assurances, it certainly is not safe, especially if you suffer from vertigo or an active imagination. Each time I approached the edge, I felt myself drawn over; the vertical became the horizontal, and a terrifying sickness took me at the stomach and throat. I have never felt this anywhere else, even when mountaineering or when I was a tree surgeon, and I wondered how many people might have been hypnotized into committing suicide unintentionally: this beautiful place openly invites you to die.

I decided that I would have to crawl if I wished to peer over the precipice, and even this set my head spinning. I then realized that there were bare patches in the grass where a multitude of others had stood and contemplated the abyss — surely some of them had survived. If they could manage it, perhaps I could, too, so I stretched out on my stomach and snaked my way to the edge. I took in as much of the view as I could before queasiness won out.

The cliff's wall, craggy with chalk, sparkled amid streaks of rust-colored ore. In places, patches of ill-advised greenery clung to the face while rock doves and fulmars made nests in crannies that did not seem spacious enough. On an outcrop halfway down the cliff lay the crushed wreckage of a small blue car, and all the way down — 550 feet, to be exact — the sea. A tiny lump of clay fell down the precipice, and my stomach seemed to follow suit.

As I inched my way back to safer ground, I couldn't help wondering what kind of damage a fall from that height might do to bones and flesh. My curiosity drove me to visit Michael Davey, Eastbourne's coroner, who deals with deaths that require explanation. Davey works in the police station, out of a small office that is disconcertingly entitled "The Aliens Clerk." Above his desk is a letter from somebody requesting the brains of the psychotic dead for research purposes. The coroner is a genial and good-humored man in early middle age who informed me that the Beachy Head corpses come covered with linear gashes filled with chalk.

It seems that long ago Davey gave up any elaborate theories about who jumps off Beachy Head and why. He told me that, in his opinion, people kill themselves because they are very unhappy, that about twelve people per annum do so on the Head, though it has been as many as twenty-eight. So far, it had been a good year, with very few deaths. No particular kind of person does it; the age range runs from sixteen to ninety. Davey used to think that it was mainly men, especially young ones who could not bear the pangs of dispriz'd love, but there are, in fact, very few teenagers. More prevalent are the menopausal women in their forties. The favorite places for self-destruction are by the two lighthouses. Notable suicides include a concert pianist and a peer of the realm.

Davey consulted his blue notebook, and I noticed that one of the entries was labeled "Accident." Apparently some idiot had been flying a kite that became snagged on the cliff face and had tried to climb down and retrieve it. Davey said that, strictly speaking, an accident would be something like being blown off by the wind, whereas fetching a kite qualifies as "misadventure." Some people fall over while drolly pretending that they are about to fall over. There was a woman who walked off unawares because she had the sun in her eyes. Particular danger attends model-airplane enthusiasts, hang-glider pilots, sheep, and unsuspecting dogs chasing seagulls and rubber balls.

Foolishly, I asked Davey all sorts of questions to which no one could possibly know the answers, such as: How many people arrive and then don't do it? I told him that people up there watch one another suspiciously, all asking themselves the same vital question. I told him that I had observed a young woman park her car, walk to the edge carrying a yellow plastic bag, and then walk straight back to her car. I wanted to ask him whether anyone makes the leap in the belief that he or she can fly.

Davey told me that the dead can't explain themselves — you can't interview them about whether they had thought they could fly. He believes that the one solid reason for jumping is that it is irrevocable, unlike an overdose. You cannot change your mind once committed, and therefore it is clear that this method of suicide is for those who genuinely long for the final peace.

The fall takes approximately six seconds. Sometimes people scream all the way down, and once or twice a falling body has nearly struck someone walking below. There was a particularly tragic case of a teenage girl who slipped while picking up a fossil. Her companion tried to save her but also fell. The girl who had slipped was saved because she landed on the body of her would-be rescuer, who was killed.

Yes, some of the victims have a history of mental illness. No, it has not become any worse since the government changed the system of health care for the mentally ill. Davey used to think that spring was the worst time of year, but now it seems to have evened out. Suicides occur in batches, possibly because potential jumpers read reports in the papers about the most recent casualty. A quarter of them visit Beachy Head in advance of their attempt in order to reconnoiter.

Is it ever a performance? Well, there was a young man who drove over on a motorcycle shouting "Geronimo!" as he went. (Here I grieve momentarily for the motorcycle. I like motorcycles. What a waste.) Others dive off with a mighty yell. But then you get the people who ease themselves over in absolute privacy. One man simply handed his driver's license to a passerby and then ran off. One woman very politely asked a passing coastguardsman if he would mind giving her a push. I suggested that some people might be stoned, but Davey shrugged noncommittally. He is opposed to generalizations and statistical extrapolations, but he admitted that alcohol is involved in about 10 percent of cases.

He informed me that the people who retrieve the bodies are all volunteers with the coast guard and was dismissive of the idea that it might be a traumatic experience. You get hardened to it, he said. How else do you think people survived the war? You recover, and all this stuff about post-traumatic stress and needing counseling is just rubbish. He belongs to the "Pull yourself together and get on with it" school of psychiatry, as do my mother and myself.

Most interestingly, Davey believes that the Beachy Headers do not commit suicide "while the balance of the mind is disturbed" but that it is a rational decision often carefully planned. People sometimes leave a bag containing their name and address, instructions as to whom to contact, how to dispose of their remains, and the whereabouts of their wills. One person asked that his body be recovered before the rats found it. Some leave two, three, even five suicide notes. They buy one-way tickets and arrange no accommodations. I told him that one of my grandfathers blew his own brains out because he could not bear the pain of his war wounds and believed that he had cancer, and that I had always thought this entirely sane and reasonable. Davey nodded in agreement and suddenly remembered a local doctor who is an expert on the Beachy Head deaths. He rifled through his cupboard and presented me with a sheaf of papers, authored by a certain Dr. S. J. Surtees.

Dr. Surtees is clearly a connoisseur. He related that in the seventh century, Saint Wilfrid found that the local savages were jumping off the cliff in despair after a three-year drought and that today some people practice hoaxes by leaving piles of clothing at the edge or driving a car to the brink and then reversing it back along its own tracks.

According to Dr. Surtees, jumpers constitute an elite 3 percent of all British suicides. It is mainly men between fifteen and forty-four who jump, and women between thirty-five and sixty. There have been two Beachy Head suicides who came all the way from New York. Sometimes a child comes to die in the same place as a parent. More people jump on Friday than on any other day of the week. Once a man looking for his model airplane found the skeleton of a woman who had been missing for five months. Another went over in a Volkswagen Beetle, which, incredibly, survived without a scratch. It had its wheels stolen before it could be salvaged, however. One anomalous woman inexplicably identified as her husband the body of a Russian sailor who had clearly been buried at sea, even though the sailor was the wrong age and size.

Not everyone dies outright. There have been deaths from inhalation of vomit, diabetic coma, and exposure. This can happen if people are caught on ledges or by vegetation. A woman of seventy-two managed to survive on a ledge, and just before I met Dr. Surtees a fifteen-year-old boy quarreled with the father of his fourteen-year-old girlfriend and endured three days on the cliff with multiple leg fractures, sucking on pebbles to keep his mouth moist.

When I returned to the cliffs, I found myself drawn not to the view but rather to the various messages scattered about, a kind of semiotic extravaganza. DANGER, CLIFF EROSION, we are repeatedly advised. There are numerous memorial benches carved with the names of the dead. Perhaps some of them died here, while others merely loved it. On a stray slab of concrete left over from the war, I read, "Mark loves Mandy," "Nat loves Dan," "Kate and Sharon," "Nadia Beachy Head," "Matthew from Twickenham woz 'ere," and "I love my mum." There is a very poignant war memorial commemorating the ROC, the RAF, the WAAF, and the immortal heroism of the young Canadians who perished in the inept Dieppe raid in 1942. One monument was erected to commemorate the International Year of Peace in 1986. I certainly do not remember much international peace that year. To me the stone was a reminder that the world contains some naive or gormless simpletons with no grasp of reality and with somebody else's money to spend. To be informed that there was once an International Year of Peace that didn't happen is pretty depressing, even if you had no intention of jumping. They should announce an International Year of Barbarism one of these days, and then none of us would be disappointed.

Next to the rescue building is a telephone box provided with the telephone number of the Samaritans, who quixotically wish to persuade us to love the world and to live longer despite the fact that one day we will all be dead. A Christian organization has placed a stone that quotes Psalm 93: "Mightier than the thunders of many waters, mightier than the waves of the sea, the Lord on high is mighty." As though conscious that this is not as effective and complete a message as they had initially hoped, and that it might not even be quite what they really meant, they added a nonscriptural postscript: "God is always greater than all of our troubles."

I had to leave Beachy Head. Every human being has known times of the most abject and implacable despair, and it was impossible not to feel profoundly what was in the hearts of those sorrowing souls. Knowing and imagining, I found it hard to keep back the tears even though the place is lovely. Either their infinite pain is imprinted upon the atmosphere or one has the illusion that it is. All about are the wings and traces of broken hearts, canceled dreams, abandoned expectations. Here are the ghosts of those who loved others too much or themselves too little, of those who lost battles with insanity, of those driven to heartsickness by an oppressive sense of futility and the apparent absence of God, of those who defiantly and courageously denied a terminal illness its final tortures. Here also are the sad small ghosts of those whose existence nobody noticed until they became a mess to clear away.

If there is any encouragement to be salvaged from all this

tragedy, it might be teased from the tale of a woman who went to Beachy Head in order to make her quietus. She had never been a drinker, but she knocked back half a bottle of gin for the sake of Dutch courage. Not long afterward she was arrested and fined for being drunk and disorderly, having decided while under the influence that life was marvelous after all.

DEBRA DICKERSON

Who Shot Johnny?

FROM THE NEW REPUBLIC

GIVEN MY LEVEL of political awareness, it was inevitable that I would come to view the everyday events of my life through the prism of politics and the national discourse. I read *The Washington Post*, *The New Republic*, *The New Yorker*, *Harper's*, *The Atlantic Monthly*, *The Nation*, *National Review*, *Black Enterprise*, and *Essence* and wrote a weekly column for the Harvard Law School *Record* during my three years just ended there. I do this because I know that those of us who are not well-fed white guys in suits must not yield the debate to them, however well-intentioned or well-informed they may be. Accordingly, I am unrepentant and vocal about having gained admittance to Harvard through affirmative action; I am a feminist, stoic about my marriage chances as a well-educated, thirty-six-year-old black woman who won't pretend to need help taking care of herself. My strength flags, though, in the face of the latest role assigned to my family in the national drama. On July 27, 1995, my sixteen-year-old nephew was shot and paralyzed.

Talking with friends in front of his house, Johnny saw a car he thought he recognized. He waved boisterously — his trademark — throwing both arms in the air in a full-bodied, hip-hop Y. When he got no response, he and his friends sauntered down the walk to join a group loitering in front of an apartment building. The car followed. The driver got out, brandished a revolver, and fired into the air. Everyone scattered. Then he took aim and shot my running nephew in the back.

Johnny never lost consciousness. He lay in the road, trying to understand what had happened to him, why he couldn't get up.

Emotionlessly, he told the story again and again on demand, remaining apologetically firm against all demands to divulge the missing details that would make sense of the shooting but obviously cast him in a bad light. Being black, male, and shot, he must apparently be involved with gangs or drugs. Probably both. Witnesses corroborate his version of events.

Nearly six months have passed since that phone call in the night and my nightmarish headlong drive from Boston to Charlotte. After twenty hours behind the wheel, I arrived haggard enough to reduce my mother to fresh tears and to find my nephew reassuring well-wishers with an eerie sang-froid.

I take the day shift in his hospital room; his mother and grandmother, a clerk and cafeteria worker, respectively, alternate nights there on a cot. They don their uniforms the next day, gaunt after hours spent listening to Johnny moan in his sleep. How often must his subconscious replay those events and curse its host for saying hello without permission, for being carefree and young while a would-be murderer hefted the weight of his uselessness and failure like Jacob Marley's chains? How often must he watch himself lying stubbornly immobile on the pavement of his nightmares while the sound of running feet syncopate his attacker's taunts?

I spend these days beating him at gin rummy and Scrabble, holding a basin while he coughs up phlegm and crying in the corridor while he catheterizes himself. There are children here much worse off than he. I should be grateful. The doctors can't, or won't, say whether he'll walk again.

I am at once repulsed and fascinated by the bullet, which remains lodged in his spine (having done all the damage it can do, the doctors say). The wound is undramatic — small, neat, and perfectly centered — an impossibly pink pit surrounded by an otherwise undisturbed expanse of mahogany. Johnny has asked me several times to describe it but politely declines to look in the mirror I hold for him.

Here on the pediatric rehab ward, Johnny speaks little, never cries, never complains, works diligently to become independent. He does whatever he is told; if two hours remain until the next pain pill, he waits quietly. Eyes bloodshot, hands gripping the bed rails. During the week of his intravenous feeding, when he was tormented by the primal need to masticate, he never asked for

food. He just listened while we counted down the days for him
and planned his favorite meals. Now required to dress himself
unassisted, he does so without demur, rolling himself back and
forth valiantly on the bed and shivering afterward, exhausted. He
"ma'am"s and "sir"s everyone politely. Before his "accident," a simple request to take out the trash could provoke a firestorm of teenage attitude. We, the women who have raised him, have changed
as well; we've finally come to appreciate those boxer-baring, oversized pants we used to hate — it would be much more difficult to
fit properly sized pants over his diaper.

He spends a lot of time tethered to rap music still loud enough
to break my concentration as I read my many magazines. I hear
him try to soundlessly mouth the obligatory "mothafuckers" overlaying the funereal dirge of the music tracks. I do not normally
tolerate disrespectful music in my or my mother's presence, but if
it distracts him now . . .

"Johnny," I ask later, "do you still like gangster rap?" During the
long pause I hear him think loudly, I'm paralyzed, Auntie, not
stupid. "I mostly just listen to hip-hop," he says evasively into his
Sports Illustrated.

Miserable though it is, time passes quickly here. We always seem
to be jerking awake in our chairs just in time for the next pill, his
every-other-night bowel program, the doctor's rounds. Harvard
feels a galaxy away — the world revolves around Family Members
Living with Spinal Cord Injury class, Johnny's urine output, and
strategizing with my sister to find affordable, accessible housing.
There is always another long-distance uncle in need of an update,
another church member wanting to pray with us, or Johnny's little
brother in need of some attention.

We Dickerson women are so constant a presence the ward nurses
and cleaning staff call us by name and join us for cafeteria meals
and cigarette breaks. At Johnny's birthday pizza party, they crack
jokes and make fun of each other's husbands (there are no men
here). I pass slices around and try not to think, Seventeen with a
bullet.

Oddly, we feel little curiosity or specific anger toward the man
who shot him. We have to remind ourselves to check in with the
police. Even so, it feels pro forma, like sending in those $2 rebate

forms that come with new pantyhose: you know your request will fall into a deep, dark hole somewhere, but still, it's your duty to try. We push for an arrest because we owe it to Johnny and to ourselves as citizens. We don't think about it otherwise — our low expectations are too ingrained. A Harvard aunt notwithstanding, for people like Johnny, Marvin Gaye was right that only three things are sure: taxes, death, and trouble. At least it wasn't the second.

We rarely wonder about or discuss the brother who shot him because we already know everything about him. When the call came, my first thought was the same one I'd had when I'd heard about Rosa Parks's beating: a brother did it. A non-job-having, middle-of-the-day malt-liquor-drinking, crotch-clutching, loud-talking brother with many neglected children born of many forgotten women. He lives in his mother's basement with furniture rented at an astronomical interest rate, the exact amount of which he does not know. He has a car phone, an $80 monthly cable bill, and every possible phone feature but no savings. He steals Social Security numbers from unsuspecting relatives and assumes their identities to acquire large TV sets for which he will never pay. On the slim chance that he is brought to justice, he will have a colorful criminal history and no coherent explanation to offer for his act. His family will raucously defend him and cry cover-up. Some liberal lawyer just like me will help him plea-bargain his way to yet another short stay in a prison pesthouse that will serve only to add another layer to the brother's sociopathology and formless, mindless nihilism. We know him. We've known and feared him all our lives.

As a teenager, he called, "Hey, baby, gimme somma that boodie!" at us from car windows. Indignant at our lack of response, he followed up with, "Fuck you, then, 'ho!" He called me a "whiteboy-lovin' nigger bitch oreo" for being in the gifted program and loving it. At twenty-seven, he got my seventeen-year-old sister pregnant with Johnny and lost interest without ever informing her that he was married. He snatched my widowed mother's purse as she waited in predawn darkness for the bus to work and then broke into our house while she soldered on an assembly line. He chased all the small entrepreneurs from our neighborhood with his violent thievery and put bars on our windows. He kept us from sitting on our own front porch after dark and laid the foundation for our periodic bouts of self-hating anger and racial embarrassment. He made our neighborhood a ghetto. He is the poster fool behind the maddening community knowledge that there are still some black mothers who raise their daughters but merely love their sons. He and his cancerous carbon copies eclipse the vast majority of us who are not sociopaths and render us invisible. He is the Siamese twin who has died but cannot be separated from his living, vibrant sibling; which of us must attract more notice? We despise and disown this anomalous loser, but for many he *is* black America. We know him, we know that he is outside the fold, and we know that he will only get worse. What we didn't know is that, because of him, my little sister would one day be the latest hysterical black mother wailing over a fallen child on TV.

Alone, lying in the road bleeding and paralyzed but hideously conscious, Johnny had lain helpless as he watched his would-be murderer come to stand over him and offer this prophecy: "Betch'ou won't be doin' nomo' wavin', mothafucker."

Fuck you, asshole. He's fine from the waist up. You just can't do anything right, can you?

In the Face

FROM THE NEW YORKER

I'VE HIT A LOT of people in the face in my life. Too many, I'm certain. Where I grew up, in Mississippi and Arkansas, in the fifties, to be willing to hit another person in the face with your fist meant something. It meant you were — well, brave. It meant you were experienced, too. It also meant you were brash, winningly impulsive, considerate of but not intimidated by consequence, admittedly but not too admittedly theatrical, and probably dangerous. As a frank, willed act, hitting in the face was a move toward adulthood, the place we were all headed — a step in the right direction.

I have likewise been hit in the face by others, also quite a few times. Usually just before or just after the former experience. Being hit in the face *goes with* doing the hitting yourself; and, while much less to be wished for, it was also important. It signaled some of those same approved character values (along with rugged resilience), and one had to be willing to endure it.

I can't with accuracy say where this hitting impulse came from, although it wasn't, I'm sure, mere peer pressure. My grandfather was a boxer, and to be "quick with your fists" was always a good trait in his view. He referred to hitting someone as "biffing." "I biffed him," he would say, then nod and sometimes even smile, which meant it was good, or at least admirably mischievous. Once, in Memphis in 1956, at a college football game in Crump Stadium, he "biffed" a man right in front of me — some drunk he got tired of and who, as we were heading up the steep concrete steps toward an exit, had kicked his heel not once but twice. The biff he delivered that day was a short, heavy boxer's punch from the shoulder.

Technically a hook. There was only one blow, but the other guy, a man in a felt hat (it was autumn), took it on the chin and went over backward and right down the concrete steps into the midst of some other people. He was biffed. We just kept going.

There were other times my grandfather did that, too: once, right in the lobby of the hotel he ran — putting a man down on the carpet with two rather clubbing blows that seemed to me to originate in his legs. I don't remember what the man had done. Another time was at a hunting camp. A man we were riding with in a pickup truck somehow allowed a deer rifle to discharge *inside* the cab with us and blow a hole through the door — a very, very loud noise. The man was our host and was, naturally enough, drunk. But it scared us all nearly to death, and my grandfather, whose boxing name was Kid Richard, managed to biff this man by reaching over me and connecting right across the truck seat. It was ten o'clock at night. We were parked in a soybean field, hoping to see some deer. I never thought about it much afterward except to think that what he, my grandfather, did was unarguably the best response.

Later, when I was sixteen and my father had suddenly died, my grandfather escorted me to the YMCA — this was in Little Rock — and there, along with the boys training for the Golden Gloves, he worked out the solid mechanics of hitting for me: the need for bodily compactness, the proper tight fist, the confident step forward, the focus of the eyes, the virtue of the three-punch combination. And he taught me to "cut" a punch — the snapping, inward quarter-rotation of the fist, enacted at the precise moment of impact, and believed by him to magnify an otherwise hard jolt into a form of detonation. Following this, I tried out all I'd learned on the Golden Gloves boys, although with not very positive effects to myself. They were, after all, stringy, small-eyed, stingy-mouthed boys from rural Arkansas, with more to lose than I had — which is to say, they were tougher than I was. Still, in years to come, I tried to practice all I'd learned, always made the inward cut, took the step forward, always looked where I was hitting. These, I considered, were the crucial aspects of the science. Insider's knowledge. A part of who I was.

I of course remember the first occasion when I was hit in my own face — hit, that is, by someone who meant to hurt me, break my cheek or my nose (which happened), knock my teeth out, ruin my vision, cut me, deliver me to unconsciousness: kill me, at least figuratively. Ronnie Post was my opponent's name. It was 1959. We were fifteen and had experienced a disagreement over some trivial school business. (We later seemed to like each other.) But he and his friend, a smirky boy named Johnny Petit, found me after class one day and set on me with a torrent of blows. Others were present, too, and I did some wild, inexpert swinging myself — nothing like what I would later learn. None of it lasted very long or did terrible damage. There was no spectacle. No one "boxed." But I got hit a lot, and I remember the feeling of the very first punch, which I saw coming yet could not avoid. The sensation was like a sound more than a shock you'd feel — two big cymbals being clanged right behind my head, followed almost immediately by cold traveling from my neck down into my toes. It didn't particularly hurt or knock me down. (It's not so easy to knock a person down.) And it didn't scare me. I may even have bragged about it later. But when I think about it now, after thirty-seven years, I can hear that cymbals sound and I go light-headed and cold again, as if the air all around me had suddenly gotten rarer.

Over the years since then, there have been other occasions for this sort of blunt but pointed response to the world's contingent signals — all occasions I think now to be regrettable. I once hit my best friend at the time flush in the cheek in between downs in a football game where we were playing shirts and skins. We were never friends after that. I once hit a fraternity brother a cheap shot in the nose, because he'd humiliated me in public, plus I simply didn't like him. At a dinner after a friend's funeral (of all places) I punched one of the other mourners, who, due to his excessive style of mourning, was making life and grief worse for everybody, and "needed" it, or so I felt. And many, many years ago, on a Saturday afternoon in the middle of May, on a public street in Jackson, Mississippi, I bent over and kissed another boy's bare butt for the express purpose of keeping him from hitting me. (There is very little to learn from all this, I'm afraid, other than where glory does not reside.)

I can hardly speak for the larger culture, but it's been true all my life that when I've been faced with what seemed to me to be an absolutely unfair, undeserved, and insoluble dilemma, I have

thought about hitting it or its human emissary in the face. I've felt
this about authors of unfair book reviews. I've felt it about other
story writers whom I considered perfidious and due for some
suffering. I've felt it about my wife on a couple of occasions. I once
took a reckless swing at my own father, a punch that missed but
brought on very bad consequences for me. I even felt it about my
neighbor across the street, who, in the heat of an argument over
nothing less than a barking dog, hit me in the face very hard,
provoking me (or so I judged it) to hit him until he was down on
the sidewalk and helpless. I was forty-eight years old when that
happened — an adult in every way.

Today, by vow, I don't do that kind of thing anymore, and pray
no one does it to me. But hitting in the face is still an act the
possibility of which I *retain* as an idea — one of those unerasable
personal facts we carry around in deep memory and inventory
almost every day, and that represent the seemingly realest, least
unequivocal realities we can claim access to. These facts are entries
in our bottom line, which for each of us is always composed of
plenty we're not happy about. Oddly enough, I don't think about
hitting much when I attend an actual boxing match, where plenty
of hitting happens. Boxing *seems* to be about so much more than
hitting — about not getting hit, about certain attempts at grace,
even about compassion or pathos or dignity. Though hitting in the
face may be *all* boxing's about — that and money — and its devo-
tees have simply fashioned suave mechanisms of language to de-
fend against its painful redundancy. This is conceivably why A. J.
Liebling wrote less about boxing than about boxers, and why he
called it a science, not an art: because hitting in the face is finally
not particularly interesting, inasmuch as it lacks even the smallest
grain of optimism.

Part of my bottom line is that to myself I'm a man — fairly, un-
fairly, uninterestingly, stupidly — who could be willing to hit you
in the face. And there are still moments when I think this or that
— some enmity, some affront, some inequity or malfeasance — will
conclude in blows. Possibly I am all unwholesome violence inside,
and what I need is therapy or to start life over again on a better
tack. Or possibly there's just a meanness in the world and, as
Auden wrote, "we are not any of us very nice." But that thought
— hitting — thrilling and awful at the same time, is still one crude

but important calibration for what's serious to me, and a guide, albeit extreme, to how I *could* confront the serious if I had to. In this way, I suppose it is a part of my inner dramaturgy, and relatable, as interior dramas and many perversions are, to a sense of justice. And in the end it seems simply better and more generally informative that I know at least this much about myself — and learn caution from it, forbearance, empathy — rather than know nothing about it at all.

FRANK GANNON

Rat Patrol: A Saga

FROM HARPER'S MAGAZINE

AS A YOUNG MAN, I liked nothing better than playing a game called Rat Patrol. It had nothing to do with rats and little to do with patrols. What it did involve was this: when I was in eighth grade, around 1966, there was on ABC an unpopular program called *The Rat Patrol*. It was canceled very quickly, and I never spent even a single minute actually watching the show. Neither did any of my fellow Rat Patrol players. What we did see (it would have been difficult to miss) was the thirty-second commercial for the show. This commercial ran virtually all day, at perhaps twenty-minute intervals. I sat in front of the television that my dad had gotten cheap because the little square that showed the channel was on sideways, and I watched this commercial, it seemed, all summer. It was always the same. This is how it went.

A deep "announcer" voice:

THEY PLAYED BY THEIR OWN RULES.

(Shot of jeeps driving very fast through the desert, making hairpin turns, throwing sand all over the camera.)

WHAT OTHER MEN CALLED
THE WASTELAND, THEY
CALLED HOME.

(Shot of some grimy-faced guys with bandannas around their necks. They are driving their jeeps very fast and making very abrupt turns that throw sand into the camera.)

THIS FALL.
THE RAT PATROL.

(Shot of a really big explosion with a giant wave of sand going all over everything.)

I watched it approximately five hundred times. I was not alone. My associates, Andy and Paul, also watched, often in my presence. Although very little was said, I am quite sure that we were all forming the same word in our eighth-grade minds. That word was "cool."

Here is how the game is played.

Near my home there is a big sloping hill. Because of some construction work done decades ago, one whole side of the hill is composed of sand. Regular beach-type sand. The hill inclines at about a forty-degree angle. So there you have it. Maybe three hundred yards of nothing but sand.

This is the official playing field.

Next, you need the equipment. You need at least one full can of lighter fluid or barbecue starter. That's easy to come by. The rest of the equipment gets a bit trickier. You need a whole bunch of aerosol cans. You need to keep your eyes open and your Rat Patrol ears cocked, particularly around the women. The big sisters and the moms are an excellent source of aerosol devices. Hair spray is the most obvious choice, but you have many others. This was, of course, the days before Sting and Greenpeace, and everybody whacked away at the ozone level on a regular basis. Deodorants. Room fresheners. Furniture polish. Nonstick cooking spray. Bug repellent.

Dads also contributed to the Rat Patrol cause. They all had those cans that they kept in the trunk of the car, canisters that were supposed to come in handy if you had a flat tire. Compressed-air devices. In the weeks of preparation for Rat Patrol, cans disappeared from Dodges and Chevys and Ramblers all over the neighborhood. After a while, we often didn't even know what we were stealing. If it had those magic words WARNING: CONTENTS UNDER PRESSURE, that was good enough for us.

The International Rules of Rat Patrol

1. You must dig a very large hole in the sand. You have to take maybe a half ton of sand out of there. If in doubt, make the hole larger. The hole can't be too big.

2. Throw all of the WARNING: CONTENTS UNDER PRESSURE canisters into the hole. As in the case of the hole, you cannot have too many cans. If you have a hundred cans, that's good. If you have, say, a googolplex cans, that's even better. An infinite number of cans would be infinitely good.

3. You must come up with some kind of fuse. The best kind is one that burns like a sparkler, with lots of little twinkly sparks as it goes along. This is best because (a) it burns slowly enough that you can get the hell out of there before zero hour, and (b) those twinkly sparks are aesthetically pleasing. If Rat Patrol isn't going to be beautiful, then why bother?

4. You have to empty a great deal of lighter fluid into the hole. Again, you can't have too much lighter fluid. Barbecue starter works just as well. A case or two of barbecue starter followed by a case or two of lighter fluid — that would maybe be the ideal formula for the platonically perfect Rat Patrol, the "Rat Patrolness" that exists in the realm of essences.

5. After the fuse has been lit, the lighter of the fuse must run away from the hole for a distance of approximately twenty-five yards. Then he, along with his fellow players, must scream loudly and dive face-down into the sand. All players should remain in said position until the explosion(s) is (are) over and there are no more flaming can fragments aloft.

6. This is optional, but the lighter of the fuse may choose to articulate some words rather than merely screaming. These are some, but not all, of the possibilities:

   A. HIT THE DECK!
   B. THAR SHE BLOWS!
   C. THEY GOT CHARLIE!
   D. EAT LEAD, COPPER!

I have not played Rat Patrol in almost thirty years. As an adult, I have found that big explosions are no longer very entertaining. I hate action movies. There is no way on earth that anyone could talk me into spending good money to watch Dennis Hopper or somebody blow stuff up.

The Fourth of July is definitely the most mediocre holiday as far as I'm concerned. Sitting outside at night while mosquitoes attack you, watching stuff explode in the sky, is just about as bad an idea for a holiday as they come. I prefer Labor Day or Columbus Day. You don't get any mail, but nothing blows up.

Last week, however, I realized that Rat Patrol is still with me. I was watching a movie on TV with my son. The movie was *The Secret Garden*. During a particularly touching moment, I looked over at my son. He appeared to be close to nausea. I asked him whether he liked the movie. He said no, very emphatically. I asked him what he didn't like.

"Heartfelt moments, Dad," he said.

"What *do* you like?" I asked.

He looked right at me.

"Explosions," he said. "That's what I like. Lots of explosions."

The next day, the boy's mother asks me to have a little talk with my son. He has been showing, she feels, an unhealthy interest in explosives, detonation, carnage, destruction, and other allegedly unhealthy aspects of life. My son is nine years old, and he has the same name — first and last — as I do.

I sit in a chair that makes me look as if I have that thing they call authority. It's a big purple chair with ugly stitching. A chair Goliath would have picked out at Haverty's if he had had the chance. Now we are ready to talk.

I clear my throat. Yes, I am the dad. My voice is deeper than his. My tone, when I begin, is somber yet vaguely intense. I tell him the most appalling stories about explosions that I can devise. After a moment I realize that if I make the stories *too* appalling, they will have the wrong effect. So I tell stories that are appalling but also a little boring. I mention grisly details, and occasionally I veer off into narrative. I tell him about the guy in the Ripley's "Believe It or Not" — the railroad worker. Just another honest workin' man putting in his time. Maybe looking to qualify for the retirement plan. About ten o'clock, though, maybe thinking about taking a break for some coffee or something, he pounds a steel railroad spike into the ground with a sledgehammer. He has done this all day every day for ten years or fifteen years. Every time, the same thing happens: the spike goes about four or five inches into the ground. Then it's time to hit it again. Do this for about five hours and it's time for lunch.

This time, though, it's not like that. This time he hits the spike, just like normal. It goes in about five inches, just like normal. Then something a little different happens. This time there's a massive, ear-shattering explosion. The spike flies back at his head at an almost unimaginable speed. It hits the side of the poor guy's chin with, of course, the flat end first. The spike, which is about two and a half inches thick, goes right through the guy's head. It leaves the mother of all exit wounds. A big, tomato-size exit wound, right on the side of his head. This poor man, making the post–Civil War equivalent of $4.25 an hour, has just had a thirty-five-pound spike driven straight through his post–Civil War head.

As I tell this, my voice gets quieter, more intense, more Clint Eastwood. I tell this as intensely as I can, trying with everything I have to convey the impression that things that explode are things that are bad. I think, with all due modesty, that I am doing this pretty well. I give myself at least a B-plus. I'm not Olivier, but I'm not Brad Pitt either.

Nevertheless, I detect in my son's eyes a need for further convincing.

I go to the big well. Vietnam. Northern Ireland. Bosnia. Hiroshima. Mangled bodies. Severed limbs. Missing eyeballs. Slow decapitations. Large pieces of metal flying through tender pieces of human flesh. Fragmentation bombs dropped near elephants. Tiny babies. Sobbing women. Everywhere anguished wails and unending human torment.

And why? Why?

I'll tell you why, my son. Because of those things that explode, that's why.

I hope I'm clear.

Then I realize I can add something very intense and personal and powerful to all this. I pull my hair back from my forehead and point to a long scar that intersects my left eyebrow.

"See this?" I ask.

He leans forward. "Yeah." I can see he's interested.

"Let me tell you how I got this." He sits down again. I begin.

"When I was in college, one night a bunch of guys and me, we got real bored. So we were looking around for something to do. One guy had a CO_2 capsule."

"What's that?"

"It's a little metal cylinder. CO_2 is carbon dioxide. They use it for scientific stuff. Anyway, he had this empty one. We decided — I forget whose idea this was — to stuff it full of match heads and make a bomb."

I look at my son's eyes. He's really interested now.

"We kept stuffing match heads in it. Finally, we couldn't fit any more in there. That's when we started pounding them in there."

I wince in recollection.

"We got a file and pliers and a hammer. We used the pliers to hold the CO_2 capsule while another guy pounded the match heads in. Finally, it got to be like a 'guts' thing. Like who had the nerve to keep pounding those things in. At the end, a guy named Bob Foundry was holding the capsule, and I pounded the last match head in."

"Then what happened?"

"It exploded. It exploded so loud I really couldn't hear it, just a crazy ringing. I looked over at myself in the mirror, and the whole left side of my face was covered in blood. They rushed me to the emergency room and gave me thirty-five stitches. The doctor said that if I was his son, he would have beaten the hell out of me. There were pieces of the capsule stuck an inch deep in the cinderblock walls of the dorm room. They never did get them out. They were still in the wall when we left at the end of the year. If the capsule had exploded a half inch lower, a fragment would have gone into my eye, and I'd either be blind or, more likely, dead, because the fragment would have just kept going until it entered my brain."

There's a pause. We both just sit there. I finally get up and get a glass of water. My mouth has gotten very dry.

About two hours later, my son starts asking me about CO_2 capsule bombs. He wants to make sure he's got the details right.

Northeast Direct

FROM THE THREEPENNY REVIEW

·

I'M ON BOARD Amtrak's number 175 to Penn Station. I've traveled by train a couple of times in the past year, but last time I discovered that each car had one electrical outlet. Besides lots of room, besides that comforting, rolling motion, it's what I think about now when I think about the train. My Powerbook has a weak battery, and I can plug in and type as long as I want.

The car is empty. Maybe three of us new passengers, two previously seated. So I do feel a little awkward taking the seat right behind this guy I saw hustling on several minutes before I did. He'd already reclined his aisle seat, thrown his day bag and warm coat on the one by the window. He was settled. I'm sure he was more than wondering why, with so many empty seats all around, I had to go and sit directly behind him. But I felt something too. Why did *he* have to pick a seat in a row in front of the electrical outlet? And if he grumbled when I bumped the back of his seat to get by, I grumbled because I had to squeeze past to get over to the window seat behind him.

I'm over it quickly because I've got my machine on and I'm working. And he seems to be into his world too. He's taken a daily planner out, and he's checking a few things. I see this because, his seat reclined, I'm given a wedge view of his face looking forward and to the side. I see his left eye and the profile of his nose when he turns toward his window. When the conductor comes by for our tickets, he asks if there's a phone, then gets up to use it. I get immersed and barely notice him return.

I pause, and my eyes float up. He's holding a thick new book.

I'm sort of looking it over with him. The way the cover feels, the way the chapters are set out. It seems like an attractively produced history book, and I bet he just bought it. He puts it down, then reaches over to the seat in front of me and brings up another.

The other book is the paperback of my novel! I *cannot* believe it! He stares at the cover for a moment, then he opens it. He's reading the acknowledgments page! When he's done he turns back to the title page for a moment, then puts the book down. He gets up and goes to a forward car, where the conductor said he'd find a phone.

How improbable is this? I mean, mine is definitely not a Danielle Steel, not a John Grisham. If it is this much shy of miraculous that I would be on a train with someone who had heard of my books at all, how much more miraculous that, because of an electrical outlet on a train, I'd be sitting inches from a person who just purchased the book and is opening it before my eyes? And look at it this way: of the possible combinations of seating arrangements in the train car, how many could give me this angle? And what if he hadn't put his seat back?

I know what you're thinking. That I should lean over and say, Hey man, you will *never* guess who's sitting behind you! No, that's not me. I don't want to do that. I won't. I want him to be my anonymous reader. How many opportunities does a writer have to learn a truthful reaction, really truthful, to his writing? How absorbed will he be? Will he smile at parts, groan at others? How about his facial expressions? Will his eyes light up or go dull?

As he's walking back, he's staring at me a little too strongly — but he can't know who I am. I'm feeling, naturally enough, self-conscious. He can't possibly know he's in the eyes of the author himself — to think it would be even *more* ridiculous than that it's true. It could be the bright yellow shirt I have on, which is a banner really, a United Farm Workers T-shirt celebrating Cesar Chavez. It reads *Cada trajabador es un organizador.* People are always looking at it, and I practically can't wear it because they do. But he's not paying attention to my shirt. It's that I'm the dude sitting behind him, typing into his ear, breathing on his neck while we're on this empty train, with so much room, so many seats, with so much possible spacing. I think he probably doesn't like me. He's probably got names for me.

He sits down. He's picked up the book! He's gone to page one and he's *reading!* Somehow I just can't believe it, and I'm typing frantically about him and this phenomenon. He's a big guy, six two. Wire glasses, blue, unplayful eyes. Grayish hair, indicating he's most likely not an undergrad, and beneath a Brown University cap, which, because he's wearing the cap, indicates he's probably not a professor. Grad student in English? Or he's into reading about the Southwest? Or maybe the cover has drawn him to the purchase. He's turned to page two! He's going! I have this huge smile as I'm typing. Bottom page two, and yes, his eyes shift to page three!

Suddenly he stops there. He gets up again. The phone is my bet. I'm taking the opportunity. I'm dying to know the name of the bookstore he's gone to, and I kind of arch upward, over the back of the seat in front of me, to see a glossy store bag when just as suddenly he's on his way back and he's eyeing me again. I squirm under the psychic weight of these circumstances, though now also from the guilty fact that I'm being so nosy. I pretend I am stretching, looking this way and that, rotating my neck — such uncomfortable seats, wouldn't you say?

He's reading the novel *again*. Page four, page five, page six! A woman walks by and he doesn't even glance up, isn't even curious about whether she is attractive or not. He's so engrossed! He's *totally* reading now. No, wait. He stops, eyes to the window where it's New England, beautifully composed and framed by this snowy winter. Those tall, boxy, two- and three-story board-and-batten houses painted colonial gray and colonial blue, two windows per floor, hip and gable roof, nubs of chimney poking up. Oh, no, he's putting the book down. Closes it, mixes it into his other belongings on the seat next to him. It's because he's moving. He must hear my manic typing and he feels crowded and so he's picking up his stuff and going up an aisle. What an astute, serious, intelligent reader I have to feel so cramped! My reader wants to read in silence, be alone with his book and the thoughts generated by it and his reaction to it and he doesn't like some dude behind him jamming up his reading time and space with this muttering keyboard sound — it just makes me *smile* thinking how keen my reader's psychic synapses are to be responding to what his conscious mind cannot know is occurring. It must be a raging psychic heat, a dizzying psychic pheromone. When he has settled comfortably into his new seat, he pulls the novel back up. He's reading again! Reading and reading! When that young woman passes through on her return, no, again, he does not look up. He's dedicated, fully concentrating. He's really reading, one page after another.

New England: white snow, silver water, leafless branches and limbs. Lumber and boat and junk yards. The bare behind of industry, its dirty underwear, so beautifully disguised by winter.

My reader has fallen asleep. We haven't been on the train an hour and my writing has made him succumb to a nap? Nah, I don't find it a bad thing. Not in the slightest. It's really a compliment. How many books do you fall asleep with? The conductor wakes him up, though. He's sorry but he found that daily planner on the seat behind him and wanted to make sure it belonged to him. But my reader goes right back to sleep. He's dead asleep now. A goner. I pass him on my way to buy myself a drink, and he's got his left thumb locked inside the book, his index finger caressing the spine, pinching. You see, my reader does not want to lose his place.

We both wake up at New Haven. Probably getting a little carried away. I thought he might get off here — walking the book into Yale. He reopens it. He's at the beginning of chapter two. He does read slowly. He's lazy? I say he's thoughtful, a careful, considerate reader, complementing precisely the manner in which I wrote the novel. It's not meant to be read quickly. He's absolutely correct to read it the way he does.

Forty-five minutes outside Penn Station, many passengers have boarded, cutting me off from my reader. He is still up there reading, but with the passage of time, and our physical distance blunted more by a clutter of other minds sitting between and around us, the shock and mystery have lessened in me. I have adjusted, accepted it. By now I am behaving as though it were ordinary that a stranger two aisles ahead is reading my work. As with every other miracle that happens in life, I am taking the event for granted already, letting it fade into the everyday of people filling trains, going home from work, going. He is reading the novel, and I am certain, by the steady force and duration of his commitment, that he fully intends to read unto the end. He and I both can look around, inside the car and out the window, and then we go back, him to the book, me to the computer keyboard, no longer writing about this.

So when the moment comes, ask what, how? Tap him on the shoulder, say excuse me, but you know I couldn't help but notice that book you're reading, and it's such an amazing coincidence, it *really* is *so* amazing how this can happen, but I was just talking with a friend about that very novel this morning — change that — I was talking to two friends, and one thought it was just great, while the other — change that — and one thought it was just great, and I wondered what you felt about it, and how did you hear of it anyway?

After the conductor announces Penn Station, we stand up and get our coats on, and, the train still swaying, move down the aisle and toward the door with our bags. I'm waiting right behind him. Can easily tap him on the shoulder. But nobody else is talking. No one, not a word. So I can't either, especially when I'd be making fake conversation. Train stops, door opens, people in front of him move forward, and a woman in an aisle steps in between me and him with her large, too-heavy-for-her suitcase. He's shot out quickly ahead of me now, up an escalator, several more people between us. When I reach the main floor of the station, get beneath the flapping electronic board that posts trains and times and departure tracks, I have caught up with him. He has stopped to get his bearings. Just as I am at his shoulder, he takes off in the same direction I'm going.

So we're walking briskly side by side in cold Penn Station. You know what? He doesn't want to talk. I am sure he has no desire to speak with me. Would definitely not want to have that conversation I'd planned. No time for me to fumble around and, maybe, eventually, tell him how I am the writer. This is New York City, no less. He's in a hurry. He'd grimace and shake his head, brush me off. He already thinks I am one of those irritating people you encounter on a trip, the one always at the edge of your sight, the one you can never seem to shake. And so as I begin a ride up the escalator toward the taxi lines, I watch him go straight ahead, both of us covered with anonymity like New England snow.

VERLYN KLINKENBORG

We Are Still Only Human

FROM THE NEW YORK TIMES MAGAZINE

I WAS RAISED to be polite, and I am polite, by default. I have learned to depend on my politeness and to hate it, because it so often feels like a hand clutching my windpipe. The politeness that afflicts me is not civility, which is an urbane quality compatible even with cynicism. To be polite in the manner of my Midwestern upbringing is to believe that humans should be judged not by their deeds but by their best intentions. And so I grew up believing in a polite past, the untainted progress of decent men and women tilling a ripe but virgin soil, building stainless, heroic cities. I was taught to imagine a polite future, too: a universal Iowa of the 1950s, but with more efficient appliances and extra longevity and even nicer people. There are worse imaginable futures, and they are all more probable.

For in reality this is a brutally impolite world where bad intentions frequently prevail, and nothing is going to change that, certainly not the passing of another hundred years. It is common to talk about the twentieth century as though it were an aberration in human history, unique in the suffering it has created. It is common to cite the Armenian massacres in the early century, the world wars, the Holocaust, to adduce Stalin's crimes and to name Bosnia and Rwanda as evidence of this century's peculiar offenses against humanity. But only the tools have changed. All of human history has been an offense, of one kind or another, against humanity. What's shocking about this century isn't the evil or the unusual efficiency of its most malevolent actors. It is the collaboration in indifference, the spiritual profiteering of the intentionless masses who are paving a road to hell with politeness.

Looking back over this century, you realize that humanity is capable of being governed but largely incapable of governing itself. Most visions of the future I have come across, utopian and dystopian alike, have tended to look like pure projections of will, of self-governance, not projections of drift. But any vision of the future that depends on the collective, interdependent self-governance of this species is essentially a delusion, for what most people contribute to their own governance is resignation. Humanity is the occasion of its own suffering. It suffers far more capably than it reasons. It endures more readily than it acts. It seems to abide without changing. The illusion of the future is that it will contain things no one has ever seen before instead of the very things we have chosen not to notice or remember. But the future will be erected from the same raw materials as the past, and whether that prospect depresses you or not depends on how you assess our native substance.

I sometimes wonder just whom the idea of the future is meant to placate — that imaginary time beyond our life span, beyond the life span of our proximate descendants. It is, I think, a luxury afforded mainly to those whose livelihoods seem pretty secure, who have a little leisure for daydreaming, though it may be a sop for the desperate, too. But the future is really the province of politicians, the men and women who speak so unrelentingly of "our children's children." Who are the children whose children are going to usher in the future? Are they the 30 percent of American children now living in poverty? What kind of future are they imagining? The beauty of making a political trope of our children's children is that it allows you to look beyond the impoverished generation on whom an insufferable present is being inflicted, to pretend that that generation — already undernourished and undereducated — will have no bearing on the shape of what's to come.

There will be no getting out of the twentieth century without carrying it with us. You will hear, as the new year in the new century in the new millennium approaches, an enormous sigh of relief and optimism, as though something shameful had been left behind and some deliverance or retribution were now at hand. The old canard — that he who forgets the past is condemned to repeat it — will be sent aloft again, almost flightless, as a caution against anyone who is a little too relieved at the onset of the twenty-first century.

It would be just as true to say that she who remembers the past is condemned to repeat it. It has become conventional to speak of memory as though it were an anodyne, to speak of the past as though its moral were apparent. But some of the most hideous acts of this century have been committed in the name of memory, and the past, as Orwell knew, is as pliable in its uses as the future. Without memory, a species is relegated to instinctive behavior. With memory, it sometimes seems, the human species has the limited advantage of contemplating its instincts at leisure without being able to do anything about them.

But I can hear my politeness welling up. It sounds like well-shod footsteps in the narthex of a Methodist church. Where is the good news, it wonders? Well, there are several varieties of good news, none of them transparently consoling. The atomic dust of which we are made is extremely ancient. We are kin to everything living on this planet. In the adaptation of our minds to the universe in which we live there is a kind of sublimity. There is beauty even in suffering.

Not consoling enough? Then try this. There is no mechanism that will somehow redeem or reform this species within the course of its secular history. Not divine grace, not the progress of science, not evolution, not even the arrival of aliens from a remote planetary system. But there is an opening, a life, allowed to each one of us, an interval of consciousness and action. What is possible is possible only within that clearing, not in some distant future. That clearing is the present, which rolls forward through the calendar, year by year, century by century. Its texture — the specificity and density of human experience — entirely outstrips the capacity to predict it.

NATALIE KUSZ

Ring Leader

FROM ALLURE

I WAS THIRTY YEARS OLD when I had my right nostril pierced, and back-home friends fell speechless at the news, lapsing into long telephone pauses of the sort that June Cleaver would employ if the Beave had ever called to report, "Mom, I'm married. His name's Eddie." Not that I resemble a Cleaver or have friends who wear pearls in the shower, but people who have known me the longest would say that for me to *draw* attention to my body rather than to work all out to *repel* it is at least as out of character as the Beave's abrupt urge for his-and-his golf ensembles. A nose ring, they might tell you, would be my last choice for a fashion accessory, way down on the list with a sag-enhancing specialty bra or a sign on my butt reading "Wide Load."

The fact is, I grew up ugly — no, worse than that, I grew up *unusual,* that unforgivable sin among youth. We lived in Alaska, where, despite what you might have heard about the Rugged Individualist, teenagers still adhere to the universal rules of conformity: if Popular Patty wears contact lenses, then you will by gum get contacts too, or else pocket those glasses and pray you can distinguish the girls' bathroom door from the boys'. The bad news was that I had only one eye, having lost the other in a dog attack at age seven; so although contacts, at half the two-eyed price, were easy to talk my parents into, I was still left with an eye patch and many facial scars, signs as gaudy as neon, telling everyone, "Here is a girl who is Not Like You." And Not Like Them, remember, was equivalent to Not from This Dimension, only half (maybe one third) as interesting.

The rest of my anatomy did nothing to help matters. I come from a long line of famine-surviving ancestors — on my father's side, Polish and Russian, on my mother's, everything from Irish to French Canadian — and thus I have an excellent, thrifty, Ebenezer Scrooge of a metabolism. I can ingest but a single calorie, and before quitting time at the Scrooge office, my system will have spent that calorie to replace an old blood cell, to secrete a vital hormone, to send a few chemicals around the old nervous system, and still have enough left over to deposit ten fat cells in my inner thigh — a nifty little investment for the future, in case the Irish potato famine ever recurs. These metabolic wonders are delightful if you are planning a move to central Africa, but for an American kid wiggling to Jane Fonda as if her life depended on it (which, in high school, it did), the luckiest people on earth seemed to be anorexics, those wispy and hollow-cheeked beings whose primary part in the locker room drama was to stand at the mirror and announce, "My God, I disgust myself, I am *so fat*." While the other girls recited their lines ("No, Samantha, don't talk like that, you're beautiful, you really *are!*"), I tried to pull on a gym shirt without removing any other shirt first, writhing inside the cloth like a cat trapped among the bedsheets.

Thus, if you add the oversized body to the disfigured face, and add again my family's low income and my secondhand wardrobe, you have a formula for pure, excruciating teenage angst. Hiding from public scrutiny became for me, as for many people like me, a way of life. I developed a bouncy sense of humor, the kind that makes people say, "That Natalie, she is always so *up*," and keeps them from probing for deep emotion. After teaching myself to sew, I made myself cheap versions of those Popular Patty clothes or at least the items (*never* halter tops, although this was the seventies) that a large girl could wear with any aplomb. And above all, I studied the other kids, their physical posture, their music, their methods of blow-dryer artistry, hoping one day to emerge from my body, invisible. I suppose I came as close to invisibility as my appearance would allow, for if you look at the yearbook photos from that time, you will find on my face the same "too cool to say 'cheese'" expression as on Popular Patty's eleven-man entourage.

But at age thirty, I found myself living in the (to me) incomprehensible politeness of America's Midwest, teaching at a small private college that I found suffocating, and anticipating the arrival of that all-affirming desire of college professors everywhere, that professional certification indicating you are now "one of the family": academic tenure. A first-time visitor to any college campus can easily differentiate between tenured and nontenured faculty by keeping in mind a learning institution's two main expectations: (1) that a young professor will spend her first several years on the job proving herself indispensable (sucking up), working to advance the interests of the college (sucking up), and making a name for herself in her field of study (sucking up); and (2) that a senior, tenured professor, having achieved indispensability, institutional usefulness, and fame will thereafter lend her widely recognized name to the school's public relations office, which will use that name to attract prospective new students and faculty, who will in turn be encouraged to call on senior professors for the purpose of asking deep, scholarly questions (sucking up). Thus, a visitor touring any random campus can quickly distinguish tenured faculty persons from nontenured ones simply by noting the habitual shape and amount of chapping of their lips.

I anticipated a future of senior-faculty meetings with academia's own version of Popular Patty — not a nubile, cheerleading fashion plate, but a somber and scholarly denture wearer who, under the legal terms of tenure, cannot be fired except for the most grievous unprofessional behavior, such as igniting plastique under the dean's new Lexus. When that official notice landed in my In box, my sucking-up days would be over. I would have arrived. I would be family.

I couldn't bear it. In addition to the fact that I possessed all my own teeth, I was unsuited to Become As One with the other tenured beings because I was by nature boisterous, a collector of Elvis memorabilia, and given to not washing my car — in short, I was and always would be from Alaska.

Even in my leisure hours, my roots made my life of that period disorienting. Having moved to the immaculate Midwest from the far-from-immaculate wilderness, I found myself incapable of understanding, say, the nature of cul-de-sacs, those little circles of pristine homes where all the children were named Chris, and where all the parents got to vote on whether the Johnsons (they were all Johnsons) could paint their house beige. I would go to potluck suppers where the dishes were foreign to me, and twelve people at my table would take a bite, savor it with closed eyes, and say, "Ah, Tater Tot casserole. Now *that* takes me back." It got to the point where I felt defensive all the time, professing my out-of-town-ness whenever I was mistaken for a local, someone who understood the conversational subtexts and genteel body language of a Min-nesotan. Moreover, I could never be sure what I myself said to these people with my subtextual language or my body. For all I knew, my posture during one of those impossible kaffeeklatsches proclaimed to everyone, "I am about to steal the silverware," or "I subscribe to the beliefs of Reverend Sun Myung Moon."

I grew depressed. Before long, I was feeling nostalgic for Alaskan eccentricities I had avoided even when I had lived there — un-shaven legs and armpits, for example, and automobiles held to-gether entirely by duct tape. I began decorating my office with absurd and nonprofessional items: velvet paintings, Mr. Potato Head, and a growing collection of snow globes from each of the fifty states. Students took to coming by to play with Legos, or to blow bubbles from those little circular wands, and a wish started to grow in my brain, a yearning for some way to transport the paraphernalia around with me, to carry it along as an indication that I was truly unconventional at heart.

So the week that I received tenure, when they could no longer fire me and when a sore nose would not get bumped during the course of any future sucking-up maneuver, I entered a little shop in the black-leather part of town and emerged within minutes with my right nostril duly pierced. The gesture was, for me, a celebra-tion, a visible statement that said, "Assume nothing. I might be a punk from Hennepin Avenue, or a belly dancer with brass knuck-les in my purse." Polite as was the society of that region, my col-leagues never referred to my nose, but I could see them looking and wondering a bit, which was exactly the thing I had wanted — a lingering question in the minds of the natives, the possibility of forces they had never fathomed.

After this, my comfort level changed some, and almost entirely for the better. I had warned my father, who lived with me those years, that I was thinking of piercing my nose. When I arrived home that day and the hole was through the side instead of the center — he had expected, I found out, a Maori-style bone beneath the nostrils — he looked at me, his color improved, and he asked if I wanted chicken for dinner. So that was all fine. At school, students got over their initial shock relatively quickly, having already seen the trailer-park ambience of my office, and they became less apt to question my judgment on their papers; I could hear them thinking, She looks like she must understand *something* about where I'm coming from. And my daughter — this is the best part of all — declared I was the hippest parent she knew, and decided it was O.K. to introduce me to her junior high friends; even Cool Chris — the Midwestern variety of Popular Patty — couldn't boast a body-pierced mom.

I have since moved away from Minnesota, and old friends (those of the aforementioned June Cleaver–type stunned silence) have begun to ask if I have decided to stop wearing a nose stud now that my initial reason for acquiring it has passed. And here, to me, is the interesting part: the answer, categorically, is no. Nonconformity, or something like it, may have been the initial reason behind shooting a new hole through my proboscis, but a whole set of side effects, a broad and unexpected brand of liberation, has provided me a reason for keeping it. Because the one-eyed fat girl who couldn't wear Popular Patty's clothes, much less aspire to steal her boyfriends, who was long accustomed to the grocery-store stares of adults and small children ("Mommy, what happened to that fat lady's face?"), who had learned over the years to hide whenever possible, slathering her facial scars with cover stick, is now — am I dreaming? — in charge. I have now, after all, deliberately chosen a "facial flaw," a remarkable aspect of appearance. Somehow now, the glances of strangers seem less invasive, nothing to incite me to nunhood; a long look is just that — a look — and what of it? I've invited it, I've made room for it, it is no longer inflicted upon me against my will.

Don't Get Comfortable

FROM HIGH PLAINS LITERARY REVIEW

THIS STORY is about a railroad detective named Charley Best. Best worked in the 1920s on the narrow-gauge lines between Pittsburgh and the lumber and mining hill towns of northwestern Pennsylvania. My father tells this story and said his father told it to him, having known Best or known others who knew him. Or maybe my grandfather rode those rails to work in the camps; I know he worked for the railroad, lighting kerosene lamps on the bridge over the Allegheny River and during winter breaking ice from cables that hoisted lanterns high above the girders.

My father tells that story too, how when he was five years old his father would take him out at night when he made his rounds on the bridge over the Allegheny in Mahoning, Pennsylvania. His father would climb over the side, hanging on to the slick catwalk while he broke cables free after an ice storm. The night would be filled with frigid gusts, and the wind was particularly strong that high above the river. On the swaying iron bridge my grandfather ordered my father to "take a holt" of the side railing. He was never frightened during these trips because his father was so strong, sure-footed, and careful. It must have been like watching an athlete, my grandfather climbing catlike over the rail, hitting the icebound cables with steady blows from the ball-peen. He was a compact man, and every movement, every swing of the hammer, seemed to come from the center of his body.

This was 1934, and my grandfather was lucky to have this bit of a job, this small paycheck, in the mountains of Pennsylvania where no farm made it, where the mines had begun to play out. So, though the job was dangerous and hard, he did it, and because I remember my grandfather as a meticulous man, I'm sure he did it well. Why he took my father along is less clear, though my grandmother may have asked him to get him out of her hair for a while, not realizing the danger, or perhaps my grandfather assumed his son would have to do the job someday. He'd been taught how to plant, to shoe horses, to make medicines, and to build outbuildings by his own father on the homestead farm. Perhaps my grandfather was teaching his son about the railroad.

Once, as my father tells it, a train crossed the bridge while they were on it. It was a bitterly cold, moonless night, and the lanterns seemed to light only the barest arc of the old iron bridge. My grandfather was hanging from a side rail, breaking ice and edging a cable through the pulley, when the headlamp of the train broke the darkness. He hollered to my father to hop over the side of the bridge and hold on, to "get a purchase and don't let go no matter what." Then, as the train caused the bridge to quake and sway, my father felt his father's arm around him and his own weight release from his arms as his father held them both by one arm, sixty feet above the icy Allegheny. "Imagine," my father says when he tells the story, "a five-year-old boy and I wasn't even scared," though I wonder if he says that in tribute to his naive courage or in acknowledgment of trusting his father so utterly that fear never occurred to him.

I don't know where my grandfather heard of Charley Best. The area was sparsely populated; it had been homesteaded in the mid-nineteenth century and remained wholly wilderness until the first oil well in the nation, the Drake Well, was drilled in Titusville. Those who worked in the lumber and mining camps, and later in oil fields and railroad yards, were all like Charley Best and my grandfather, raised on hardscrabble farms in the Allegheny Mountains, farms now part of the Allegheny National Forest, a mixed old growth–second growth wilderness replacing their hard-won clearings and plantings. They were coarse, often violent people for whom fighting was merely another kind of work. For Charley Best, his work became violence. Best had a fierce reputation, and my father, who used to see him at Walker's store in Mahoning, said he looked the part. The railroad detective bought cigars at Walker's, and even there he carried a sidearm, what my father thought was an enormous Colt. He was a big man, and my father also remembers his wide hat, the high leather boots with the pant cuffs tucked inside, and the huge chain stretched across his chest, Prince Albert style, upon which hung a nickel-plated railroad watch my father thought was as big as an alarm clock. Mostly, though, he remembers that handgun and a handlebar mustache Best had cultivated to curl around his wide face. My father poses as Best as he tells the story, striding the catwalks and tops of railcars, wind whipping his mustache back like flames. But it's the same picture he paints of his grandfather, Doc, one of the original homesteaders in Forest County. We have a photograph of him, published in a volume of local history, his reportedly immense size diminished by a team of oxen behind him, that same mustache flaring like horns.

My father heard a story about Doc at the funeral of one of his uncles, and in it his mustache and oxen are part of the scenery. Doc Leslie had taken cattle into Brookville, Pennsylvania, to sell. Later, while he was having a drink at the Sigel Hotel, one of the men from town said, "Aren't you scared traveling all the way back to Blue Jay Ridge with that much money on you, Doc?"

My father doesn't say what Doc said back — some grunt or mumble through his mustache — but later, on Blood Road in his oxcart, Doc was jumped by three men wearing bandannas, like the outlaws they had read about in dime novels.

It was only a joke. These were friends of Doc's, out only to put a scare in him, but when one of them said "Stick 'em up," Doc replied, "Stick 'em up, hell. There'll be feet up and shit flying," as he leaped from the cart, scattering the men with his bullwhip. When my father tells it, he pantomimes rolling up one sleeve to signify the fight, his eyes fierce and fixed. The story is frozen at that point: Doc poised for action, the flight of the men inevitable.

Part of Charley Best's story is arrested as well. Best patrolled the tops of railcars as they sped across the hills toward the coal fields. My father said those who hopped trains rode Charley's line only twice: the first time you were warned, and if you took Detective Best's warning with humility, you got where you wanted to go. But Best remembered, and the second time he caught you riding free, you were off.

"Off?" I once asked, interrupting my father for once as he told the story. His irritation was clear.

"Yeah, *off,*" he said, his arms poised in the act of grabbing some-one by the scruff of the neck and back of the trousers. I remem-bered a postcard drawn by Wobbly leader Joe Hill, a comic portrait of himself being booted from a train, and had less admiration for Best and more sympathy for the hoboes who just wanted a ride and ended up flying.

I could see them soaring, sprawling like skydivers over the empty air of the railroad cut, over the sixty-foot drop from the bridge in Mahoning. I've always been hesitant about heights — not actually frightened, only concerned and reluctant about climbing, a con-trollable vertigo. Not that I have suffered many spectacular falls. Once I fell off, or more accurately, ran off, the top of an extension ladder when a wasp landed on my nose. I simply turned around, stepped off the top of the ladder, and began to run, heading straight down to a gravel parking lot of the car dealership where I was working. I was pretty skinned up, landing on my forearms to protect my face from the gravel, and my coworker, a young biker named Rocky, said, "Man, did you crash 'n' burn!" Perhaps I got this timidity from my mother, who also shied from heights. I remember my father, mother, older sister, and myself climbing a fire tower in the Allegheny Mountains. My mother and I made it about halfway up when the open sides and the lack of a railing sent me back down. My father and sister made it to the top, and I watched from the ground as they laughed and climbed impossibly higher.

My sister trusted my wild and unpredictable father and would follow him, while my trust in him had limits. Probably he had learned not to fear heights from his father on that railroad bridge; he even took a job as a tree-topper for a lumber company and later as a lineman for the power company. When he was sixteen he got a job as a ground hand, or "ground squirrel," as they called the young boys who dragged limbs by the butt to the burn pile. He grew to love the work, part of the postwar rural electrification program, and when not piling brush he watched the men high in trees worrying off limbs with bow saws.

Finally he got his own climbing gear: long hooks like bayonets that strapped to his high-topped boots and a wide leather belt to wrap around tree trunks. He got so good he'd climb a tree, and eventually a utility pole, with only his hooks and hands on the trunk, using the belt only when he reached the top. He said he loved heights; on top of a tree on a mountain he said he could see all of Forest County, see deer move in herds and bears trailing cubs on the ridge miles away. Working for the power company, my father climbed poles on wide rights of way cut across the mountains, high power lines carrying thousands of volts from transformer substations to light lamps in a farmhouse on remote Blue Jay Ridge.

But he fell. Twice. The first time, he says, they were putting up new lines on poles in residential Brookville. Poles were originally treated with creosote to prevent decay, a dark, oil-based coating that smelled vaguely of kerosene and urine, now outlawed in favor of a pressure treatment with brine. These were old poles, put up at the turn of the century during the first wave of utility construction, and that morning my father climbed the first one. He says he had just hooked on his belt and was looking up at the late autumn sky, a mix of clouds and high blue. He thought, "Those clouds sure are moving fast," and then he realized it was he who was moving, not the clouds, as the pole was falling, breaking off at the rotten base. He tells how he managed to take off his belt and scamper to the other side, riding the pole to the ground as it bent, then snapped.

The other time he fell was more dangerous, and more miraculous. He was at the top of a forty-five-foot pole, and according to the newspaper article from the *Oil City Derrick* his belt snapped and he pitched backward. My father says that after he felt the belt give he reached for the crossarm. His fingertips barely reached the glass insulators on his right, but he was unable to grasp them or the wooden beam, and he fell. He flipped backward twice in the air, landed on his feet, bounced, and fell on his side. He stood up, apparently unhurt, but when he tried to unbuckle his tool harness he found the fingers on his left hand would not work; he had broken his wrist in two places. Later he would develop severe back problems and would suffer years of pain, caused I'm sure by that jarring fall, though he never seemed to connect the two.

He doesn't tell either of those stories often. You don't tell stories that could have ended so finally. I heard him once admit to waking up in the middle of the night, years later, a dream of fingertips grazing the crossarm tearing him into sweaty wakefulness. And these stories are among the few illustrating a point or a moral. My father would sometimes say, after telling one of these stories, that there's only one thing you need to know to do "high work": "Don't get comfortable." What he means goes beyond the commonplace "Keep your wits about you." It's the lesson I forgot when I ran off the top of that ladder — whenever doing anything high up, do it with the knowledge of where you are. I use this advice whenever I work on ladders or roofs — whenever I am moving about and stop thinking about being up high, I force myself to remember; I stop and say aloud, "Don't get comfortable."

Charley Best would not have told his own story either. Perhaps that's why others told the story for him. My father claims he grew mean and that his father did not like Best, not because he threw men off trains but because he shot a twelve-year-old boy in the back for stealing coal from the railyard at night. The boy, a homeless child the railroad workers called Hard Rock Pete, hung around the railyards, and the gandy dancers and switch operators often shared their lunches with him, casually adopting him. My grandfather said he was shy and weak, and they all assumed he slept in abandoned work shacks or boxcars in the yard. Best, my grandfather claimed, saw the boy at night, stooping over and pulling lumps of coal into a shirt hooped to make a sack. Best claimed at the investigation that he couldn't tell it was Hard Rock Pete — the boy was tall and wore bulky clothes that late fall evening, hiding his frail frame. When he stood up and lit a cigarette, Best saw him, and when the detective's menacing voice called out, the boy ran. That's when Charley Best shot him with the big Colt.

But that's not the story of Charley Best my father often tells; that's another story, or actually part of the longer version of the story, because it shows how mean Best got afterward, how what happened changed him. I remember once my father was telling the story at my grandmother Harnish's house, a gathering of men in his mother-in-law's parlor listening, among them Sam, her second husband, who in the last year had been forced to sit on the couch with an oxygen tank beside him, alternately reaching for the hose and mask to give him the oxygen black lung denied him and bending over, panting with effort, to spit tobacco juice into a plastic bucket.

My father began telling the story sitting down, but was standing by the time he began describing Best, the Harnish men listening

closely though they had heard the story before, while I sat watching the story being retold as I leaned forward in the straight-
backed chair moved into the room and parked near the television.
I had recently turned thirteen and was splitting my time between
the room where adult men sat, talking slowly, and the cousins
outside exploring the forty-acre farm I had already mapped over
the years of visits. Sam's son Warren had finally finished a long-
winded story that made my father edgy and restless, and how he
had managed to get to the story of Charley Best I'm not sure, but
the story was well under way.

Best had been assigned jurisdiction, lacking any other police,
over several mining camps in northwestern Pennsylvania, and was
sent to arrest a miner in Chickasaw, near the New York border,
who was accused of stealing. My father added that he probably only
had stolen coal from the railyard, as everyone did in the 1930s.
Warren interrupted briefly to tell how he and his brothers stole
coal from the Clarion yards, but my father skillfully steered the
conversation back to Best.

"Chickasaw was a rough mining camp, just up the river from
Mahoning, and Charley Best was sent there, where there was no
other law, to arrest that miner," he began again, and everyone
leaned comfortably back into the story, glad Warren had been
stopped. He explained how Best arrived in town, Colt revolver
displayed prominently, cigar under his ample mustache, and how
he walked over to the tavern, a slapped-up, long and low shed
affair, where he assumed he would find the thief. The men inside
sat on rough stools, and the ceiling of plank was held up with
twelve-inch rough-cut beams. "One of them eyes Best, and Best
figured that was him and that he'd have to slug it out with the
miner to take him." My father's eyes grew narrow and menacing.

I'd heard this story many times and knew the men in the room
had heard it too; they were sitting through the telling as though
it were a ritual, a stage in their conversation they always reached,
and passed. But then an unexpected reaction from Sam drew their
attention from my father, who was perched on his knees at the
end of the story. Sam did not speak much in those last years
because speech was breath, and each breath was bought with larger
portions of his strength. Yet there in the room filled with his sons
and the husbands of his daughters, he pushed out a hurried "Yes,"

and quickly drawing on the oxygen as the heads of the men turned to him, added, "I drove those miners to Chickasaw every day in an old buckboard — they were usually drunk. A rough, wild bunch," he said, spitting a brown stream and reaching for the hose again. "Yes, that's how it happened."

My father never worked in the mines, so was spared the black lung from which Sam and so many others suffered, but he often spoke of the mines as though he had worked there, as he had lived among the miners, played with their children, fought with their sons, and eventually drunk and laughed with them after work on the power lines. In his father's day the miners began forming unions, and these hardened men formed even harder coal-black clumps of strikers. One of them, Piercy MacIntyre, was an organizer and therefore was even rougher than most. The bosses in Chickasaw claimed he had been sent in from the outside, an agitator, but some of the men said he came from around Blue Jay Ridge, from a hill farm so far back "the owls carried knapsacks."

My father had met Piercy MacIntyre, but he knew his son Jackie better. The miners said Piercy had been a boxer in France during World War I, and whether true or not, he did teach his son Jackie how to box. He'd take the boy, eight or nine years old, down to Walker's store, and men would clear a makeshift ring in the corner, moving stock to form a rough square. Walker would then hold the bets as Jackie's opponent, usually an older boy of twelve or so, was announced. My father claims Jackie beat all comers, and my father, younger by two or three years, always rooted for him as fervently as he did for Joe Louis when his father would struggle to pick up Louis's fights through the static on KDKA radio. He tells how Louis knocked out Max Schmeling, the Nazi superman, so quickly that once they got the station in, all they heard was the count to ten.

Twenty-five years later, after my father had moved one hundred miles away to work in the mills of Ohio, he ran into Jackie MacIntyre at Republic Steel. He spoke to him, and though Jackie, now John, didn't remember him as one of his youngest fans among the dozens or more who had watched him fight as a kid, my father said they talked briefly of people they knew, even about Charley Best. My father said he was puzzled to see how the guys in the mill picked on him, and MacIntyre didn't seem to care. My father thought, "You guys don't know who you're dealing with."

Although my father had moved to the edge of the industrial Midwest, the mountains and forests remained home to him, and we went back every weekend to visit. And he hunted in Pennsylvania, not along the industrial riverbanks of Ohio. My father liked only two sports, boxing and hunting, and he tried to teach me both. I never caught on to boxing, partly because my father couldn't coach me while we sparred without beginning to fight in earnest, burying me in a flurry of open-palmed combinations and jabs. I liked the fluidity of the movements, the backpedaling, the duck-and-jab; however, I was not destined to be a boxer. I have a glass jaw, a nerve positioned in my face that makes a knockout a matter of one punch. My father found this fatal flaw one day while we sparred in the living room. One quick jab to my left jaw and I felt nothing — I saw pinpoints of light and awoke to my father shaking his head and saying, "The kid's got a glass jaw." As a boxer I was finished.

But hunting was another matter. Early on, my father declared I was a natural good shot, that I had a "good eye" that made up, I suppose, for my bad jaw. I could pick off pennies at twenty-five yards with a .22-caliber rifle, and after I got a shotgun, a 16-gauge, my father spent one long afternoon throwing clay pigeons, which I shot out of the air. He threw more than seventy, and I missed two. I enjoyed target shooting not only because I was good at it but because I did it without thinking. I simply knew when I was on target and then pulled the trigger. I guess it was instinct or something reflexive.

Yet, by age eighteen, I had pretty much lost interest in hunting. Animals made poor targets; they were hard to find, but when found, too big and easy. For a target shooter, walking all day for one shot at an easy target was not much of a thrill. I still went hunting with my father when in my teens, but I had no real enthusiasm for the sport, as he did. I tried to find it; I remember not eating one day, thinking that it would make me a keener hunter, but it only made me a hungry one. What I liked was the evening, getting comfortable down at Archie's camp, near his stone fireplace, listening to hunting stories.

The last time I went hunting with my father I was eighteen. I hadn't been deer hunting that last fall because the season fell during final exam week at college, and it was with some relief that

I realized this would happen every year. However, I went hunting for turkey that spring. I think I liked turkey hunting most because the hunt occurred in midautumn and midspring, the two most beautiful times of the year to be in the forest. You also could go deeper into the woods because, unlike a deer, once a turkey was shot it was not hard to pull it out of the woods. Dragging a hundred pounds of deer carcass over several miles of rough terrain quickly dampened the thrill of the hunt.

It was a cold April in the mountains that year; patches of snow still clung to rocks and roots in the forest, and springs remained frozen, even in the bright sunshine. My father led the way through the woods we hunted north of Brookville, stepping around the icy stones and fallen limbs with sure-footed grace and speed. Every hour or so we would stop and cradle our shotguns, and my father would bring out the wooden turkey call, a cedar box with a top that wagged loosely when shaken, chalk between box and lid giving off a decent gobble.

The turkey call was a new addition to our hunting gear. My father had never gone in for gimmicks as a hunter, although he thought my aunt Clair's trick of rubbing apple cores on her boots to attract deer might account for her yearly success. However, in the over twenty-five years he had been hunting, he had never bagged a wild turkey. He was well known among the locals for regularly bringing out a deer. He'd have a deer within the first couple of hours of the opening day of the season and could be found down at Archie's camp or at the Sigel Hotel by early afternoon, telling how the deer, never a trophy buck but respectable, would have risen from his bed twenty-five yards from my father's stand at first light. But turkeys had always eluded him, so he bought the call and had been practicing for months, brief chirps and throaty gobbles rising from our basement ever since September.

That day we had walked farther into the woods than usual, so far that we found ourselves on Windfall Ridge, or so it was called on my father's topo map. The ridge was steep and treeless, and the North Fork Creek ran noisily below. My father had noticed a stand of beech, and knowing turkeys like beechnuts, we had stopped to look for signs. Sure enough, my father found a large patch where turkeys had been scratching the winter-decayed leaves, a large flock probably discovered and broken up by other hunters earlier in the morning. The turkeys would still be in the area, scattered over Windfall, calling out to regroup. We stood and listened, but all I heard was the icy North Fork and a high wind in the trees.

So my father decided to try calling them in, making first a few hesitant chirps, then a long and short gobble that he'd heard was the turkey equivalent of "I'm over here."

And a turkey answered. The bird sounded like it was on the edge of the ridge, about fifty yards in front of us, but neither of us could see it. We walked cautiously toward the sound, my heart pounding for my father, hoping he'd at long last get a shot at the turkey. As we reached the ridge we split, my father wandering to the right of a tall pine growing in the fragile earth of the rim of the ridge, I to the left. The turkey flew out of the tree in a great bluster of wings. It flew left and was clearly my shot.

I snapped up my shotgun and found him quickly, flying high but in range. Then I thought about it. I wished the bird had flown right, to give my father the shot, wished it was not flying over the ice-filmed North Fork into which I would surely have to wade, waist high, to retrieve the bird. And I knew I did not want to kill the turkey; I had no need of it.

So I shot behind it, the bird's wings flapping comically faster after the sound echoed over the ridge. The turkey flew higher, out of range of another shot from me or my father, not landing until it reached the next ridge. I turned to look at my father, who said, "How'd you miss him?"

"Jerked the trigger, I think," I said, still looking over at the ridge where the bird had disappeared. "Or I choked; I don't know," I added.

"Hell, a good shot like you must have hit him," he said. "Maybe he went down with a few shot in him."

"Nah, he was too high up, out of range," I answered, not wanting to have to wade the creek anyway and hike the next ridge looking for the bird.

But we did cross the creek, over the back of a windfallen tree, and after searching for the bird for a while decided we had had our shot for the day and gave up. It was midafternoon, and it was a long way back, and I, having slipped into the North Fork on the return crossing, wearily tramped behind my father, one boot sloshing with creek water.

By the time we arrived at the Sigel Hotel my father was convinced I had hit the gobbler but that, as he said, "death is invisible, while life can be seen." A slain animal is still, and the natural camouflage is perfect. He believed we didn't find a dead turkey because it blended in with the rocks and undergrowth.

At the Sigel Hotel we sat at the long bar, adding our hunting outfits of red wool caps and canvas game vests to those of other hunters gathered there. My father began telling the story of our hunt to the man at his right elbow, and eventually to two or three down the counter. "The boy here got a shot, and I know he hit him — you should have seen the feathers fly! This kid is a great wingshot," he continued, telling of my slaughter of clay pigeons.

The other men answered his story with others, and through that, through the progress of stories to the next, he began telling the story of Charley Best. "He walked into this bar, a smoky place with a low ceiling supported by big, twelve-inch rough-cut post," he said, his hands surrounding one in the air, "rough like everything else in those camps."

Best looked around the smoky room, and when he spotted the man eyeing him he said, "You'd better finish that drink, because you're coming with me. You're under arrest."

The man sat with his stool tipped backward against a post, and when Best approached he said, "Well, I guess you're going to have to pull that big revolver, because I'm not going anywhere." Best was standing over him, and my father was on his feet in the Sigel Hotel, doing his best to look down at me as Best must have glared at the miner.

Then my father said, "The guy suddenly pulls a knife, cuts Best across the gut, and slips behind the thick post." My father's knees buckle.

Best was not used to working in the camps, so he was out of his element and forgot to watch himself. He was too comfortable, my father would say, and should have reminded himself that Chickasaw was a rough mining camp and that the man he sought could be armed and was drunk, that he was not simply approaching a frightened hobo on top of a rushing train. At this point my father's voice became a little squeezed, imitating the pain of the knife wound, but he continued, "He cut Best clear across the stomach, and his guts bulged and began to spill. With his left arm Best reached down and pulled his own guts back in, and with the right drew his gun and shot the miner." My father was fully on his knees now, his arm and hand holding in intestines, his other arm raising a Colt revolver.

"He hit him in the mouth. Killed him deader than hell."

This is where the story of Charley Best generally ends, though sometimes my father tells how they took him by train to a hospital in Brookville, how he got mean after that. But with my father on his knees, clutching his stomach in agony, this is when Charley Best appeared, or should have. He could have been a little fellow, age having shrunken him, a glass of clay-colored liquor in front of him at the bar, his mustache trimmed to a salt-and-pepper line under his nose. He'd sit near the opposite end of the counter, listening to but not telling his own story.

Best wouldn't wear hunting clothes. He'd stand up and, pulling out his flannel shirttails, say, "That's just the way it happened." Then he'd raise his shirt quickly, and we'd see the brutish pucker circling his waist. When Best sat back down he would drain the liquor in front of him, no one noticing that his left arm rested across his lap and against his body, holding the organs in, still trying to get comfortable with the wound.

THOMAS McGUANE

Twenty-Fish Days

FROM SPORTS AFIELD

IT WAS A WARM DAY in mid-October at Sakonnet Point, Rhode
Island. I was staying again at my uncle Bill's old house at the point,
with its view over the low weathered roofs to the harbor and the
old cove where we swam as children. There were still roses bloom-
ing along the stone fences, and the air was full of swallows and
gulls. When I was growing up, we often visited family along the
Massachusetts and Rhode Island shores, where great importance
was placed on the benefits of "salt air." As I recall, it was believed
to contribute not only to good health but to salutary morals as
well.

Today I sat on the wide wooden porch with my morning coffee,
waiting to go fishing with my cousin Fred, and vividly pictured,
really saw before me, scenes from long ago, of my aunts and uncles,
brother and sister, cousins and parents, gathered on that damp
and fragrant grass in sight of the sea and blue skies.

The harbor was an active commercial fishing place in those
days, with a number of swordfish boats from whose pulpits swordfish and white marlin, called "skillygallee," were harpooned. The
swordfishermen were our heroes. We made model swordfish boats,
with needles and thread for harpoon and line, tied "choggy"
minnows across their decks for a triumphant return to port. I
remember my businessman father heading out in his long-billed
cap for a day of swordfishing with the great Gus Benakes aboard
a beautiful Nova Scotia boat, the *Bessie B.* Those people are almost
all gone. But much else has stayed the same. Even the old harbor
tender, the *Nasaluga,* is still there.

As if to bless my fishing, a gold-crowned kinglet (probably dazed) landed on my shoulder while I drank my coffee and contemplated the striped bass fishing ahead. My cousin Fred came and we set out across the lawn to go fishing. We were doing this forty-five years ago, carrying handlines and fiddler crabs. Now we bore graphite flyrods and bar stock aluminum flyreels. It felt the same. More to the point, we had arranged to fish with Fred's friend Dave Cornell, who in his well-set-up open fisherman, guides these waters he has grown up with and knows so well.

I had come from across the country and we were making a late start. The wind was already blowing hard. Nevertheless, we quickly headed out through the harbor, around the breakwater and running between granite ledges past the ruins of the West Island Club, where sports of the Gilded Age cast baby lobsters for tackle-smashing striped bass. Club logs reveal their astounding catches followed by a rapid decline, paralleling the industrial pollution of their spawning rivers. Where once were their fishing stations, grande luxe living quarters, and kitchen gardens, there remained only gull-whitened rocks and the nervous attendance of the green Atlantic.

The sea was rough. We made a few stabs at schooling albacore and worked our way east toward Westport, finally tying off to a mooring buoy and eating our lunch. Dave was thinking in defensive terms, based on our uncooperative weather and the gentlemanly hours of his guests. He untied us from the buoy and we headed up a saltwater river, turning into a fairly busy marina. He positioned us just outside the pilings of some empty slips along a finger pier. In a very short time, I could hear bass popping along the seawall. We caught several small fish before facing that our options that day were sharply limited. We headed back to Sakonnet.

The next day, Fred and I were better behaved and we headed out at daybreak, with Dave far more optimistic. We rounded Warren's Point and looked east toward the Massachusetts shore. The wooded land looked remarkably unpopulated except for a church steeple sticking up above the trees. Between the green landmass and the Atlantic was a pure white line of low surf, sparkling with sea birds.

The ocean looked as wide and level as a snooker table. At a

number of places, birds were diving into schools of bait, which was
in turn pushed by predatory fish underneath. There would be a
patch of roughed water with a stream of birds trailing from it like
drifting white smoke. This looked suspiciously like the good old
days.

We skirmished with a couple of schools of false albacore without success, casting from the drifting boat into the bait, the albacore cutting through like fighter planes in the clear water,
succeeding through speed rather than maneuverability. It was
hit-or-miss, with little opportunity to tease them into taking. We
missed.

Dave Cornell fishes like a prowler. Even when he is in fish he is
looking for more fish. I who am most often confined by riverbanks
was fascinated by this wide-angled view. I was soon made comfortable by our fishing along the rocks, the ocean gulping and foaming
around their bases. It looks right when a big green and white
Deceiver drops into this turmoil and is drawn into the fishy darkness. No dice.

Dave spotted a school of stripers. By the time we reached them,
they had strung out in a line and one of Dave's friends was already
fishing the far end of that line. This was suddenly not difficult
fishing. To say that it was like taking candy from a baby would be
to defame the baby. We had tied on Clouser Minnows, a pattern
of nearly universal effectiveness, and striped bass see them as opportunity.

Every once in a while, angling provides an episode that we can
keep for life. It is not necessarily of big fish, though sometimes it
is, or of great difficulty overcome; rather, it is a kind of poetic sin-
gularity. Sometimes you even know it when it happens.

This was such an event. We drifted along the school of feeding
stripers, my cousin in one end of the boat, me in the other, Dave
Cornell making such adjustments as were needed to keep us lined
up to the drift.

It was a big school of bass and their feeding was creating what
looked like a low breaker traveling steadily over the surface. A dark
mass of bait like a shadow full of silver flashes moved ahead of this
breaking wave, marked along its length by silver and black stripes
of fish. Along the front of the wave, the length of it, were . . .
mouths. Above the wave, again, all down its length, terns hovered,

forked tails touching the water while they sighted bait, caught it, and swept away.

We hooked and released bass continuously. Stripers were so hard to come by when Fred and I were kids that I looked at each of these handsome native fish as though I'd never seen one before.

Dave radioed to his colleague at the other end of the school and asked how he was doing. His friend said he thought they'd put the rods away and "just lip them from the boat."

When the sun came up fully, a beautiful sea haze spread across the land to the north. We poked around for a while, had lunch off Goose Wing Beach at Little Compton, then headed for the Elizabeth Islands, where we saw Highlander cattle walking on the beach and beautiful stands of hardwood trees just beginning to turn color.

Dave ran us through Quicks' Holes between Pasque and Nashawena and pulled us around a beautiful bay on the north side of Nashawena. There were ultra-alert false albacore finning around this quiet bay, but we found no takers. Dave was thinking of lateral moves at the line of scrimmage.

We headed back to Sakonnet Point and put the boat back on the trailer. Fred and I changed clothes, then followed Dave to his house in South Dartmouth, where we put his canoe on top of his car. Through judicious use of car, canoe, and sandy roads, we found ourselves in a remarkable world illuminated by sea light. Through a long bank of dunes, the ocean had made a hidden inlet. Once inside, the tidal channel formed a salt marsh. On the high ground circling the marsh, old houses looked on, their windows shining in the late sun.

The tide channel made its serpentine way through the cattails. It was the size of a trout stream, which it resembled in other ways, excepting the blue crabs that backed away from us and the stone-heavy quahogs revealed by our sinking feet.

We spread out along the stream, finding places where sandbars faced the deep flowing water on the outside of bends and their undercut banks: easy casting and an absorbing world. It seems a matter of wonder that from beneath those banks, oceangoing striped bass took our streamers and fought the good fight. Looking across the cattails and spartina, I could see Dave, then Fred, with deep bows in their rods.

I slept well that night, with all the windows open so that the fog could creep around my bedclothes and I could better hear the sonorities of the sea buoy. All night long I received cheerful visits from family ghosts and remembered how I once longed for even one striped bass. I wondered how my life might have gone had I known at twelve that at fifty-five I'd have a twenty-fish day. Perhaps Fred can tell me.

CULLEN MURPHY

Backlogs of History

FROM THE ATLANTIC MONTHLY

ONE MORNING a few years ago an envelope arrived from my parents containing the bill from New Rochelle Hospital for my delivery, in 1952. The contents of a basement or attic were being culled, and the bill had turned up in one of the many cardboard reliquaries that have long lent a kind of ballast to my childhood home. The hospital's total charge for a five-day stay, including drugs and phone calls, came to $187.86. I was amazed at the cost, to be sure. But I was also struck by something else: that among all those decades' worth of family documents my parents had looked through, the delivery bill was the only thing they thought of sufficient interest to pass along.

This episode came to mind last fall when the U.S. National Archives and Records Administration announced its decision about whether, in addition to the vast numbers of government documents that it was already required to store, it would keep copies, paper or electronic, of all the government's E-mail. The decision came after years of debate among historians, public-interest groups, and government officials over a question that individual American households also ask themselves: How much stuff is worth saving? Opponents of E-mail storage argued that it would preserve at great expense a lot of useless clutter. Proponents noted that these days E-mail is sometimes the only "paper" trail that survives, and pointed to the role it played in the case of Oliver North and the Iran-contra arms-for-hostages deal.

Last fall the proponents won: the government's E-mail is now being saved.

* * *

At some point most of us realize that having a personal archival strategy is an inescapable aspect of modern life: one has to draw the line somewhere. What should the policy be toward children's drawings and report cards? Toward personal letters and canceled checks? Toward family photographs and wedding mementos? Toward favorite but no longer usable articles of clothing? People work out ad hoc answers to such questions, usually erring, I suspect, on the side of overaccrual. My father, who is an artist, still has all his art school sketchbooks from when he was in his early teens, and he has some ten thousand Polaroid photographs of himself that he took over the years in order to capture details of lighting and drapery. He has a file of newspaper clippings about Fordham football games from the 1930s. Almost everyone seems to save — or "curate," as archaeologists say — issues of *National Geographic*. That is why in garbage landfills copies of that magazine are rarely found in isolation; rather, they are found in herds, when an entire collection has been discarded after an owner has died or moved.

I happen to be an admirer of the archiving impulse and an inveterate archivist at the household level. Though not quite one of those people whom public-health authorities seem to run across every few years, with a house in which neatly bundled stacks of newspaper occupy all but narrow aisles, I do tend to save almost everything that is personal and familial, and even to supplement this private hoard with oddities of a more public nature — a calling card of Thomas Nast's, for instance, and a baseball bat of Luis Aparicio's, and Kim Philby's copy of *The Joy of Cooking*.

I cannot help wondering, though, whether as a nation we are compiling archives at a rate that will exceed anyone's ability ever to make sense of them. A number of observers have cited the problem of "information overload" as if it were a recent development, largely the consequence of computers. In truth, the archive backlog has been a problem for millennia. The excavation of thousands of cuneiform tablets in the ancient archives of Ebla, in what is now Syria, was hugely important, but it will be many decades before the tablets are fully translated, and by then further discoveries will no doubt have dug scholars more deeply, as it were, into a hole. A few years ago a Vatican official spent a morning taking me through the rich labyrinths and frescoed recesses of the Vatican Library. "Do you even know what you have?" I asked at one point. He shrugged

and said that although the name of every item probably existed in
the records somewhere — "Here, like this," he said, pulling out an
eighteenth-century ledger and pointing to an entry in an elegant
hand — he guessed that no one had actually opened up and
looked at two thirds of the collection.

Writing's great advantage over memory has ever been that it
allows one to "remember" what one can then forget about — an
invitation to warehousing. The process keeps speeding up, and Roy
Williams, a researcher at the California Institute of Technology's
Center for Advanced Computing Research, has attempted to cal-
culate how fast. He notes that the amount of information now
stored in all printed sources everywhere in the world is roughly
equivalent to two hundred "petabytes," a petabyte being one quad-
rillion bytes. In contrast, Williams has calculated, the amount of
information that will have accumulated in online media alone by
the year 2000 — that is, in the course of a mere couple of decades
— is expected to be two and a half times as much as that, and he
conceded that this figure may be a gross underestimation.

Historians obviously have problems when information is scarce,
but it's not hard to see a very different problem emerging as source
material becomes spectacularly overabundant. The great historian
R. G. Collingwood addressed this issue in 1926 in his *Lectures on
the Philosophy of History,* pointing out why historians at the time
approached ancient Greece differently from ancient Rome. For
example, he wrote,

> Greek history in the fifth century B.C. is a valuable study for the be-
> ginner in historical work because there are so few sources for it that
> the beginner can grasp them as a whole, and proceed to the work of
> interpreting them for himself. . . . When, on the other hand, he deals
> with Roman history of the early Empire, he is embarrassed by the
> immense mass of the available sources, especially those derived from
> epigraphy; here, therefore, he is confronted with the opposite problem,
> the problem of acquiring a sound scholarship or acquaintance with the
> sources, and the work of interpreting them falls comparatively into the
> background.

Imagine how much more daunting the work of interpretation
becomes with the development of modern national bureaucracies
and the national archives they have supplied. The historian Derek

Beales, writing recently about the immense task facing any chroni-
cler of the nearly sixty-eight-year reign of the Emperor Franz Josef
of Austria-Hungary, observed, "What remains of the remorseless
bureaucratic record is far too large for any one person to master."
Leave aside the task of assessing an entire epoch and consider what
is required in purely physical terms to preserve even a single
prominent person's lifetime documentary output. Benjamin Dis-
raeli's correspondence survived down to the level of what today
would be an E-mail message: "My darling, I shall be home for
dinner at 1/2 pt 7. In haste, Your, Dis." Woodrow Wilson left so
much behind that the historian Arthur S. Link spent his entire
career at Princeton University annotating and publishing Wilson's
personal papers, in sixty-nine volumes.

The National Archives in Washington now has about five billion
documents in storage. Nationwide, federal repositories have another nineteen million cubic feet of them, which in boxes set end
to end would stretch from coast to coast. (Thirty years ago the
boxes would have reached only from Washington to Wichita.)
There are thousands of other data hoards, public and private, all
around the country. Electronic storage, despite its incomparable
vastness, may eventually make finding some specific things easier,
if one knows what one is looking for, and the Library of Congress
and the National Archives have ambitious projects under way. But
electronic storage also has some major drawbacks, such as the fact
that deterioration and technological obsolescence will require that
all electronic data be copied onto new systems every ten years. In
any event, the cadre of people available to look into all this material is not getting much larger. The number of professors of American history, for instance, has been relatively constant for years.
(There are currently about six thousand.)

Is it preposterous to begin thinking of some of our archives as
the new tels? Tels are the mounds that layer upon layer of former
cities make; they are everywhere in the Middle East, harboring the
archaeological record of thousands of years of human history. But
there are too many of them for more than a few ever to be exca-
vated systematically, and understanding what's in even those few
takes decades if not centuries. For the rest, the occasional explora-
tory shaft or trench must suffice. I thought of those shafts and
trenches when a historian friend mentioned that some of his col-

leagues, confronted with too great a bulk of sources, resign themselves to "sampling," and others increasingly narrow the focus of their academic inquiries until they find something manageable.

Don't get me wrong: I am not proposing that we discard anything at all. One rarely knows in advance what will turn out to be of interest or importance and what should have gone directly into the oubliette. It is always delightful when something is discovered unexpectedly, as the biblical city Urkesh of the Horites was just a few months ago (inside a tel). But information does have its natural predators, and it may be that sometimes natural processes work out for the best.

A professor of mine once said that the only thing enabling him to complete his study of medieval France was that so many of the records he would otherwise have had to look at were destroyed during the Wars of Religion and the French Revolution. I called him up recently to ask if I remembered his remark correctly. He said yes, I did. And he recalled with particular gratitude a certain bonfire in Carcassonne.

CYNTHIA OZICK

A Drugstore Eden

FROM THE NEW YORKER

IN 1929, my parents sold their drugstore in Yorkville — a neighborhood comprising Manhattan's East Eighties — and bought a
pharmacy in Pelham Bay, in the northeast corner of the Bronx. It
was a move from dense city to almost country. Pelham Bay was at
the very end of a relatively new stretch of elevated train track that
extended from the subway of the true city all the way out to a
small-town enclave of little houses and a single row of local shops:
shoemaker's, greengrocer, drugstore, grocery, bait store. There
was even a miniature five-and-ten where you could buy pots, house-
dresses, and thick lisle stockings for winter. Three stops down the
line was the more populous Westchester Square, with its bank and
post office, which old-timers still called "the village" — Pelham Bay
had once lain outside the city limits, in Westchester County.

This lost little finger of the borough was named for the broad
but mild body of water that rippled across Long Island Sound to
a blurry opposite shore. All the paths of Pelham Bay Park led down
to a narrow beach of rough pebbles, and all the surrounding
streets led, sooner or later, to the park, wild and generally deserted.
Along many of these streets there were empty lots that resembled
meadows, overgrown with Queen Anne's lace and waist-high weeds
glistening with what the children termed "snake spit"; poison ivy
crowded between the toes of clumps of sky-tall oaks. The snake
spit was a sort of bubbly botanical excretion, but there were real
snakes in those lots, with luminescent skins, brownish-greenish,
crisscrossed with white lines. There were real meadows, too: acres
of downhill grasses, in the middle of which you might suddenly

come on a set of rusty old swings — wooden slats on chains — or a broken red-brick wall left over from some ruined and forgotten Westchester estate.

The Park View Pharmacy — the drugstore my parents bought — stood on Colonial Avenue between Continental and Burr: Burr for Aaron Burr, the vice president who killed Alexander Hamilton in a duel. The neighborhood had a somewhat bloodthirsty Revolutionary flavor. You could still visit Spy Oak, the venerable tree, not far away, on which some captured Redcoats had been hanged; and now and then Revolutionary bullets were churned up a foot or so beneath the front lawn of the old O'Keefe house, directly across the street from the Park View Pharmacy. George Washington had watered his horses, it was believed, in the ancient sheds beyond Ye Olde Homestead, a local tavern that well after Prohibition was still referred to as "the speakeasy." All the same, there were no Daughters of the American Revolution here: Pelham Bay was populated by the children of German, Irish, Swedish, Scottish, and Italian immigrants, and by a handful of the original immigrants themselves. The greenhorn Italians, from Naples and Sicily, kept goats and pigs in their back yards and pigeons on their roofs. Pelham Bay's single Communist — you could tell from the election results that there was such a rare bird — was the Scotsman who lived around the corner, though only my parents knew this. They were privy to the neighborhood's opinions, ailments, and family secrets.

In those years, the drugstore seemed one of the world's permanent institutions. Who could have imagined that it would one day vanish into an aisle in the supermarket, or reemerge as a kind of supermarket itself? What passes for a pharmacy nowadays is all open shelves and ceiling racks of brilliant white neon suggesting perpetual indoor sunshine. The Park View, by contrast, was a dark cavern lined with polished wood cabinets rubbed nearly black and equipped with sliding glass doors and mirrored backs. The counters were heaped with towering ziggurats of lotions, potions, and packets, and under them ran glassed-in showcases of the same sober wood. There was a post office (designated a "substation") that sold penny postcards and stamps and money orders. The prescription area was in the rear, closed off from view: here were scores of labeled drawers of all sizes and rows of oddly shaped brown bottles. In one of those drawers traditional rock candy was stored, in two flavors, plain and maple; it dangled on long strings. And finally there was the prescription desk itself, a sloping, lecternlike affair on which the current prescription ledger always lay, like some sacred text.

There was also a soda fountain. A pull at a long black handle spurted out carbonated water; a push at a tiny silver spout drew forth curly drifts of whipped cream. The air in this part of the drugstore was steamy with a deep coffee fragrance, and on wintry Friday afternoons the librarians from the Travelling Library, a green truck that arrived once a week, would linger, sipping and gossiping on the high-backed fountain chairs or else at the little glass-topped tables nearby, with their small three-cornered seats. Everything was fashioned of the same burnished chocolate-colored wood, except the fountain counters, which were heavy marble. Above the prescription area, sovereign over all, rose a symbolic pair of pharmacy globes, one filled with red fluid, the other with blue. My father's diploma, class of 1917, was mounted on a wall; next to it hung a picture of the graduates. There was my very young father, with his round pale eyes and widow's peak — a fleck in a mass of black gowns.

Sometime around 1937, my mother said to my father, "Willie, if we don't do it now we'll never do it."

It was the trough of the Great Depression. In the comics, Pete the Tramp was swiping freshly baked pies set out to cool on windowsills, and in real life tramps (as the homeless were then called) were turning up in the Park View nearly every day. Sometimes they were city drunks — "Bowery bums" — who had fallen asleep downtown on the subway and ended up in Pelham Bay. Sometimes they were exhausted Midwesterners who had been riding the rails and had rolled off into the cattails of the Baychester marsh. But always my father sat them down at the fountain and fed them a sandwich and soup. They smelled bad, and their eyes were red and rheumy; often they were very polite. They never left without a meal and a nickel for carfare.

No one was worse off than the tramps, or more desolate than the family who lived in an old freight car on the way to Westchester Square; but no one escaped the Depression. Seven days a week, the Park View opened at 9 A.M. and closed at two the next morn-

ing. My mother scurried from counter to counter, tended the fountain, unpacked cartons, climbed ladders; her varicose veins oozed
through their strappings. My father patiently ground powders and
folded the white dust into translucent paper squares with elegantly
efficient motions. The drugstore was, besides, a public resource:
my father bandaged cuts, took specks out of strangers' eyes, and
once removed a fishhook from a man's cheek — though he sent
him off to the hospital, on the other side of the Bronx, immediately afterward. My quiet father had cronies and clients, grim
women and voluble men who flooded his understanding ears with
the stories of their sufferings, of flesh or psyche. My father mur-
mured and comforted, and later my parents would whisper sadly
about who had "the big C," or, with an ominous gleam, they would
smile over a geezer certain to have a heart attack: the geezer would
be newly married to a sweet young thing. (And usually they were
right about the heart attack.)

Yet, no matter how hard they toiled, they were always in peril.
There were notes to pay off: they had bought the Park View from
a pharmacist named Robbins, and every month, relentlessly, a note
came due. They never fell behind, and never missed a payment
(and in fact were eventually awarded a certificate attesting to this
feat), but the effort — the unremitting pressure, the endless anxiety — ground them down. "The note, the note," I would hear, a
refrain that shadowed my childhood, though I had no notion of
what it meant.

What it meant was that the Depression, which had already
crushed so many, was about to crush my mother and father:
suddenly their troubles intensified. The Park View was housed in
a building owned by a woman my parents habitually referred to,
whether out of familiarity or resentment, only as Tessie. The pharmacy's lease was soon to expire, and at this moment, in the cru-
ellest hour of the Depression, Tessie chose to raise the rent. Her
tiger's eyes narrowed to slits; no appeal could soften her.

It was because of those adamant tiger's eyes that my mother said,
"Willie, if we don't do it now we'll never do it."

My mother was aflame with ambition, emotion, struggle. My
father was reticent and far more resigned to the world as given.
Once, when the days of the Travelling Library were over and a
real library had been constructed at Westchester Square — you

reached it by trolley — I came home elated, carrying a pair of books I had found side by side. One was called *My Mother Is a Violent Woman*, the other was *My Father Is a Timid Man*. These seemed a comic revelation of my parents' temperaments. My mother was all heat and enthusiasm. My father was all logic and reserve. My mother, unrestrained, could have run an empire of drugstores. My father was satisfied with one.

Together they decided to do something revolutionary, something virtually impossible in those raw and merciless times. One street over — past McCardle's sun-baked gas station, where there was always a Model A Ford with its hood open for repair, and past the gloomy bait store, ruled over by Mr. Isaacs, a dour and reclusive veteran of the Spanish-American War, who sat reading military histories all day under a mastless sailboat suspended from the ceiling — lay an empty lot in the shape of an elongated lozenge. My parents' daring plan — for young people without means it was beyond daring — was to buy that lot and build on it, from scratch, a brand-new Park View Pharmacy.

They might as well have been dreaming of taking off in Buck Rogers's twenty-fifth-century rocket ship. The cost of the lot was a stratospheric $13,500, unchanged from the boom of 1928, just before the national wretchedness descended. And that figure was only for the land. Then would come the digging of a foundation and the construction of a building. What was needed was a miracle.

One sad winter afternoon, my mother was standing on a ladder, concentrating on setting out some newly arrived drug items on a high shelf. (Although a typical drugstore stocked several thousand articles, the Park View's unit-by-unit inventory was never ample. At the end of every week, I would hear my father's melodious, impecunious chant on the telephone, as he ordered goods from the jobber: "A sixth of a dozen, a twelfth of a dozen . . .") A stranger wearing a brown fedora and a long overcoat entered, looked around, and appeared not at all interested in making a purchase; instead, he went wandering from case to case, picking things up and putting them down again, trying to be inconspicuous, asking an occasional question or two, all the while scrupulously observing my diligent parents. The stranger turned out to be a mortgage officer from the American Bible Society, and what he saw, he explained afterward, was a conscientious application of the work ethic; so it was the American Bible Society that supplied the financial foundation of my parents' Eden, the new Park View. They had entertained an angel unawares.

The actual foundation, the one to be dug out of the ground, ran into instant biblical trouble: flood. An unemployed civil engineer named Levinson presided over the excavation; he was unemployed partly because the Depression had dried up much of the job market but mostly because engineering firms in those years were notorious for their unwillingness to hire Jews. Poor Levinson! The vast hole in the earth that was to become the Park View's cellar filled up overnight with water; the bay was near, and the water table was higher than the hapless Levinson had expected. The work halted. Along came Finnegan and rescued Levinson: Finnegan the plumber, who for a painful fee of fifty dollars (somehow squeezed out of Levinson's mainly empty pockets) pumped out the sea.

After the Park View's exultant move, in 1939, the shell of Tessie's old place on Colonial Avenue remained vacant for years. No one took it over; the plate-glass windows grew murkier and murkier. Dead moths were heaped in decaying mounds on the inner sills. Tessie had lost more than the heartless increase she had demanded, and more than the monthly rent the renewed lease would have brought: there was something ignominious and luckless — tramplike — about that fly-specked empty space, now dimmer than ever. But, within its freshly risen walls, the Park View redux gleamed. Overhead, fluorescent tubes — an indoor innovation — shed a steady white glow, and a big square skylight poured down shifting shafts of brilliance. Familiar objects appeared clarified in the new light: the chocolate-colored fixtures, arranged in unaccustomed configurations, were all at once thrillingly revivified. Nothing from the original Park View had been left behind — everything was just the same, yet zanily out of order: the two crystal urns with their magical red and blue fluids suggestive of alchemy; the entire stock of syrups, pills, tablets, powders, pastes, capsules; tubes and bottles by the hundred; the fountain, with its marble top; the prescription desk and its sacrosanct ledger; the stacks of invaluable cigar boxes stuffed with masses of expired prescriptions; the locked and well-guarded narcotics cabinet; the post office and the safe in which the post office receipts were kept. Even the great, weighty, monosyllabically blunt hanging sign — "Drugs" — had been brought over and rehung, and it, too, looked different now. In the summer heat it dropped its black rectangular shadow over Mr. Isaacs's already shadowy headquarters, where vials of live worms were crowded side by side with vials of nails and screws.

At around this time, my mother's youngest brother, my uncle Rubin, had come to stay with us — no one knew for how long — in our little house on St. Paul Avenue, a short walk from the Park View. Five of us lived in that house: my parents, my grandmother, my brother, and I. Rubin, who was called Ruby, was now the sixth. He was a bachelor and something of a family conundrum. He was both bitter and cheerful; effervescence would give way to lassitude. He taught me how to draw babies and bunnies, and could draw anything himself; he wrote ingenious comic jingles, which he illustrated as adroitly, it struck me, as Edward Lear; he cooked up mouthwatering corn fritters and designed fruit salads in the shape of ravishing unearthly blossoms. When now and then it fell to him to put me to bed, he always sang the same heartbreaking lullaby — "Sometimes I fee-eel like a motherless child, a long, long way-ay from ho-ome" — in a deep and sweet quaver. In those days, he was mostly jobless; on occasion, he would crank up his tin lizzie and drive out to upper Westchester to prune trees. Once he was stopped at a police roadblock, under suspicion of being the Lindbergh-baby kidnapper — the back seat of his messy old Ford was strewn with ropes, hooks, and my discarded baby bottles.

Ruby had been disappointed in love, and was somehow a disappointment to everyone around him. When he was melancholy or resentful, the melancholy was irritable and the resentment acrid. As a very young man, he had been single-minded in a way that none of his immigrant relations, or the snobbish mother of the girlfriend who had been coerced into jilting him, could understand or sympathize with. In czarist Russia's restricted Pale of Settlement, a pharmacist was the highest vocation a Jew could attain to. In a family of pharmacists, Ruby wanted to be a farmer. Against opposition, he had gone off to a farm school in New Jersey — one of several Jewish agricultural projects sponsored by the German philanthropist Baron Maurice de Hirsch. Ruby was always dreaming up one sort of horticultural improvement or another, and sometimes took me with him to visit a certain Dr. McClean, at the

New York Botanical Garden, whom he was trying to interest in one of his inventions. He was kindly received, but nothing came of it. Despite his energy and originality, all Ruby's hopes and strivings collapsed in futility.

His presence now was fortuitous: he could assist in the move from Tessie's place to the new location. But his ingenuity, it would soon develop, was benison from the goddess Flora. The Park View occupied all the width but not the entire depth of the lot on which it was built. It had, of course, a welcoming front door, through which customers passed, but there was also a back door, past a little aisle adjoining the prescription room in the rear of the store, and well out of sight. When you walked out this back door, you were confronted by an untamed patch of weeds and stones, some of them as thick as boulders. At the very end of it lay a large flat rock, in the center of which someone had scratched a mysterious X. The X, it turned out, was a surveyor's sign; it had been there long before my parents bought the lot. It meant that the property extended to that point and no farther.

I was no stranger either to the lot or to its big rock. It was where the neighborhood children played — a sparse group in that sparsely populated place. Sometimes the rock was a pirate ship; sometimes it was a pretty room in a pretty house; in January it held a snow fort. But early one summer evening, when the red ball of the sun was very low, a little girl named Theresa, whose hair was as red as the sun's red ball, discovered the surveyor's X and warned me against stamping on it. If you stamp on a cross, she said, the Devil's helpers climb right out from inside the earth and grab you and take you away to be tortured. "I don't believe that," I said, and stamped on the X as hard as I could. Instantly, Theresa sent out a terrified shriek; chased by the red-gold zigzag of her hair, she fled. I stood there abandoned — suppose it was true? In the silence all around, the wavering green weeds seemed taller than ever before.

Looking out from the back door at those same high weeds, my mother, like Theresa, saw hallucinatory shapes rising out of the ground. But it was not the Devil's minions that she imagined streaming upward; it was their very opposite — a vision of celestial growths and fragrances, brilliant botanical hues, golden pears and yellow sunflower faces, fruitful vines and dreaming gourds. She imagined an enchanted garden. She imagined a secret Eden.

What she did not imagine was that Ruby, himself so unpeaceable, would turn out to be the viceroy of her peaceable kingdom. Ruby was angry at my mother; he was angry at everyone but me — I was too young to be held responsible for his lost loves and aspirations. But he could not be separated from his love of fecund dirt. Dirt — the brown dirt of the earth — inspired him; the feel and smell of dirt uplifted him; he took an artist's pleasure in the soil and all its generative properties. And though he claimed to scorn my mother, he became the subaltern of her passion. Like some wizard commander of the stones — they were scattered everywhere in a wild jumble — he swept them into orderliness. A pack of stones was marshaled into a low wall. Five stones were transformed into a perfect set of stairs. Seven stones surrounded what was to become a flower bed. Stones were borders, stones were pathways, stones — placed just so — were natural sculptures. And, finally, Ruby commanded the stones to settle in a circle in the very center of the lot. Inside the circle there was to be a green serenity of grass, invaded only by the blunders of violets and wandering buttercups. Outside the circle, the earth would be a fructifying engine. It was a dreamer's circle, like the moon or the sun, or a fairy ring, or a mystical small Stonehenge, miniaturized by a spell.

The back yard was cleared, but it was not yet a garden. Like a merman combing a mermaid's weedy hair, my uncle Ruby had unraveled primeval tangles and brambles. He had set up two tall metal poles to accommodate a rough canvas hammock, with a wire strung from the top of one pole to the other. Over this wire a rain-faded old shop awning had been flung, so that the hammock became a tent or cave or darkened den. A backyard hammock! I had encountered such things only in storybooks.

And then my uncle was gone — drafted before the garden could be dug. German tanks were biting into Europe. Weeping, my grandmother pounded her breast with her fist: the British White Paper of 1939 had declared that ships packed with Jewish refugees would be barred from the beaches of Haifa and Tel Aviv, and returned to a Nazi doom. In P.S. 71, our neighborhood school, the boys were drawing cannons and warplanes; the girls were drawing figure skaters in tutus; both boys and girls were drawing the Trylon and the Perisphere. The Trylon was a three-sided pyramid. The Perisphere was a shining globe. They were already as sublimely legendary as the Taj Mahal. The "official" colors of the 1939 World's Fair were orange and blue: everyone knew this; everyone had ridden in the noiselessly moving armchairs of the Futurama into the fair's City of Tomorrow, where the elevated highways of the impossibly futuristic 1960s materialized among inconceivable suburbs. In the magical lanes of Flushing, you could watch yourself grin on a television screen as round and small as the mouth of a teacup. My grandmother, in that frail year of her dying, was taken to see the Jewish Palestine Pavilion.

Ruby sent a photograph of himself in army uniform and a muffled recording of his voice, all songs and jolly jingles, from a honky-tonk arcade in an unnamed Caribbean town. It was left to my mother to dig the garden. I have no inkling of when or how. I lived inside the hammock all that time, under the awning, enclosed; I read and read. Sometimes, for a treat, I would be given two nickels for carfare and a pair of quarters, and then I would climb the double staircase to the train and go all the way to Fifty-ninth Street: you could enter Bloomingdale's directly from the subway, without ever glimpsing daylight. I would run up the steps to the book department, on the mezzanine, moon over the Nancy Drew series in an agony of choosing (*Password to Larkspur Lane*, *The Whispering Statue*, each for fifty cents), and run down to the subway again with my lucky treasure. An hour and a half later I would be back in the hammock, under the awning, while the afternoon sun broiled on. But such a trip was rare. Mostly, the books came from the Travelling Library; inside my hammock cave the melting glue of new bindings sent out a blissful redolence. And now my mother would emerge from the back door of the Park View, carrying — because it was so hot under the awning — half a cantaloupe with a hillock of vanilla ice cream in its scooped-out center. (Have I ever been so safe, so happy, since? Has consciousness ever felt so steady, so unimperiled, so immortal?)

Across the ocean, synagogues were being torched, refugees were in flight. On American movie screens Ginger Rogers and Fred Astaire whirled in and out of the March of Time's grim newsreels — Chamberlain with his defeatist umbrella, the Sudetenland devoured, Poland invaded. Meanwhile, my mother's garden grew. The wild raw field Ruby had regimented was ripening now into a luxuriant and powerful fertility: all around my uncle's talismanic ring of stones the ground swelled with thick, savory smells. Corn tassels hung down over the shut green-leaf lids of pearly young cobs. Fat tomatoes reddened on sticks. The bumpy scalps of cucumbers poked up. And flowers! First, as tall as the hammock poles, a flock of hunchbacked sunflowers, their heads too weighty for their shoulders — huge, heavy heads of seeds and a ruff of yellow petals. At their feet, rows of zinnias and marigolds, with tiny violets and the weedy pink buds of clover sidling between.

Now and then a praying mantis — a stiffly marching fake leaf — would rub its skinny forelegs together and stare at you with two stern black dots. Or there would be a sudden blizzard of butterflies — mostly white and mothlike, but sometimes a great black-veined monarch would alight on a stone, in perfect stillness. Year by year, the shade of a trio of pear trees widened and deepened.

Did it rain? It must have rained — it must have thundered — in those successive summers of my mother's garden, but I remember a perpetual sunlight, hot and honeyed, and the airless boil under the awning, and the heart-piercing scalliony odor of library glue (so explicit that I can this minute re-create it in my very tear ducts, as a kind of mourning), and the fear of bees.

No one knew the garden was there. It was utterly hidden. You could not see it, or suspect it, inside the Park View, and because it was nested in a wilderness of empty lots, it was altogether invisible from any surrounding street. It was a small secluded paradise.

And what vegetable chargings, what ferocities of growth, the turbulent earth pushed out! Buzzings and dapplings. Birds dipping their beaks in an orgy of seed lust. It was as if the ground itself were crying peace, peace; and the war roared on. In Europe, the German death factories were pumping out smoke and human ash from a poisoned orchard of chimneys. In Pelham Bay, among bees and white-wing flutterings, the sweet brown dirt pumped ears of corn.

Though I was mostly alone there, I was never lonely in the garden. But, on the other side of the door, inside the Park View, an unfamiliar churning had begun — a raucous teeming, the world turning on its hinge. In the aftermath of Pearl Harbor, there was all at once a job for nearly everyone, and money to spend in any cranny of wartime leisure. The Depression was receding. On week-ends, the subway spilled out mobs of city picnickers into the green fields of Pelham Bay Park, bringing a tentative prosperity to the neighborhood — especially on Sundays. I dreaded and hated this new Sunday frenzy, when the Park View seemed less a pharmacy than a carnival stand, and my isolation grew bleak. Open shelves sprouted in the aisles, laden with anomalous racks of sunglasses, ice coolers, tubes of mosquito repellent and suntan lotion, paper cups, colorful towers of hats — sailors' and fishermen's caps, celluloid visors, straw topis and sombreros, headgear of every conceivable shape. Thirsty picnickers stood three deep at the fountain, clamoring for ice cream cones or sodas. The low, serious drugstore voices that accompanied the Park View's weekly decorum were swept away by revolving, laughing crowds — carnival crowds. And at the close of these frenetic summer Sundays my parents would anxiously count up the cash register in the worn night of their exhaustion, and I would hear their joyful disbelief: unimaginable riches, almost seventy-five dollars in a single day!

Then, when the safe was locked up and the long cords of the fluorescent lights pulled, they would drift in the dimness into the garden to breathe the cool fragrance. At this starry hour, the katydids were screaming in chorus, and fireflies bleeped like errant semaphores. In the enigmatic dark, my mother and father, with their heads together in silhouette, looked just then as I pictured them looking on the Albany night boat, on June 19, 1921, their wedding day. There was a serial photo from that long-ago time I often gazed at — a strip taken in an automatic photo booth in fabled, faraway Albany. It showed them leaning close, my young father quizzical, my young mother trying to smile, or else trying not to; the corners of her lips wandered toward one loveliness or the other. They had brought back a honeymoon souvenir: three sandstone monkeys joined at the elbows — see no evil, hear no evil, speak no evil. And now, in their struggling forties, standing in Ruby's circle of stones, they breathed in the night smells of the garden, onion grass and honeysuckle, and felt their private triumph. Seventy-five dollars in seventeen hours.

Nearly all the drugstores of the old kind are gone, in Pelham Bay and elsewhere. The Park View Pharmacy lives only in a secret Eden behind my eyes. Gone are Bernardini, Pressman, Weiss, the rival druggists on the way to Westchester Square. They all, like my father, rolled suppositories on glass slabs and ground powders with brass pestles. My mother's garden has returned to its beginning: a wild patch, though enclosed now by brick house after brick house. The houses have high stoops; they are city houses. The meadows are striped with highways. Spy Oak gave up its many ghosts long ago.

But under a matting of decayed pear pits and thriving ragweed back of what used to be the Park View, Ruby's circle of stones stands frozen. The earth, I suppose, has covered them over, as — far off, in an overgrown old cemetery on Staten Island — it covers my dreaming mother, my father, my grandmother, my resourceful and embittered farmer uncle.

My Father

FROM UNDER THE SUN

I HAVE NO RECOLLECTION of a time when I was not afraid of my father. He was critical of everyone and everything, and especially of his children.

He was born in Brooklyn, New York, on August 9, 1906. One night when he was a baby, his father shot himself through the head with a pistol. The boss of the printing shop where he worked had fired him that morning for coming in late and hung over. His friends believed it was an accident. They said, "He didn't mean to kill himself. He was just cleaning the gun."

Two years later, Billy, a thin and silent little boy, was walking with his mother, whose name was Daisy, and a gentleman friend of hers on the beach at Coney Island. The man had made Billy a little boat, out of a wooden box, to float around in. They watched the midday sun glisten on tiny waves and seagulls squawk and flap around the barnacled pilings along the fishing pier. Old men squatted on dirty tackle boxes and boys dangled their brown legs, holding out lines, waiting for a catch. Laughter shrieked from the boardwalk behind the beach, and in the distance music from the merry-go-round came and went amid the tumbling roar and screams from what was, in my father's time, the world's biggest roller coaster. That day his mother pushed the boat from the beach, then pushed it again farther out. The man had gone to buy them lemonade. She pushed till Billy started drifting off in the changing tide. Her companion returned, scowling at Daisy, and he quickly took off his shoes and socks, rolled up his pants, and waded out to the box to guide it back to shore. But in the time it took him to get there, my father, who watched his mother on the beach, knew she had tried to kill him. She left home soon after that, and he never heard from her again.

Beyond telling me this story, Father never talked much about his childhood, except to speak fondly of his aunt Kate, who took care of him after Daisy left. She was a widow with no children of her own and provided a home for him and his older sisters, Alice and Kathryn. She was big-bosomed and not more than five feet tall, and walked with her back straight and chin held high. She wore long dresses with detachable linen collars. For church on Sunday, she attached lilac and white silk flowers to a wide-brimmed hat that threw a shadow across her brown eyes.

One day decades later, when Father was seventy and visiting me in New York, he took a taxi out to Bedford-Stuyvesant to see the brownstone house on Herkimer Street where he had lived with Kate. At the beginning of the twentieth century, when they were there, it was a middle-class neighborhood of mostly English, Scottish, and Irish: some new immigrants, but also some more-established families who had come to America a century earlier. Those who became lawyers and doctors and successful businessmen moved away to more affluent neighborhoods: Brooklyn Heights, Prospect Park, parts of Manhattan. The street remained much the same as when he was a boy: rows of Victorian brownstones, front stoops rising from well-tended rose gardens of pink, yellow, and white. The entire street had a sweet, delicious smell. When the blossoms died in late June, petals scattered down the bluestone sidewalk like confetti. Now tall sycamore trees lined Herkimer Street and two girls were skipping rope in front of the stoop where my father had his photograph taken on his twelfth birthday, in his first pair of knickers, a new shirt, and a bow tie.

Father rang the doorbell and a black man nearly his age peeked from behind a lace curtain. He smoked a pipe and wore red suspenders. When the door opened Father explained he had lived there many years before, and added wistfully that a pear tree used to grow in a garden out back. The gentleman invited him to come inside. They walked through the house and into the garden behind it. There they visited for the afternoon, sitting under a tree ripe with pears.

Father had gone to P.S. 23, and each Sunday he sang in the

choir at Grace Episcopal Church, where Aunt Kate took all the children. For a few summers she sent him to a boys' choir school in the Adirondack Mountains, where he fished and swam and walked in the woods. I think this is where his love for music must have originated. What I recall for sure now is the way, in church, he tilted his head back, closed his eyes, and sang the music deeply. The rich sounds seemed to soothe and energize him like a narcotic, to make him feel peaceful, kinder to those around him. I think that music must have eased his melancholy and insecurity, so it was useful for the rest of his life.

At the age of sixteen, bored with school, he went to work at the *Brooklyn Eagle* newspaper, as a messenger boy first, then a cub reporter, finally a sports reporter, covering his beloved Brooklyn Dodgers. When he was seventeen he began attending a different church, Christ Episcopal in Brooklyn Heights, traveling some distance by trolley to attend services and sing in the choir. From his seat in the back of the choir stall he could see colored sunlight streaming through the church's stained-glass windows. He was befriended by people there who were more educated than any he had ever known. The minister gave him books. He became a more avid reader, and he began going to art museums, orchestra concerts, and jazz clubs as often as he could afford to.

Photographs from then show he was skinny as a young man, but nice looking, and a stylish dresser. He wore English tweeds of the finest quality, which he could not afford, but he bought them anyway. He grew to be six three. He had dark curly hair and big blue eyes. In his late thirties he began a mustache, believing this gave him an aristocratic appearance. From my earliest memories, he was a large and imposing figure. I remember when he walked into a room, people noticed him and found him charming.

In 1927 he married my mother, Louise Haley, at the Little Church Around the Corner, on Fifth Avenue in Manhattan. He was twenty-one, she was twenty-three. Father was writing for good pay by then, Mother was becoming a very successful fashion illustrator, and while they made a great deal of money, they spent every cent of it. They had a penthouse on the West Side, a Chinese house servant, a Stutz Bearcat roadster, and a country house in Bethel, Connecticut. They traveled abroad by steamer several times, and twice

Father went off alone to shoot grouse and play golf in Scotland. They went with friends to speakeasies and jazz clubs, in Harlem and Greenwich Village, to dance and drink bootleg whiskey. They collected art and antiques. This was the Roaring Twenties.

They didn't really settle down until 1935, when I was born and they moved with my older brother, Billy, and me to a country house near New Hope, Pennsylvania. Three years later mother asked for a divorce. The following year, when he was thirty-six, father married Ann Mangum, a twenty-one-year-old debutante from Charleston, South Carolina.

His professional achievements were such that I was always proud of him, even as I struggled to have a personal relationship with him. He was also mysterious, unpredictable, and contradictory, always elegant, intellectual. In 1946 *Time* magazine sent him to Paris, on the *Gripsholm* sailing from New York, with Ann and their sons, my half-brothers Ben, four, and John, two, and a new Ford sedan. They lived in an old house with a maid and nanny, traveled throughout France, and a third son, Alexander, was born there. In 1948 Father made a film, *The Cradle of Man's Art,* about the Lascaux cave paintings. After they returned to the States, he joined the first editorial staff of *Sports Illustrated,* later worked as the arts editor for *Look* magazine, then was food and wine editor of *House and Garden,* his favorite job of all. He loved visiting the best restaurants in New York, becoming friends with such great chefs as Julia Child and James Beard. After writing in New York for ten years, he took Ann and the sons to live with him on the Standing Rock Indian Reservation, in Wakpala, South Dakota, where he directed an Episcopal boarding school for Sioux Indian children, then directed the first Outward Bound school, in Marble, Colorado, in 1961. He wrote a book about the Indians, *Remember the Wind,* then he and Ann retired to Charleston. After she died, in 1975, he became a recluse, except for twice-a-year trips he made to New York to serve on the wine-tasting committee of the Century Club.

Father's career ventures are documented by photographs I recently found in albums Ann had assembled carefully over the years. I had not seen them and was surprised by the sudden nauseated feeling they caused in me not long ago — tightness pulling across my back, forgotten tensions suddenly recurring — a few weeks before my sixtieth birthday. There is one picture of him sitting at his desk in Paris. He looks right into the camera, right at me, and I realize I barely knew him. He never intended to harm his children, but it happened.

The house my parents moved to after I was born lay on the Delaware River two miles south of New Hope. It was a river tavern before the Revolutionary War, fieldstone and clapboard, painted white, and sat on a grassy slope next to woods filled with birds. A clear brook, alive with tadpoles and noisy bullfrogs, ran across the property, under the river road and into the canal behind a leaning stone barn and cow shed.

In this house, I remember entering the living room cautiously. I was hardly tall enough to reach the arm of Father's club chair, where he sat surrounded by books and magazines and mail, reading. I feared that just my passing through would make him angry, as it so often did.

"What are you doing here, sneaking around?" he said once without looking up from his *New York Times*. "Get out of here."

Yet, another time he smiled warmly, said, "Give a kiss, Lucy Locket," and hiked me to his lap. With his large hands, he smoothed my dress down, then he bounced me on his knee, singing, "Trot, trot to Boston, trot, trot to Lynn, see little Lukie tumble in." He pretended to drop me to the floor and we laughed.

"Do it again, Papa," I begged.

But in an instant his mood darkened and he pushed me back on my feet, saying, "Go off."

By the time he was thirty, my father was an alcoholic, not the all-day-sipper kind, but a determined drunk, every night. He required me to know how to mix different cocktails, and by the time I was fourteen I could make most of them.

"Now, come with me to the kitchen, Lucia," he called, "and I will show you how to make a perfect dry martini." I dreaded this particular demonstration, which I had seen many times. Silently, I followed him to the kitchen and perched on a stool, resting my elbows on the counter.

"First you take the cold shaker from the icebox," he said, lifting it from where it was wedged above the ice trays. Grinning, he unscrewed the top of a Gilbey's gin bottle. "Fill a two-ounce jigger

twice," he instructed, "and pour it into the frosty silver shaker —
carefully and slowly, so you don't bruise the gin." He slowly rubbed
his thumb and first finger together like a scientist contemplating
the success or failure of an experiment. Then, for the second time
in ten minutes, he measured a jigger of gin, held it up to the
overhead light, looked at it carefully, brought it under his nose,
breathed deeply, and said, "Well, bottoms up, daughter, down the
hatch." I watched him empty the jigger in one gulp, a familiar
ritual. He rinsed the glass and put it in the sink. "Pass me that
green bottle of Martini Rossi, sweetie," he mumbled. "Just a whisper of vermouth goes in the shaker now, hardly a drop — like this."
He spent minutes carefully peeling a lemon into narrow strips,
placing one piece into each stemmed martini glass. He looked to
be sure I was watching attentively as he added a few ice cubes to
the shaker and stirred the mixture gently with a long silver spoon.
"Ah-ha. Now we have something wonderful, a perfect martini." He
poured the clear, cold mixture into the glasses, put the drinks on
a small silver tray, and carried it into the living room, announcing,
"Cocktails are served!"

Dinner was always late, often after nine o'clock, and Father
served everyone else first. He poured himself a goblet of wine,
sniffed the glass, took a mouthful, and held it for a minute. He
swallowed half, swished the rest around his teeth with his tongue,
closed his eyes, and drank. He looked at his plate of food, then at
the quiet faces of me, my half-brothers, and my stepmother around
the table, and heard only the sounds of hungry chewing.

"Well, for God's sake," he barked, slapping his hands flat on the
table, "what kind of heathens are you?" Knives and forks dropped
in a dissonant clang on the bone china. No one moved.

"Yes, Papa," John said in a small, serious voice. "We forgot to say
the blessing." He was balanced on two telephone books.

"Grab hands," Father said. "We will say grace, for this meal which
my lovely wife, whom I taught how to cook, has prepared." My
stepmother did not blink. His eyes were puffy and bloodshot as he
bowed his head and muttered a blessing I never quite understood.
"Amen!" was heard immediately around the table.

Having served each plate from his position at the head, he
often, especially to my brothers, served little meat, heaping huge
amounts for himself, then second and third helpings. To them he

said, "If you're still hungry, have some bread and butter," and poured himself another glass of Beaujolais from the tarnished silver coaster. From a white Italian ceramic pitcher we were served Starlac powdered milk. At dinner, drinking, he seemed to grow larger, getting red in the face, with his big blue eyes popping out of the sockets.

"Let me tell you something," he said. He began a lecture on opera. No one dared interrupt. Then he played an entire opera recording late into the night. I listened hard, tried to get it as he lectured, "Maria Callas is the greatest fucking singer in the world, right?"

"Yes, Father," I nodded. I held my head in my hands. None of us, including my stepmother, ever stopped it or asked to go to bed. He did not stop until the last drop of wine was gone.

He belittled his children and, as far as I could tell, his wife. More often than not, he was hard, driven. In the summer he sent my brothers out all day to weed the garden, to pick beans, to clear brush on the hill behind the house, while he sat in his reading chair, watching them through the window. They were allowed a quick lunch before he sent them out to another job. When their work failed to please him, they were beaten with a switch from the forsythia bush until red welts rose. He seemed to have no expectations that any of us should want to become anything in our lives, someone of worth. Or perhaps he feared just that — that one of his children might one day grow equal to his intelligence and success. No matter. I learned to hate him, and as I grew older, I avoided him. I never had any idea how he would react to anything, be it a Christmas gift or a personal opinion I offered him, or anything else: how I dressed, parked the car, filled the ice tray, or whom I chose to marry or the names I gave my children. I could not please him, although I tried. I would have done cartwheels if I thought that would make him like me. But I never succeeded in getting his approval. In his life, he never told me he loved me.

After mother divorced him (I was four), I never lived in my father's house, though he insisted I visit often — at least one weekend a month, longer during school holidays. Yet he never seemed really to want me there. The room he provided had only a bed, nothing else, no drawer or closet where I might leave something of my own. It was always cold, especially at night. I put two sweaters on over my nightgown and asked for a second blanket, but was told I didn't need it: "Too hot." Sometimes I snuck one from the linen closet, then returned it early the next morning before anyone could notice. I wrapped the blanket around me and looked at the window frost.

But I must also own that Father gave me, somehow, a love of great literature, music, theater, and art. He opened my ears and eyes to symphonies and ballet. When I was ten he took me to Carnegie Hall, and we sat in special seats with his friend Winthrop Sargent, the *New Yorker*'s music critic. Two years later he took me to the Metropolitan Opera for a performance of *Carmen* and, afterward, backstage to meet the diva, Rise Stevens. We had my picture taken with her. I still have it.

It was not just operas my brothers and I were compelled to listen to during those torturous evenings we sat at the dinner table, not daring to doze off, as he played recordings until after midnight. One night during World War II, Billy and I stayed up to hear the folksinger Leadbelly sing in our living room. He had just been released from a state penitentiary in Mississippi, into the custody of a friend of Father's who was writing a book about him and recording his music. I was very small, but I loved every bit of it, including his twelve-string guitar. When it was time for us to sleep, Leadbelly made up a song about Billy and Lukie going to bed. Another time, Father came home with a new 45 of Tex Ritter's "Do Not Forsake Me, Oh My Darlin'," from the movie *High Noon,* and one snowy Christmas Eve he stepped off the train from New York waving a recording of Gene Autry singing "Rudolph the Red-Nosed Reindeer." When I was fourteen, he snuck me into Jimmy Ryan's Dixieland jazz club, on West Fifty-second Street, to hear Wilbur de Paris play the trombone. The room was dark, smelled of whiskey and cigarette smoke, and was filled with black men and women. Ignorant as I was, I was afraid of the place at first, until Father introduced some of them as friends of his. We sat in a corner for an entire set. The building shook as everyone stomped on the floor when the band played "When the Saints Go Marching In." On the last chord, people leaped to their feet clapping and hollering over Wilbur and the boys.

Later he took me to art galleries on Fifty-seventh Street where he knew the owners, and once, after I'd just turned seventeen, to the Museum of Modern Art, where I was quizzed on who painted what. I believe he'd planned this outing as another tutorial session for me, during the Christmas holiday. He didn't know I had just finished dedicating myself to an art history course at school. I'd earned an A-plus on my term paper. We took the escalator to the second-floor gallery and immediately he pointed to a huge canvas on the first wall. "Know who painted that?" he asked, authority in his voice. I felt my heart jump. He began to speak again, to tell me, as I blurted out, "Henri Rousseau. It's *The Peaceable Kingdom*."

He looked startled, said nothing more as we passed into the next gallery. We walked around the room slowly and he pointed to other pictures. I felt suddenly like the world's greatest art expert as I said correctly, "That's called *Jazz* by Matisse, and I love it, don't you?" I followed with "Modigliani. Picasso. Braque. Paul Klee." He raised his eyebrows, looked at me, shrugged his shoulders. He was pleased, but he would not say it. My final moment came when he led me into the garden and, standing next to a huge stone sculpture, I said slowly, looking right at him, "*Reclining Nude* by Henry Moore."

He never asked how I knew these works. A few weeks later, back at school, I received a poster of *Jazz*. It arrived from the museum, with no note. The lingering thought always in my mind was to please him at any cost. It was, of course, impossible, and time with him wore at me. I began to realize there was always tension when he was around me, even if we were only having lunch in the garden of the museum.

Father made some arrangement which allowed that he would have no financial responsibility for me or Billy after the divorce. The four years I was at boarding school in New Hampshire he never came to visit, not even for my graduation, nor for those of my brothers. He disdained formal education, felt it was a waste of time. Since no education at all had been good enough for him, none was worth providing for his children. None of us made it through college: Billy eloped in high school, John and Ben joined the navy, and Alex, after one semester of college with no money, became a hippie. I believe Father must have smiled at these outcomes, ever more certain that none of his children could threaten to become as wise as he was. He had bought no life insurance, spent more money than he made, eventually was forced to give up the New Hope house to cover his unpaid bills, and wound up living with Ann and her mother in Charleston. For over thirty-five years Ann had served his every whim. She suffered his absences and his drinking, and took care of him until she died, in 1975, of cancer. Four years later, still outraged at the inconvenience her departure had caused him, he suffered a stroke and had to move to a nursing home, where he lived to become a lonely old man, visited occasionally by his children and some grandchildren, who also tried to amuse him. For my part, I had arranged to have the *New York Times* delivered to him daily. I couldn't do more.

In April 1981, when I was forty-five, I drove my thirteen-year-old twins, Tony and Jane, from New York to Charleston for a spring vacation reunion with my half-brothers and their families. John, his wife Claudette, and daughters Liz and Chris came from Pennsylvania. Alex, divorced, drove down from Atlanta with Eliza, Christian, and Rebekah. Ben and his wife and two daughters had moved into Ann's house after Father went to the nursing home.

The day after everyone arrived, we all went to the home to visit him. He had suffered that stroke, was strapped in a wheelchair, and looked so diminished I hardly recognized him. His shoulders were hunched forward. Heavy blue veins streaked the back of his unsteady hands reaching for ours. We leaned over to kiss the old man on the cheek. He did not speak. I looked away with tears in my eyes. I wondered how this could be the same man who had terrified me. But I was soon reminded of his power. He opened a bag of jellybeans we had brought him and spilled them onto the tray in his lap. One by one he asked each of us a question, and the answer was rewarded with a candy he selected. I stood at the end of the line. I was never asked a question. Several days later when I boarded the plane for home, I knew that I would never see him again.

In October, Jane and Tony asked me to take them on a Saturday trip to Bromley Mountain's alpine slide, in southern Vermont, to celebrate their fourteenth birthday. That Wednesday, they invited some friends; I was to be an appropriately inconspicuous mother and drive the station wagon. It was going to be fun.

Friday morning I got the phone call telling me Father had died.

It was another stroke, not a big surprise. What surprised me more was that I felt no sense of loss then, no sadness. I shed no tears. Rather, I hated him for spoiling the good weekend I'd planned with my children. I slammed the phone down, took a deep breath, lit a cigarette. I wondered what kind of daughter I could be, to feel only irritation on hearing my father was dead.

My daughter wanted to head for Charleston with me. She had never been to a funeral before and she was curious. He was her grandfather. She called him "Boom Boom." Tony refused to go, since a friend had invited him to a Mets playoff game that Sunday.

The funeral was at St. Michael's Episcopal Church in downtown Charleston. Except for his children and their families, few other people came. Ben, John, Alex, and three of their friends were the pallbearers. A gathering of tourists stood outside along the iron gates and watched.

We followed the hearse south out of town on the Savannah Highway, turning off toward Yemesee, then onto a narrow dirt road along old rice fields. This led to his wife's family cemetery, a small clearing surrounded by overgrown woods and tangles of wisteria and camellias and huge old live oak trees dripping with Spanish moss. It was a beautiful day and a peaceful place for us to leave him. We drove back to Charleston, and though we relaxed together in Father's house with Ben and his wife and their daughters, and told stories about Father well into the night, his place at the head of the dining table remained vacant. Nobody, it seemed, wanted to sit there.

I know that Father suffered from severe melancholy all his life, and booze may have eased this. With it he hurt all of us. I've just turned sixty. I still hope, believe, that he loved me, that he was proud of me. I believe he was just afraid to show it or tell me so. He seemed so often to feel I was trying to put something over on him; especially as he became older, he became paranoid. He even, once, at the nursing home, accused me of stealing a blue and white teapot from him. By then I could no longer even try to be kind to him, to have a conversation. He forgot I was his only daughter. He raged at me as if I were supposed to take it, a rage at all women, perhaps, or perhaps just at Daisy, his mother, who had thrown him away years ago, and whom he could never forgive.

My daughter and I flew from Charleston back to New York, nonstop, Sunday evening, and I watched the blue sky turn to orange, to pink, then to a deep purple as the sun fell below the horizon. Clouds gathered below us. The sky turned black. The plane's overhead lights went off and only a few reading lights came on. Jane was asleep, curled up with her knees under her chin, cheek resting on the palm of one hand, the other clutching a yellow Walkman.

I leaned my head against the window, looked into the blackness outside, and pulled the airline blanket more tightly around me. A chill was coming from deep within me that I could not stop. I was tired and wanted to sleep, but it made me ache. My whole body hurt. I could not move. I began to feel terribly afraid, a fear so strong I felt paralyzed in it. My forehead hurt, my eyes watered, but they were not really tears, not a release, I was not crying. Instead, I felt, I couldn't even blink. I couldn't close my eyes.

My father was there in that cold darkness, watching me. I felt vulnerable, exposed, as if now he finally had the power really to hurt me. I thought I might pray against this. I began, Our Father who art in heaven, hallowed be thy name. I couldn't continue it. Often before, I had begun this prayer, then stopped. What good could it do me? I fear Bill Chapman. I fear he has the ability now to see my thoughts, to understand I do not like him. He may yet punish me. Does he know all that I've said about him? The stories and jokes I've told about him, to put laughter onto memories of him that are painful to me?

I do not think I am afraid to die. But I live with a sense that he may be waiting for me. In dreams I see him embrace me in his huge arms, and I forget and am happy for a moment close to him. Then he will push me away, stand back, look at me, and begin to tell me what a dreadful, stupid girl I always was and that he has been waiting for this moment to tell me so. He has waited for years. I grow old. I turn eighty. I dread this moment, the moment of my death, when I am taken against my will, which dies with me, to where he is. My mother and stepmother sit silently next to each other, their heads down, their hands folded in their laps. They appear calm, even serene. Are they indifferent? What is this place? They say nothing, they nod. I think they believe I am getting what I deserve. They are going to let him have at me and I am scared. Where is God in this place? Is he?

LUC SANTE

Living in Tongues

FROM THE NEW YORK TIMES MAGAZINE

THE FIRST THING you have to understand about my childhood is that it mostly took place in another language. I was raised speaking French, and did not begin learning English until I was nearly seven years old. Even after that, French continued to be the language I spoke at home with my parents. (I still speak only French with them to this day.) This fact inevitably affects my recall and evocation of my childhood, since I am writing and primarily thinking in English. There are states of mind, even people and events, that seem inaccessible in English, since they are defined by the character of the language through which I perceived them. My second language has turned out to be my principal tool, my means for making a living, and it lies close to the core of my self-definition. My first language, however, is coiled underneath, governing a more primal realm.

French is a pipeline to my infant self, to its unguarded emotions and even to its preserved sensory impressions. I can, for example, use language as a measure of pain. If I stub my toe, I may profanely exclaim, in English, "Jesus!" But in agony, such as when I am passing a kidney stone, I become uncharacteristically reverent, which is only possible for me in French. *"Petit Jésus!"* I will cry, in the tones of nursery religion. When I babble in the delirium of fever or talk aloud in my sleep, I have been told by others, I do so in French. But French is also capable of summoning up a world of lost pleasures. The same idea, expressed in different languages, can have vastly different psychological meanings. If, for example, someone says in English, "Let's go visit Mr. and Mrs. X," the concept is neutral, my reaction determined by what I think of Mr. and Mrs. X. On the other hand, if the suggestion is broached in French, *"Allons dire bonjour,"* the phrasing affects me more power-fully than the specifics. *"Dire bonjour"* calls up a train of associations: for some reason, I see my great-uncle Jules Stelmes, dead at least thirty years, with his fedora and his enormous white mustache and his soft dark eyes. I smell coffee and the raisin bread called *cramique,* hear the muffled bong of a parlor clock and the repetitive commonplaces of chitchat in the drawling accent of the Ardennes, people rolling their *r*'s and leaning hard on their initial *h*'s. I feel a rush-caned chair under me, see white curtains and starched tablecloths, can almost tap my feet on the cold ceramic tiles, per-haps the trompe-l'oeil pattern that covered the entire floor sur-face of my great-uncle Albert Remacle's farmhouse in Viville. I am sated, sleepy, bored out of my mind.

A large number of French words and turns of phrase come simi-larly equipped with dense associative catalogues, which may con-tain a ghostly impression of the first time I understood their use in speech. On the other hand, nearly all English words and phrases have a definite point of origin, which I can usually recall despite the overlaying patina acquired through years of use. Take that word "patina," for example. I don't remember how old I was when I first encountered it, but I know that I immediately linked it to the French *patiner,* meaning "to skate," so that its use calls up an image of a crosshatched pond surface.

Other English words have even more specific histories. There is "coffee," which I spotted on a can of Chock Full o' Nuts in our kitchen in Westfield, New Jersey, in 1960, when I was six. I learned to spell it right away because I was impressed by its insistent doub-ling of *f*'s and *e*'s. The creative spellings reveled in by commerce in the early 1960s tended to be unhelpful. I didn't know what to make of "kleen" or "Sta-Prest," and it took me some time to ap-preciate the penguin's invitation on the glass door of the phar-macy: "Come in, it's KOOL inside." Then there was the local dry-cleaning establishment whose signs promised "one-hour Marti-nizing." I struggled for years to try and plumb that one, coming up with increasingly baroque scenarios.

* * *

When I started first grade, my first year of American schooling —
I had begun school in Belgium at three and a half, in a pre-kin-
dergarten program that taught basic reading, writing, and arith-
metic — I knew various words in English, but not how to construct
a sentence. My first day remains vivid in its discomfort: I didn't
know how to ask to go to the toilet. In addition, my mother had
dressed me in a yellow pullover over a white shirt-collar dickey. It
was a warm day, and the nun in charge suggested I take off my
sweater. Since I didn't understand, she came over and yanked it
off me, revealing my sleeveless undershirt.

As the weeks and months went on, I gradually learned how to
speak and comprehend the new language, but between home and
school, and school and home, I would pass through a sort of
fugue state lasting an hour or two during which I could not use
either language. For a while, my mother tackled this problem by
tutoring me in French grammar and vocabulary as soon as I got
home. It never crossed my parents' minds that we should begin
employing English as the household tongue. For one thing, my
parents' command of it was then rudimentary — I was rapidly
outpacing them — and for another, they were never certain that
our American sojourn was to be permanent. We were economic
refugees, to use the current expression, victims of the collapse of
the centuries-old textile industry centered in my native city of
Verviers, but my parents' loyalty to their own country was unques-
tioned.

For several years our family kept up a sort of double role. We were
immigrants whose income bobbed just above the poverty line,
thanks to my father's capacity for working swing shifts and double
shifts in factories (and thanks to the existence of factory jobs); but
we were also tourists. As soon as we could afford a used car we
began methodically visiting every state park, historical site, and
roadside attraction within a reasonable radius, taking hundreds of
snapshots — some to send to my grandparents, but many more
that were intended for our delectation later on, when we were
safely back in Belgium, recalling our fascinating hiatus in the land
of large claims and vast distances. This was not to be, owing to
family deaths and diverse obligations and uneasily shifting fi-
nances, but my parents kept up their faith in an eventual return,

and a concomitant relative detachment from the American way of life.

Our household was a European outpost. My parents made earnest attempts to replicate Belgian food, a pursuit that involved long car trips to the then rural middle of Staten Island to purchase leeks from Italian farmers, and expeditions to German butcher shops in Union and Irvington, New Jersey, to find a version of *sirop* — a dense concentrate of pears and apples that is the color and texture of heavy-gauge motor oil and is spread on bread — and various unsatisfactory substitutions. Neither cottage cheese nor ricotta could really pass for the farmer cheese called *makée* (*sirop* and *makée* together make *caca de poule*), but we had little choice in the matter, just as club soda had to stand in for *eau gazeuse,* since we lived in suburbs far from the seltzer belt, and parsley could only ever be a distant cousin to chervil. Desires for gooseberries and red currants, for familiar varieties of apricots and strawberries and potatoes and lettuce, for "real" bread and "real" cheese and "real" beer, simply had to be suppressed.

It wasn't easy constructing a version of Belgium in an apartment in a wooden house, with wood floors and Salvation Army furniture and sash windows and no cellar — not that the situation didn't present certain advantages, such as central heating, hot running water, and numerous appliances, none of which my parents could afford in Belgium, where we had actually been more prosperous. "Belgium" became a mental construct, its principal constituent material being language. We spoke French, thought in French, prayed in French, dreamed in French. Relatives kept us supplied with a steady stream of books and periodicals, my father with his Marabout paperbacks, my mother with the magazine *Femme d'Aujourd'hui* (Woman of Today), and me with history books for kids and comic magazines, in particular *Spirou,* which I received every week. Comics occupy a place in Belgian popular culture roughly comparable to that held in America by rock-and-roll, and like every other Belgian child, I first aspired to become a cartoonist. The comics I produced were always in French and clearly set in Belgium. (I couldn't abide American superhero adventures, although I did love *Mad* and the Sunday funnies, which were more commensurate with a Belgian turn of mind.) Somehow, though, I decided I wanted to become a writer when I was ten, and having made that decision never thought of writing in any language but English. Even so, I continued to conduct my internal monologues in French until late adolescence. For me the French language long corresponded to the soul, while English was the world.

My parents learned the language of their adopted country not without some difficulty. My father could draw on what remained of his high school English, complete with pronunciation rules that wavered between Rhenish German and the BBC, but otherwise my parents had arrived equipped only with the 1945 edition of a conversation manual entitled *L'Anglais sans peine* (English Without Toil). This volume, published by the Assimil firm of Paris and Brussels, is sufficiently embedded in Francophone consciousness that you can still raise a snicker by quoting its opening phrase, "My tailor is rich." (English speakers, of course, will have no idea what you are talking about.) The book could not have been much help, especially since its vocabulary and references were attuned not to 1960s America but to Britain in the 1930s: "The Smiths had wired ahead the time of their arrival, and were expected for lunch at Fairview." This was also true of their other textbook, a reader called *Short Narratives* published in Ghent: "The proprietor of an eating-house ordered some bills to be printed for his window, with the words, 'Try our mutton pies!' " There were also some evening classes at the YMCA in Summit, New Jersey, where we eventually settled, but I don't recall their lasting very long.

My parents' circle of acquaintances was almost entirely Belgian. My father had grown up in a tenement apartment in Verviers downstairs from the Dosquet family, whose children became his closest friends. The second daughter, Lucy, married an American GI after the war and they went to live in his native northern New Jersey. In 1953, her younger brother, Léopold (known as Pol), who was the same age as my father, followed suit with his wife, Jeanne. They were enthusiastic about the States and wrote rapturous letters. In 1957, when the prospects of my father's employer, an iron foundry that manufactured wool-carding machinery, were beginning to look grim, Jeanne Dosquet returned on a visit, and we all spent a week at the seaside resort of De Panne, at a socialist hostelry called the Hôtel Germinal, where plans were made for our own emigration.

After our arrival, we briefly shared an apartment with the Dosquets, a tight and uncomfortable situation. They introduced my parents to such Belgians as they had met by chance, in particular the three Van Hemmelrijk sisters and their mother, bourgeois French-speaking Antwerpers who had somehow ended up in America in straitened circumstances. There were others, too: a couple from Dolhain, near Verviers, who worked as caretakers of an estate in Tuxedo Park, New York, and another French-speaking Fleming, whom I only ever knew as Marie-Louise *"du facteur,"* because she had once been married to a mailman. She contributed another item to my burgeoning English vocabulary. One evening, while we were all watching television, Cesar Romero appeared on the screen: "Such a handsome man!" Marie-Louise exclaimed in English. To this day, any appearance of the word "handsome" calls up, in my mind's eye, the faint but unmistakable impression of Cesar Romero.

Even non-Belgian acquaintances tended to be foreigners whose grasp of the local tongue was as limited as ours. In Summit, our downstairs neighbors for a while were Hungarians named Szivros, who had fled their country after the doomed Budapest uprising of 1956. Since we did not yet own a television, Mrs. Szivros would stand at the foot of the stairs of an evening and call up, "Missis, missis! *Million Dollar Movie!*" Given the landscape, then, it is not surprising that my parents were somewhat at sea, knocked about among languages.

Sometimes, especially under pressure, my parents would reach for one tongue or the other and find themselves instead speaking Walloon, the native patois of southern Belgium. Walloon, now moribund, is usually identified as a dialect of French, whereas it is actually as old as the patois of Île-de-France, which became the official language — the eleventh edition of the *Encyclopedia Britannica* in fact describes it as the northernmost Romance language. Like English, Walloon incorporates a substantial body of words that derives from Old Low German, so that it could, if unconsciously, seem like the middle ground between English and French. An often-told story in my family related how Lucy Dosquet, when her GI suitor arrived looking like a slob, angrily ordered him in Walloon, *"Louke-tu el mireu!"* He understood perfectly, and studied his reflection.

*   *   *

Walloon was the household tongue of all the relatives of my grand-parents' generation. Their parents in turn might have spoken nothing else; that no one bothered to establish rules for the writing of Walloon until the very beginning of this century, just in time for its decline in currency, partly accounts for the fact that nearly everyone in the family tree before my grandparents' time was illiterate. Walloon enjoyed a brief literary flowering that started in the 1890s but was largely killed off by World War I. My paternal grandfather acted in the Walloon theater in Verviers during its heyday, and my father followed in his footsteps after World War II, but by then it had largely become an exercise in nostalgia. To-day, only old people still speak Walloon, and poor ones at that, since its use is considered rude by merchants, businessmen, and the middle class in general, and young people simply don't care. Young Walloons nowadays have been formed by television, movies, and pop music, much of it emanating from France, and they have seemingly acquired the Parisian accent *en bloc.*

I was raised in a Belgian bubble, though, which means, among other things, that my speech is marked by the old Verviers Walloon accent, which causes observant Belgians some confusion. They can't reconcile that accent with the American flavor that has in-evitably crept in, nor with my age and apparent class status. My French speech is also peppered with archaisms; I find myself un-consciously saying, for example, *"auto"* instead of *"voiture"* to mean "car," or *"illustré"* instead of *"revue"* to mean "magazine," expres-sions redolent of the thirties and forties, if not earlier.

The sound of Walloon, on those rare occasions when I hear it, affects me emotionally with even more force than French does. Hearing, as I did a few months ago, an old man simply greeting his friend by saying, *"Bôdjou, Djôsef,"* can move me nearly to tears. But, of course, I hear much more than just "Hiya, Joe" — I hear a ghostly echo of my maternal grandfather greeting his older brother, Joseph Nandrin, for one thing, and I also hear the table talk of countless generations of workers and farmers and their wives, not that I particularly wish to subscribe to notions of col-lective ethnic memory. Walloon is a good-humored, long-suffer-ing language of the poor, naturally epigrammatic, ideal for both choleric fervor and calm reflection, wry and often psychologi-cally acute — reminiscent in some ways of Scottish and in some

ways of Yiddish. Walloon is often my language of choice when,
for instance, I am sizing up people at a party, but I have no one
to speak it with at home. (My wife hails from Akron, Ohio.) I
sometimes boast that, among the seven million people in New
York City, I am the only Walloon speaker, which may or may not
be true.

My three languages revolve around and inform one another. I
live in an English-speaking world, of course, and for months on
end I may speak nothing else. I do talk with my parents once a
week by phone, but over the years we have developed a family
dialect that is so motley it amounts to a Creole. I cannot snap back
and forth between languages with ease, but need to be surrounded
by French for several days before I can properly recover its rhythm,
and so recover my idiomatic vocabulary — a way of thinking rather
than just a set of words — and not merely translate English idioms.
This means that I am never completely present at any given moment, since different aspects of my self are contained in different
rooms of language, and a complicated apparatus of air locks prevents the doors from being flung open all at once. Still, there
are subterranean correspondences between the linguistic domains
that keep them from stagnating. The classical order of French, the
Latin-Germanic dialectic of English, and the onomatopoeic-peas-
ant lucidity of Walloon work on one another critically, help en-
hance precision, and reduce cant.

I like to think that this system helps fortify me in areas beyond
the merely linguistic. I am not rootless but multiply rooted. This
makes it impossible for me to fence off a plot of the world and
decide that everyone dwelling outside those boundaries is "other."
I am grateful to the accidents of my displaced upbringing, which
taught me several kinds of irony. Ethnically, I am about as homo-
geneous as it is possible to be: aside from one great-grandmother
who came from Luxembourg, my gene pool derives entirely from
an area smaller than the five boroughs of New York City. I was born
in the same town as every one of my Sante forebears at least as far
back as the mid-sixteenth century, which is as far back as the
records go. Having been transplanted from my native soil, though,
and having had to construct an identity in response to a double
set of demands, one from my background and one from my environment, I have become permanently "other." The choice I am

faced with is simple: either I am at home everywhere or I am nowhere at all; either I realize my ties to human beings of every
race and nationality or I will die, asphyxiated by the vacuum. Mere
tolerance is idle and useless — if I can't recognize myself in others,
no matter how remote in origin or behavior they might appear, I
might as well declare war upon myself.

PAUL SHEEHAN

My Habit

FROM THE NEW YORKER

THE MORNING AFTER New York's great January blizzard, I took a long walk to the places where I often explore my arcane little niche of the drug world. I walked up Central Park West from the Nineties to Harlem and Morningside Park, passed under the lee of the Cathedral of St. John the Divine, and crossed over to Riverside Park. All are fertile drug sites for me.

The city looked gloriously serene and cleansed, but I was curious to see if my specialty, the crack trade, had paused during the previous day and night of heavy snow. The crack epidemic still rages quietly, even though it has largely slipped from public concern, and a popular myth has grown that the trade is burning itself out because so many crack addicts became zombies. But the police don't see any burnout among hard-core users. And from my peculiar perch I find that the trade seems as busy as ever. I wanted to see what the snow would reveal.

It revealed that the crack trade had not paused. In two hours, I found a dozen vials newly discarded on the fresh snow. Each had been used in the narrow space of time since the blizzard had dissipated. Most of the vials had been used outside, but a few had been thrown out of windows and had landed upright in the powdery snow, like little missiles.

Every New Yorker has stepped over empty crack vials, yet most people tell me they don't even know what a crack vial looks like. I look, and so I find. During my walk after the blizzard, I also came upon a man lighting his crack pipe in Morningside Park. It was ten o'clock in the morning, and the park was filled with children and parents playing in the snow. He was clearly, as they say on the street, "thirsty."

I waited until he left, then walked to his spot and saw something I had hoped to find. Lying bright on a snowdrift was a small glass tube, not quite an inch long, with a blue plastic cap inserted in the top. The inside surface of the glass was coated with the white residue of crack. I don't know why the man had neatly reinserted the cap before throwing the vial away, but a lot of crack addicts have that fastidious habit. I watched him walking away, then examined the slender vial. I knew I held a totem of the quenchless thirst for crack in my hand, but I did not feel sorry for him, because he had left a type of crack vial I had not seen before. I was thrilled.

I write for a living, but I am also the owner and curator of what is almost certainly the world's largest collection of crack vials. The crack vial first turned up in New York and Florida, and was invented specifically as a package for crack cocaine, which comes in a pebble form that must be handled with care. For a decade, the vials have been made illegally in an abundance of styles, and they have been discarded by the tens of thousands on the streets of New York. My collection is a measure of this abundance, and a small monument to it.

Inevitably, it has become more difficult to find new vials as the collection has grown into the hundreds, so my search has widened, and the terrain has become more unfamiliar and sometimes dangerous. Last November, I was surrounded by drug dealers in the notorious Cabrini-Green housing project in Chicago. I had gone there looking for Chicago crack vials and had not found any, and so had begun to root around the buildings, until I became an object of inspection for every lookout and enforcer at work in the project that day. They kept asking me, "Wassup, slick boy?" This was an unnecessary risk, an obsessional predicament, and all for something that most people would regard as worthless. I smiled and introduced myself as "Father Sheehan from St. Joseph's," and, with a measured, priestly gait, continued on my way out of Cabrini. (I am not a priest.) And I discovered belatedly that addicts don't use crack vials in Chicago; they use tiny plastic bags.

As I have wandered around rough neighborhoods, talking to addicts and cops and scholars, the underground world of crack has revealed some of itself to me. I learned about "mills," where heroin and cocaine are processed for street distribution. The cocaine powder is cooked into the more potent form of crack cocaine: teams of women, sometimes naked, I was told, fill hundreds of vials a day — an operation known as "bottling up." The idea that naked women are employed to fill crack vials seemed a patently absurd urban myth, but serious people, among them several urban ethnographers, assured me that it was true. Drug dealers are paranoid about pilfering. "A naked woman can't steal it, because she's got nowhere to put it" is how one source explained it.

I learned the street names of many of the vials: bunnies, crazies, supers, skinnies, flavors, bullets, and Taj Mahals. The word "vial" carries the heavy connotation of poison, and it is a term that users avoid, preferring to call the vials "caps." Users in need of the drug are "thirsty" or are "looking for Scotty" (as in "Beam me up, Scotty," from *Star Trek*) or looking for "rock" or "ready rock." New crack vials are usually sold in bags of fifty at grocery stores and bodegas, and the wholesale business appears to be dominated by immigrants from Yemen. "The crack-vial manufacturers have eluded us so far," Inspector William Taylor, of the New York Police Department drug squad, told me. "The information we have is that the vials are brought in from overseas." When I told him I had heard that they are brought in from the Bronx and Queens, he conceded that that may also be true. The police occasionally conduct sweeps against the paraphernalia industry and confiscate display boards, which are kept under shops' counters and used to show drug dealers the available range of vials' colors and designs.

The colors can denote a selling crew or a supplier or a product or a gang territory, or they can simply be random. I have heard dealers on Amsterdam Avenue shouting "We got blue!" or "Blue is up!" to alert buyers that blue-capped crack vials are on the street. Crack is price-driven, and the price is generally three to five dollars per vial, sometimes as low as two. The whole point of crack, which in its most common form is a cooked mixture of cocaine, lidocaine (a synthetic crystalline compound used in anesthetics), and baking soda, is to create more value out of a kilo of cocaine powder by making a drug that can produce an intense high at a very low price, thus vastly expanding the market downward. The more intensely addictive quality of crack is simply a bonus.

Blue caps? I have seventy different ones, blue being the most common color in a collection that at the time of writing contains 562 different crack vials. They are displayed in five Riker Specimen Mounts, thin cases with glass fronts which can be hung on the wall; the cases were designed to hold insects. Each of my cases has a name:

1. The Main Collection. A large case densely overcrowded with plastic vials — no glass vials — representing three quarters of the collection and gathered entirely on the Upper West Side and mostly within a ten-block radius of my apartment building, on West Ninety-eighth Street, off Riverside Drive.

2. The Taj Mahal Annex. A set of fifty-six plastic vials with ornate colored caps. I originally called this collection the Crown Annex, because the caps look like little crowns, but then learned that their street name is Taj Mahals.

3. The Newark Annex. Glass vials collected during two visits to Newark. Everything there was glass, no plastic. Because glass vials break easily and perish quickly once they're discarded, they are much harder to find.

4. The Harlem Annex. A mixture of both glass and plastic vials and caps that are unique to Harlem. They include "jumbo" vials — larger glass vials, developed for the suburban trade.

5. The Gold and Silver Annex. Thirty different vials, either glass or plastic, whose caps are either gold or silver plastic. This is my favorite case.

Among the 562 vials are eighty different cap designs, possibly suggesting eighty different manufacturers, and each cap is usually produced in ten or twelve different colors. The vials themselves have numerous variations — hexagonal, bullet-shaped, long, squat, thin, thick, plastic, glass — totaling more than four dozen different types, but all of them are transparent, so the contents can be seen. Vials produced a frisson of excitement in me last summer when they appeared in tinted versions for the first time: green vials, then blue, then red. Most of the cap and vial designs in the collection are no longer made and will never be on the streets again.

I clean all the vials except those which contain crack residue: I don't touch that. (I also have eight vials with deep teeth indentations, which I keep in a plastic bag, out of sight.)

* * *

Why bother? What is the worthiness? Isn't this collection a variation on the parasitism that crack already represents? Similar brutal questions are posed by Geoff Nicholson in *Hunters and Gatherers,* his novel about bizarre and exceptionally useless collections and collectors:

> What was collecting, anyway? You took one thing and you took another thing, you put them next to each other and somehow their proximity was supposed to create a meaning. You put certain artifacts together, drew an artificial boundary around them, and there you were with a collection. So what?
>
> As for the people themselves, I suspected that collectors were deeply inadequate human beings, compensating for a lack of personality, intelligence or love. I pictured them as a bunch of unsocial dullards: shy, oafish, unhip.

I am comfortable with these questions. I asked them myself long ago, and I have the answers.

The collection began as evidence. In 1991, the West 97/98th Street Block Association filed suit to block the reopening, by Volunteers of America, of a residence for homeless people, including some who were mentally ill, at 305 West Ninety-seventh Street. Two years later, the New York State Court of Appeals rejected a "fair share" argument that there were already thirty-eight shelters and treatment centers between West Ninetieth Street and West 110th Street, and almost none on the Upper East Side or on the West Side below Ninetieth Street. Meanwhile, the center reopened in 1992, and neighborhood activists predicted that drug-taking, panhandling, and car break-ins would increase. Whether or not crack users did move into the building — Volunteers of America always said they did not — I did notice more crack vials between Ninety-seventh and Ninety-eighth Streets and began gathering them as tangible evidence that the block association was right. One of the denizens of West Ninety-seventh Street, a stick-figure junkie with bleached blond hair who always seemed to be crying, parked herself at the entrance to the Ninety-sixth Street subway station every day and panhandled. For the first time, I found vials on the pavement outside the entrance to my building. I felt that the courts and the city government were pushing the tide of drugs right to my front door.

Once I started seeing crack vials, I noticed their extraordinary variety. Then the writer Allen Kurzweil came to visit, still basking in the success of his first novel, *A Case of Curiosities,* and he suggested that I put the crack vials in a display case — a case of curiosities. He then brought me a small Riker Specimen Mount from Maxilla & Mandible, on Columbus Avenue. After we mounted the vials, we discovered that when crack vials are massed in multicolored ranks they are charismatic. They have something to say. I put them on the wall, and when people came by they always looked at the crack case before even noticing any of the other art in my living room.

I can't explain why, but collecting became important to me. I stopped worrying about who lived at 305 West Ninety-seventh Street. Besides, the crying junkie had disappeared, the building had been cleaned up, and crack vials had become rare on my street. I felt safe wandering around some of the city's worst neighborhoods, especially after I noticed that people were calling me "Officer." Once, in Morningside Heights, a man came out of the bushes with his hands up when he saw me approaching. In Harlem, while I was on my knees sifting through a scattering of crack vials under a park bench, a young woman lolling on the bench, who was high on something, said to me, "You don't care what people think about you, do you?"

I have seen the entire panoply of New York's addiction debris: hundreds of discarded butane lighters, hypodermic needles, "cooker" bottles, tubes of glue, used condoms, empty handbags, empty bottles of Night Train, baking-soda boxes, rubbing-alcohol bottles, razor blades, and broken crack pipes.

In a paper that Doug Goldsmith, a New York ethnographer, delivered last year to the Society for Applied Anthropology, he compared crack vials to the detritus found at archaeological digs. Not long afterward, I spoke with him. "I've been on digs in the Southwest," he told me, "and I know those indestructible colored tops are the things that will remain behind, like pottery shards in ancient dwellings."

One day, there will be no more crack vials. And one day, perhaps soon, crack itself will be replaced. When the hard pebbles created by cooking cocaine were first sold, in the early 1980s, dealers used small perfume bottles or contact-lens cases to distribute them. Today's small, cheap, transparent, sturdy vials were developed as the market expanded, and the packaging of crack continues to evolve. Dealers are increasingly replacing vials with tiny Ziploc plastic bags, because they are easier to obtain, sell, carry, and, most important, conceal. When there are no more crack vials, I suppose my collection will have genuine anthropological value.

Artists have tinkered with drug paraphernalia to make aesthetic moral statements. The composer Philip Glass owns a work entitled *Found Dope* #2, which was made by a friend of his, and which consists of crack vials and caps stuck on parchment. The most common reaction to my collection has been that it is beautiful, so I took some of my cases of vials to a friend, a distinguished art historian, because I thought he would find layers of meaning that had not occurred to me. He loved the collection. "It's like looking at a little graveyard, little tombs," he said. "Except it has these childlike colors from Toys R Us, a compound of juvenilia and death. It reminds me of the collection of Dr. Ruysch, a Dutch anatomist who draped fetuses in lace and preserved them in jars. Staggeringly horrible oxymorons. But compelling oxymorons. They ended up in the collection of Peter the Great."

CHARLES SIMIC

Dinner at Uncle Boris's

FROM CREATIVE NONFICTION

ALWAYS PLENTY of good food and wine. The four of us at the table take turns uncorking new bottles. We drink out of water glasses the way they do in the old country. "More bread," somebody yells. There's never enough bread, never enough olives, never enough soup. We are eating through our second helping of thick bean soup after having already polished off a dozen smoked sausages and a couple of loaves of bread.

And we argue with mouths full. My uncle Boris would make Mother Teresa reach for a baseball bat. He likes to make big pronouncements, to make the earth tremble with his political and artistic judgments. You drop your spoon. You can't believe your ears. Suddenly, you are short of breath and choking as if you swallowed a big fly.

"Is he kidding?" I hear myself say, my voice rising to a falsetto.

I am the reasonable type. I try to lay out the pros and cons as if I were a judge making a summation to the jury. I believe in the calming effect of an impeccable logical argument. Before I can get very far, my brother interrupts to tell me that I'm full of shit. His philosophy is: The more reasonable it sounds, the less likely it is that it's true. My father, on the other hand, always takes the Olympian view. "None of you know what the fuck you're talking about," he informs us, and resumes slurping his soup.

Before we can all gang up on him, the pork roast is served. The skin is brown and crusty with a bit of fat underneath. There are potatoes and onions in the pan, soaked in the drippings. We are in heaven. The new bottle of wine is even better. Nuit Saint Geor-

ges is my father's favorite wine, since his name is George. That's
the only one he buys when he is flush.

For a while we don't say anything. We just grunt with our faces
in our plates. My aunt is carving more meat while my uncle runs
into the kitchen to get those hot little red Mexican peppers he
forgot all about.

Unfortunately, one of us starts on politics. Immediately we are
arguing again. In the last few years Boris has become very conser-
vative. He loves Barry Goldwater. He loves Nixon. As for Bobby
Kennedy, he's a Russian agent, if you ask him. Boris even warned
the *New York Times* about that, but they didn't print the letter,
of course. Tonight he shouts that I am a Communist, too. He has
suspected it for years and now has had his final proof just two
minutes ago.

I have no idea what I said to make him think that, so I ask him
to please repeat it. He's appalled. "No guts," he says. "Feigning
innocence, backtracking. Jesus Christ!" He calls on the heavens to
witness.

"It's what you said about Hoover," my brother says, guffawing.
Both he and my father are enjoying themselves, while I'm debating
whether to punch Boris in the mouth. He's really pissed, too. He
says I even look like Trotsky with my wire-rim glasses. "Get me the
FBI on the phone," he yells to my aunt. He's going to speak to J.
Edgar personally about me.

It's hard to tell with Boris if he's entirely serious. He loves scenes.
He loves opera. It's the third act, we are all dead on the stage, and
he is caterwauling. Without histrionics life is boring. This is bliss,
as far as he's concerned.

Watching him rant like that, I get an inspiration. I rise from the
table, walk over, and solemnly kiss him on the top of his bald head.
He's stunned speechless. It takes him some time to collect himself.
Finally, he smiles sheepishly and embraces me in turn.

"Forget about the FBI," he yells to my aunt in the kitchen.

She comes out with enough different cheeses to open a store.
We eat and drink and converse politely. The old guys are reminisc-
ing about the war.

Is it true that one grows nostalgic even about the horrors as one
grows old? Probably. I'm nostalgic about an August afternoon after
the war. My mother, brother, and I were being escorted at gunpoint

and on foot from one prison to another. At some point we walked past an apple orchard, and our guard let us stop and pick apples. Not a care in the world. Munching the apples and chatting with the guard.

As for my father and Boris, it seems, when they were in Trieste they used to pull this stunt. My father would invite friends to a fancy restaurant, but when the time came to pay the bill, he'd send Boris to break the news to the unsuspecting owner that they were completely broke.

"You were very good at it," my father assured him.

Boris, when he's not raving, looks like an English gentleman and has the appropriate clothes and fine manner to go along with his face. The owner of the restaurant would accept his apologies and his promise to settle the bill expeditiously, and would even permit his financially strapped guests to order another round of brandies before going off into the night.

"It's his smile," we all agree. Boris has the sweetest, shiest smile when he's happy. Old ladies, especially, adore him. Nobody knows how to bow and kiss their hands like he does. It's hard to believe he was once a guard in a maximum-security penitentiary in Australia. Come to think of it, none of us, individually or collectively, make much sense. We are all composite characters, made up of a half-dozen different people, thanks to being kicked around from country to country.

Boris, for instance, right now is singing. He studied opera singing for years, tried to make a career of it, and failed. Now he sings only when he's happy. He has a huge, beautiful tenor voice, but no ear. When he starts hitting the high notes, you have to run for your life. It's no use. He can be heard across the street. He has the world's loudest voice, and it's off-key.

He sings for us an aria from *Otello*. We survive that somehow, but he's not through yet. We are going to hear Tristan's death scene. Across the table my father looks grim. My brother has vanished. I am lying on the floor at Tristan's feet, trying my best to keep a straight face. Boris paces up and down, conducting the Berlin Philharmonic as he sings. From time to time he stops to translate for us. "Tristan is going mad," he whispers. No doubt about that. This Tristan is ready for the loony bin. His tongue is lolling, and his eyes are popping out of his head. He's standing on the sofa and leaning against the wall, arms spread, as if he is about to be crucified.

"*Verflucht wer dich gebrant!*" he shrieks.

"Stop it, Boris," my aunt says calmly, coming in from the kitchen with the cake.

"Please let him sing the death scene, Auntie," I say, and now even my father has to grin.

You have to admire the man's love of the music. Boris confessed to me once that he could never sing in a real opera house. He'd get so excited on the stage, he'd jump into the orchestra pit at the conclusion of his aria.

Now we applaud him. We are thirsty and hungry again, and so is he, luckily. My brother has reappeared.

"I'm going to bed," my aunt announces after she brings back the cheese and cold cuts. She knows this is not going to end soon. We are on our favorite topic, the incredible stupidity of our family.

I don't know if all large families indulge in such orgies of self-abuse, but we make a specialty of it. I don't think it's pretense either. I mean, it's not like we believe secretly we are really superior and this is just talk. Our family is a story of endless errors of judgment, of bad situations made even worse by bickering.

"Imagine this," my father says. "There's a war on, the Nazis, the Ustashi, the Hungarians, the Romanians, the Chetniks, the Italians, the Bulgarians, the Communists are killing us, and even the English and the Americans are dropping bombs. So, what do we do to make things really interesting? We all take different sides in that war so we can really make life miserable for each other."

We are silent with the weight of our drunkenness and the sad truth of my father's last remark. Finally, Boris looks up and says, "How about a really great bottle of wine?"

We all look at Boris, puzzled, but he explains that this wine is supposed to be very special, very old, very expensive.

"What is it?" we want to know.

He's not telling. He's going to decant it in the cellar so we can taste it blind and guess its origins.

Very well. Off he goes, and he's gone so long we are beginning to think the bastard sneaked off to bed. Instead, he returns with an air of mystery, carrying a bottle wrapped in a towel. The last time Boris had a bottle of expensive wine, he had us sip it from a teaspoon. He went around the table pouring drops of a fine old Margaux into a spoon and making us all in turn say "Aaaaaahh" like a baby doctor.

This time we just get clean glasses, and he pours everybody a little taste. It's red wine. There's no doubt about that, even at three in the morning. We twirl it in our glasses, sniff it like real pros, and take a sip. I think it's a Chianti, my father says it's a Burgundy, my brother mentions Spanish wine, but is not sure.

Boris is triumphant! Here's the final proof! Serbs as a people, and the members of this family especially, are all know-nothings, showoffs, and the world's biggest phonies.

Then, to rub it in, he tells us how he found out recently that the Sicilian who pumps his gas in Brooklyn makes his own wine. "Probably in the same bathtub where he washes his ass," he adds for effect. Anyway, the man gave him a bottle for Christmas, and this is what we are drinking.

It still tastes pretty good, but on second thought, we have to admit, we made complete fools of ourselves. Of course, we can barely keep our eyes open. The day is breaking. For the moment we have run out of talk. We just look at each other, yawning occasionally. The house is quiet. The city is quiet. Even the cops are catching forty winks in their patrol car on the corner.

"How about some ice cream?" Boris asks.

LAUREN SLATER

Black Swans

FROM THE MISSOURI REVIEW

THERE IS SOMETHING satisfying and scary about making an angel, lowering your bulky body into the drowning fluff, stray flakes landing on your face. I am seven or eight and the sky looms above me, gray and dead. I move my arms and legs — expanding, contracting — sculpting snow before it can swallow me up. I feel the cold filter into my head, seep through the wool of my mittens. I swish wider, faster, then roll out of my mold to inspect its form. There is the imprint of my head, my arms which have swelled into white wings. I step back, step forward, pause and peer. Am I dead or alive down there? Is this a picture of heaven or hell? I am worried about where I will go when I die, that each time I swallow, an invisible stone will get caught in my throat. I worry that when I eat a plum, a tree will grow in my belly, its branches twining around my bones, choking. When I walk through a door I must tap the frame three times. Between each nighttime prayer to Yahweh I close my eyes and count to ten and a half.

And now I look down at myself sketched in the snow. A familiar anxiety chews at the edges of my heart, even while I notice the beauty of the white fur on all the trees, the reverent silence of this season. I register a mistake on my angel, what looks like a thumbprint on its left wing. I reach down to erase it, but unable to smooth the snow perfectly, I start again on another angel, lowering myself, swishing and sweeping, rolling over — no. Yet another mistake, this time the symmetry in the wingspan wrong. A compulsion comes over me. I do it again, and again. In my memory hours go by. My fingers inside my mittens get wrinkled and raw. My breath comes heavily and the snow begins to blue. A moon rises, a perfect crescent pearl whose precise shape I will never be able to re-create. I ache for something I cannot name. Someone calls me, a mother or a father. *Come in now, come in now.* Very early the next morning I awaken, look out my bedroom window, and see the yard covered with my frantic forms — hundreds of angels, none of them quite right. The forms twist and strain, the wings seeming to struggle up in the winter sun, as if each angel were longing for escape, for a free flight that might crack the crystal and ice of her still, stiff world.

Looking back on it now, I think maybe those moments in the snow were when my OCD began, although it didn't come to me full-fledged until my mid-twenties. OCD stands for obsessive-compulsive disorder, and some studies say more than three million Americans suffer from it. The "it" is not the commonplace rituals that weave throughout so many of our lives — the woman who checks the stove a few times before she leaves for work, or the man who combs his bangs back, and then again, seeking symmetry. Obsessive-compulsive disorder is pervasive and extreme, inundating the person's life to the point where normal functioning becomes difficult, maybe even impossible.

For a long time my life was difficult but not impossible. Both in my childhood and my adulthood I'd suffered from various psychiatric ailments — depressions especially — but none of these were as surreal and absurd as the obsessive-compulsive disorder that one day presented itself. Until I was twenty-five or so, I don't think I could have been really diagnosed with OCD, although my memory of the angels indicates I had tendencies in that direction. I was a child at once nervous and bold, a child who loved trees that trickled sap, the Vermont fields where grass grew the color of deep-throated rust. I was a child who gathered earthworms, the surprising pulse of pink on my fingers, and yet these same fingers, later in the evening, came to prayer points, searching for safety in the folds of my sheets, in the quick counting rituals.

Some mental health professionals claim that the onset of obsession is a response to an underlying fear, a recent trauma, say, or a loss. I don't believe that is always true because, no matter how hard I think about it, I remember nothing unusual or disorienting before my first attack, three years out of college. I don't know exactly

why at two o'clock one Saturday afternoon what felt like a seizure
shook me. I recall lying in my apartment in Cambridge. The floors
were painted blue, the curtains a sleepy white. They bellied in and
out with the breezes. I was immersed in a book, *The Seven Storey
Mountain,* walking my way through the tale's church, dabbing holy
water on my forehead. A priest was crooning. A monk moaned.
And suddenly this: a thought careening across my cortex. I CAN'T
CONCENTRATE. Of course the thought disturbed my concentration, and the monk's moan turned into a whisper, disappeared.

I blinked, looked up. I was back in Cambridge on a blue floor.
The blue floor suddenly frightened me; between the planks I could
see lines of dark dirt and the sway of a spider crawling. Let me get
back, I thought, into the world of the book. I lowered my eyes to
the page, but instead of being able to see the print, there was the
thought blocking out all else: I CAN'T CONCENTRATE.

Now I started to panic. Each time I tried to get back to the book
the words crumbled, lost their sensible shapes. I said to myself, *I
must not allow that thought about concentration to come into my mind
anymore,* but, of course, the more I tried to suppress it, the louder
it jangled. I looked at my hand. I ached for its familiar skin, the
paleness of its palm and the three threaded lines that had been
with me since birth, but as I held it out before my eyes, the phrase
I CAN'T CONCENTRATE ON MY HAND blocked out my hand,
so all I saw was a blur of flesh giving way to the bones beneath,
and inside the bones the grimy marrow, and in the grimy marrow
the individual cells, all disconnected. Shattered skin.

My throat closed up with terror. For surely if I'd lost the book,
lost language, lost flesh, I was well on my way to losing the rest of
the world. And all because of a tiny phrase that forced me into a
searing self-consciousness, that plucked me from the moment into
the meta-moment, so I was doomed to think about thinking instead of thinking other thoughts. My mind devouring my mind.

I tried to force my brain onto other topics, but with each mental
dodge I became aware that I was dodging, and each time I itched
I became aware that I was itching, and with each inhalation I
became aware that I was inhaling, and I thought, *If I think too much
about breathing, will I forget how to breathe?*

I ran into the bathroom. There was a strange pounding in my
head, and then a sensation I can only describe as a hiccup of the

brain. My brain seemed to be seizing as the phrase about concentration jerked across it. I delved into the medicine cabinet, found a bottle of aspirin, took three, stood by the sink for five minutes. No go. Delved again, pulled out another bottle — Ativan, a Valium-like medication belonging to my housemate, Adam. Another five minutes, my brain still squirting. One more Ativan, a tiny white triangle that would put me to sleep. I would sleep this strange spell off, wake up me again, sane again. I went back to my bed. The day darkened. The Ativan spread through my system. Lights in a neighboring window seemed lonely and sweet. I saw the shadow of a bird in a tree, and it had angel wings, and it soared me someplace else, its call a pure cry.

"What's wrong with you?" he said, shaking my shoulder. Adam stood over me, his face a blur. Through cracked eyelids I saw a wavering world, none of its outlines resolved: the latticed shadow of a tree on a white wall, my friend's face a streak of pink. I am O.K., I thought, for this was what waking up was always like, the gentle resurfacing. I sat up, looked around.

"You've been sleeping for hours and hours," he said. "You slept from yesterday afternoon until now."

I reached up, gently touched a temple. I felt the faraway nip of my pulse. My pulse was there. I was here.

"Weird day yesterday," I said. I spoke slowly, listening to my words, testing them on my tongue. So far so good.

I stood up. "You look weird," he said, "unsteady."

"I'm O.K.," I said, and then, in that instant, a surge of anxiety. I had lied. I had not been O.K. *Say "God I'm sorry" fourteen times,* I ordered myself. *This is crazy,* I said to myself. *Fifteen times,* a voice from somewhere else seemed to command. "You really all right?" Adam asked. I closed my eyes, counted, blinked back open.

"O.K.," I said. "I'm going to shower."

But it wasn't O.K. As soon as I was awake, obsessive thoughts returned. What before had been inconsequential behaviors, such as counting to three before I went through a doorway or checking the stove several times before bed, now became imperatives. There were a thousand and one of them to follow: rules about how to step, what it meant to touch my mouth, a hot consuming urge to fix the crooked angles of the universe. It was constant, a cruel nattering. *There, that tilted picture on the wall. Scratch your head with your left hand only.* It was noise, the beak of a woodpecker in the soft bark of my brain. But the worst by far were the dread thoughts about concentrating. I picked up a book but couldn't read, so aware was I of myself reading, and the fear of that awareness, for it meant a cold disconnection from this world.

I began to avoid written language because of the anxiety associated with words. I stopped reading. Every sentence I wrote came out only half coherent. I became afraid of pens and paper, the red felt tip bleeding into white, a wound. What was it? What was I? I could not recognize myself spending hours counting, checking, avoiding. Gods seemed to hover in their air, inhabit me, blowing me full of their strange stellar breaths. I wanted my body back. Instead, I pulsed and stuttered and sparked with a glow not my own.

I spent the next several weeks mostly in my bedroom, door closed, shades drawn. I didn't want to go out because any movement might set off a cycle of obsessions. I sat hunched and lost weight. My friend Adam, who had some anxiety problems of his own and was a real pooh-pooher of "talk therapy," found me a behaviorist at McLean.

"These sorts of conditions," the behavioral psychologist, Dr. Lipman, told me as I sat one day in his office, "are associated with people who have depressive temperaments, but unlike depression, they do not yield particularly well to more traditional modes of psychotherapy. We have, however, had some real success with cognitive/behavioral treatments."

Outside it was a shining summer day. His office was dim, though, his blinds adjusted so only tiny gold chinks of light sprinkled through, illuminating him in patches. He was older, maybe fifty, and pudgy, and had tufts of hair in all the wrong places, in the whorls of his ears and his nostrils. I had a bad feeling about him.

Nevertheless, he was all I had right now. "What is this sort of condition exactly?" I asked. My voice, whenever I spoke these days, seemed slowed, stuck, words caught in my throat. I had to keep touching my throat, four times, five times, six times, or I would be punished by losing the power of speech altogether.

"Obsessive-compulsive disorder," he announced. "Only you," he said, and lifted his chin a little proudly, "have an especially difficult case of it."

This, of course, was not what I wanted to hear. "What's so especially difficult about my case?" I asked.

He tapped his chin with the eraser end of his pencil. He sat back in his leather seat. When the wind outside blew, the gold chinks scattered across his face and desk. Suddenly the world cleared a bit. The papers on his desk seemed animated, rustling, sheaves full of wings, books full of birds. I felt creepy, despondent, and excited all at once. Maybe he could help me. Maybe he had some special knowledge.

He then went on to explain to me how most people with obsessive thoughts — *my hands are filthy,* for instance — always follow those thoughts with a compulsive behavior, like hand washing. And while I did have some compulsive behaviors, Dr. Lipman explained, I had also reported that my most distressing obsession had to do with concentration, and that the concentration obsession had no clear-cut compulsion following in its wake.

"Therefore," he said. His eyes sparkled as he spoke. He seemed excited by my case. He seemed so sure of himself that for a moment I was back with language again, only this time it was his language, his words forming me. "Therefore, you are what we call a primary ruminator!"

A cow, I thought, chewing and chewing on the floppy scum of its cud. I lowered my head.

He went on to tell me about treatment obstacles. Supposedly, primary ruminators are especially challenging because, while you can train people to cease compulsive behaviors, you can't train them nearly as easily to tether their thoughts. His method, he told me, would be to use a certain instrument to desensitize me to the obsessive thought, to teach me not to be afraid of it, so when it entered my mind, I wouldn't panic and thereby set off a whole cycle of anxiety and its partner, avoidance.

"How will we do it?" I asked.

And that is when he pulled "the instrument" from his desk drawer, a Walkman with a tiny tape in it. He told me he'd used it with people who were similar to me. He told me I was to record my voice saying "I can't concentrate I can't concentrate" and then wear the Walkman playing my own voice back to me for at least two hours a day. Soon, he said, I'd become so used to the thought it would no longer bother me.

He looked over at the clock. About half the session had gone by.

"We still have twenty more minutes," he said, pressing the red Record button, holding the miniature microphone up to my mouth. "Why don't you start speaking now."

I paid Dr. Lipman for the session, borrowed the Walkman and the tape, and left, stepping into the summer light. McLean is a huge, stately hospital, buildings with pillars, yawning lawns. The world outside looked lazy in the sweet heat of June. Tulips in the garden lapped at the pollen-rich air with black tongues. A squirrel chirped high in the tuft of a tree. For a moment the world seemed lovely. Then, from far across the lawn, I saw a shadow in a window. Drawn to it for a reason I could not articulate, I stepped closer, and closer still. The shadow resolved itself into lines — two dark brows, a nose. A girl, pressed against glass on a top-floor ward. Her hands were fisted on either side of her face, her curls in a ratty tangle. Her mouth was open, and though I could not hear her, I saw the red splash of her scream.

Behavior therapy is in some ways the antithesis of psychoanalysis. Psychoanalysis focuses on cause, behavior therapy on consequence. Although I've always been a critic of old-style psychoanalysis with its fetish for the past, I don't completely discount the importance of origins. And I have always believed in the mind as an entity that at once subsumes the body and radiates beyond it, and therefore in need of interventions surpassing the mere technical — interventions that whisper to mystery, stroke the soul.

The Walkman, however, was a purely technical intervention. It had little red studs for buttons. The tape whirred efficiently in its center like a slick dark heart. My own voice echoed back to me, all blips and snaky static. I wondered what the obsession with concentration meant. Surely it had some significance beyond the quirks in my neuronal wiring. Surely the neuron itself — that tiny pulse of life embedded in the brain's lush banks — was a God-given charge. When I was a girl, I had seen stalks of wheat filled with a strange red light. When I was a girl, I once peeled back the corn's green clasps to find yellow pearls. With the Walkman on, I closed my eyes, saw again the prongs of corn, the wide world, and myself floating out of that world, in a place above all planets, severed even from my own mind. And I knew the obsession had something to do with deep disconnection and too much awe.

"There may be no real reasons," Dr. Lipman repeated to me during my next visit. "OCD could well be the result of a nervous system that's too sensitive. If the right medication is ever developed, we would use that."

Because the right medication had not yet been found, I wore the Walkman. The earplugs felt spongy. Sometimes I wore it to bed, listening to my own voice repeat the obsessive fear. When I took the earphones off, the silence was complete. My sheets were damp from sweat. I waited. Shadows whirled around. Planets sent down their lights, laying them across the blue floor. Blue. Silver. Space. *I can't concentrate.*

I did very little for the next year. Dr. Lipman kept insisting I wear the Walkman, turning up the volume, keeping it on for three, now four hours at a time. Fear and grief prevented me from eating much. When I was too terrified to get out of bed, Dr. Lipman checked me into the local hospital, where I lay amidst IV drips, bags of blood, murmuring heart machines that let me know someone somewhere near was still alive.

It was in the hospital that I was first introduced to psychiatric medications, which the doctors tried out on me, to no avail. The medications had poetic names and frequently rhymed with one another — nortriptyline, desipramine, amitriptyline. Nurses brought me capsules in miniature paper cups or oblong shapes of white that left a salty tingle on my tongue. None of them worked, except to make me drowsy and dull.

And then one day Dr. Lipman said to me, "There's a new medication called Prozac, still in its trial period, but it's seventy percent effective with OCD. I want to send you to a Dr. Stanley, here at McLean. He's one of the physicians doing trial runs."

I shrugged, willing to try. I'd tried so much, surely this couldn't hurt. I didn't expect much though. I certainly didn't expect what I finally got.

In my memory, Stanley is the Prozac Doctor. He has an office high in the eaves of McLean. His desk gleams. His children smile out from frames lined up behind him. In the corner is a computer with a screen saver of hypnotic swirling stars. I watch the stars die and swell. I watch the simple gold band on Stanley's hand. For a moment I think that maybe in here I'll finally be able to escape

the infected repetitions of my own mind. And then I hear a clock
tick-tick-ticking. The sound begins to bother me; I cannot tune it
out. *The clock is ruining my concentration,* I think, and turn toward
it. The numbers on its face are not numbers but tiny painted pills,
green and white. A chime hangs down, with another capsule,
probably a plastic replica, swinging from the end of it. Back. Forth.
Back. Back.

The pads of paper on Stanley's desk are all edged in green and
white, with the word "Prozac" scripted across the bottom. The pen
has "Prozac" embossed in tiny letters. He asks me about my symptoms for a few minutes, and then uses the Prozac pen to write out
a prescription.

"What about side effects?" I ask.

"Very few," the Prozac Doctor answers. He smiles. "Maybe some
queasiness. A headache in the beginning. Some short-term insom-
nia. All in all it's a very good medication. The safest we have."

"Behavior therapy hasn't helped," I say. I feel I'm speaking
slowly, for the sound of that clock is consuming me. I put my hands
over my ears.

"What is it?" he asks.

"Your — clock."

He looks toward it.

"Would you mind putting it away?"

"Then I would be colluding with your disease," he says. "If I put
the clock away, you'll just fixate on something else."

"Disease," I repeat. "I have a disease."

"Without doubt," he says. "OCD can be a crippling disease, but
now, for the first time, we have the drugs to combat it."

I take the prescription and leave. I will see him in one month
for a follow-up. Disease. Combat. Collusions. My mind, it seems, is
my enemy, my illness an absurdity that has to be exterminated. I
believe this. The treatment I'm receiving, with its insistence upon
cure — which means the abolition of hurt instead of its transfor-
mation — helps me to believe this. I have, indeed, been invaded
by a virus, a germ I need to rid myself of.

Looking back on it now, I see this belief only added to my panic,
shrunk my world still smaller.

On the first day of Prozac I felt nothing, on the second and third
I felt nauseated, and for the rest of that week I had headaches so

intense I wanted to groan and lower my face into a bowl of crushed ice. I had never had migraines before. In their own way they are beautiful, all pulsing suns and squeezing colors. When I closed my eyes, pink shapes flapped and angels' halos spun. I was a girl again, lying in the snow. Slowly, one by one, the frozen forms lifted toward the light.

And then there really was an angel over me, pressing a cool cloth to my forehead. He held two snowy tablets out to me, and in a haze of pain I took them.

"You'll be all right," Adam said to me. When I cried it was a creek coming from my eyes.

I rubbed my eyes. The headache ebbed.

"How are you?" he asked.

"O.K.," I said. And waited for a command. *Touch your nose, blink twelve times, try not to think about think about concentrating.*

The imperatives came — I could hear them — but from far far away, like birds beyond a mountain, a sound nearly silent and easy to ignore.

"I'm . . . O.K.," I repeated. I went out into the kitchen. The clock on the stove ticked. I pressed my ear against it and heard, this time, a steady, almost soothing pulse.

Most things, I think, diminish over time, rock and mountain, glacier and bone. But this wasn't the nature of Prozac, or me on Prozac. One day I was ill, cramped up with fears, and the next day the ghosts were gone. Imagine having for years a raging fever, and then one day someone hands you a new kind of pill, and within a matter of hours sweat dries, the scarlet swellings go down, your eyes no longer burn. The grass appears green again, the sky a gentle blue. *Hello hello. Remember me?* the planet whispers.

But to say I returned to the world is even a bit misleading, for all my life the world has seemed off-kilter. On Prozac, not only did the acute obsessions dissolve; so too did the blander depression that had been with me since my earliest memories. A sense of immense calm flooded me. Colors came out, yellow leaping from the light where it had long lain trapped, greens unwinding from the grass, dusk letting loose its lavender.

By the fourth day I still felt so shockingly fine that I called the Prozac Doctor. I pictured him in his office, high in the eaves of McLean. I believed he had saved me. He loomed large.

"I'm well," I told him.

"Not yet. It takes at least a month to build up a therapeutic blood level."

"No," I said. "It doesn't." I felt a rushing joy. "The medicine you gave me has made me well. I've — I've actually never felt better."

A pause on the line. "I suppose it could be possible."

"Yes," I said. "It's happened."

I became a "happening" kind of person. Peter Kramer, the author of *Listening to Prozac,* has written extensively on the drug's ability to galvanize personality change as well as to soothe fears or elevate mood. Kramer calls Prozac a cosmetic medication, for it seems to reshape the psyche, lift the face of the soul.

One night, soon after the medication had kicked in, I sat at the kitchen table with Adam. He was stuck in the muck of his master's thesis, fearful of failure.

"It's easy," I said. "Break the project down into bits. A page a day. Six days, one chapter. Twelve days, two. One month, presto." I snapped my fingers. "You're finished."

Adam looked at me, said nothing. The kitchen grew quiet, a deliberate sort of silence he seemed to be purposefully manufacturing so I could hear the echo of my own voice. Bugs thumped on the screen. I heard the high happy pitch of a cheerleader, the sensible voice of a vocational counselor. In a matter of moments I had gone from a fumbling, unsure person to this — all pragmatism, all sure solutions. For the first time on Prozac I felt afraid.

I lay in bed that night. From the next room I heard the patter of Adam's typewriter keys. He was stuck in the mire, inching forward and falling back. Where was I? Who was I? I lifted my hand to my face, the same motion as before, when the full force of obsession had struck me. The hand was still unfamiliar, but wonderfully so now, the three threaded lines seams of silver, the lights from passing cars rotating on my walls like the swish of a spaceship softly landing.

In space I was then, wondering. How could a drug change my mind so abruptly? How could it bring forth buried or new parts of my personality? The oldest questions, I know. My brain wasn't wet clay and paste, as all good brains should be, but a glinting thing crossed with wires. I wasn't human but machine. No, I wasn't machine but animal, linked to my electrified biology more completely than I could have imagined. We have lately come to think of machines and animals, of machines and nature, as occupying opposite sides of the spectrum — there is IBM and then there's the lake — but really they are so similar. A computer goes on when you push its button. A gazelle goes on when it sees a lynx. Only humans are supposedly different, above the pure cause and effect of the hard-wired primitive world. Free will and all.

But no, maybe not. For I had swallowed a pill designed through technology, and in doing so, I was discovering myself embedded in an animal world. I was a purely chemical being, mood and personality seeping through serotonin. We are all taught to believe it's true, but how strange to feel that supposed truth bubbling right in your own tweaked brainpan. Who was I, all skin and worm, all herd? For the next few weeks, amidst feelings of joy and deep relief, these thoughts accompanied me, these slow, simmering misgivings. In dreams, beasts roamed the rafters of my bones, and my bones were twined with wire, teeth tiny silicon chips.

I went to Drumlin Farm one afternoon to see the animals. A goose ate grass in an imperturbable rhythm. Sheep brayed robotically, their noses pointing toward the sky. I reached out to touch their fur. Simmering misgivings, yes, but my fingers alive, feeling clumps of cream, of wool.

Every noon I took my pill. Instead of just placing it on my tongue and swallowing with water, I unscrewed the capsule. White powder poured into my hands. I tossed the plastic husk away, cradled the healing talc. I tasted it, a burst of bitterness, a gagging. I took it that way every day, the silky slide of Prozac powder, the harshness in my mouth.

Mornings now, I got up early to jog, showered efficiently, then strode off to the library. I was able to go back to work, cutting deli part-time at Formaggio while I prepared myself for divinity school the next year by reading. I read with an appetite, hungry from all the time I'd lost to illness. The pages of the books seemed very white; the words were easy, black beads shining, ebony in my quieted mind.

I found a book in the library's medical section about obsessive-compulsive disorder. I sat in a corner, on a corduroy cushion, to read it. And there, surrounded by pages and pages on the nature of God and mystery, on Job who cried out at his unfathomable pain, I read about my disorder from a medical perspective, followed the charts and graphs and correlation coefficients. The author proposed that OCD was solely physical in origin, and had the same neurological etiology as Tourette's. Obsessive symptoms, the author suggested, are atavistic responses left over from primitive grooming behaviors. We still have the ape in us; a bird flies in our blood. The obsessive person, linked to her reptilian roots, her mammalian ancestors, cannot stop picking parasites off her brother's back, combing her hair with her tongue, or doing the human equivalent of nest building, picking up stick after stick, leaf after leaf, until her bloated home sits ridiculously unstable in the crotch of an old oak tree.

Keel keel, the crow in me cries. The pig grunts. The screen of myself blinks on. Blinks off. Darkens.

Still, I was mostly peaceful, wonderfully organized. My mind felt lubed, thoughts slipping through so easily, words bursting into bloom. I was reminded of being a girl on the island of Barbados, where we once vacationed. My father took me to a banquet beneath a tropical sky. Greased black men slithered under low poles, their liquid bodies bending to meet the world. Torches flared, and on a long table before me steamed food of every variety. *A feast,* my father said, *all the good things in life.* Yes, that was what Prozac was first like for me, all the good things in life: roasted ham, delicate grilled fish, lemon halves wrapped in yellow waxed paper, fat plums floating in jars.

I could, I thought, do anything in this state of mind. I put my misgivings aside — how fast they would soon come back! how hard they would hit! — and ate into my days, a long banquet. I did things I'd never done before: swimming at dawn in Walden Pond, writing poetry I knew was bad and loving it anyway.

I applied for and was awarded a three-month grant to go to Appalachia, where I wanted to collect oral histories of mountain women. I could swagger anywhere on the Zack, on Vitamin P. Never mind that even before I'd ever come down with OCD I'd been the anxious, tentative sort. Never mind that unnamed trepidations, for all of my life, had prevented me from taking a trip to New Hampshire for more than a few days. Now that I'd taken the cure, I really could go anywhere, even off to the rippling blue mountains of poverty, far from a phone or a friend.

A gun hung over the door. In the oven I saw a roasted bird covered with flies. In the bathroom, a fat girl stooped over herself, without bothering to shut the door, and pulled a red rag from between her legs.

Her name was Kim, her sister's name was Bridget, and their mother and father were Kat and Lonny. All the females were huge and doughy, while Lonny was a single strand of muscle tanned to the color of tobacco. He said very little, and the mother and daughters chattered on, offering me Cokes and Cheerios, showing me to my room, where I sat on a lumpy mattress and stared at the white walls.

And then a moon rose. A storm of hurricane force plowed through fields and sky. I didn't feel myself here. The sound of the storm, battering just above my head, seemed far far away. There was a whispering in my mind, a noise like silk being split. Next to me, on the night table, my sturdy bottle of Prozac. I was fine. So long as I had that, I would be fine.

I pretended I was fine for the next couple of days, racing around with manic intensity. I sat heavy Kat in one of her oversized chairs and insisted she tell me everything about her life in the Blue Ridge Mountains, scribbling madly as she talked. *I am happy happy happy,* I sang to myself. I tried to ignore the strange sounds building in my brain, kindling that crackles, a flame getting hot.

And then I was taking a break out in the sandy yard. It was near one hundred degrees. The sun was tiny in a bleary sky. Chickens screamed and pecked.

In one swift and seamless move, Lonny reached down to grab a bird. His fist closed in on its throat while all the crows cawed and the beasts in my bones brayed away. He laid the chicken down on a stump, raised an ax, and cut. The body did its dance. I watched the severing, how swiftly connections melt, how deep and black is space. Blood spilled.

I ran inside. I was far from a phone or a friend. Maybe I was reminded of some pre-verbal terror: the surgeon's knife, the violet umbilical cord. Or maybe the mountain altitudes had thrown my chemistry off. I don't really know why, or how. But as though I'd never swallowed a Prozac pill, my mind seized and clamped and the obsessions were back.

I took a step forward and then said to myself, *Don't take another step until you count to twenty-five.* After I'd satisfied that imperative, I had to count to twenty-five again, and then halve twenty-five, and then quarter it, before I felt safe enough to walk out the door. By the end of the day, each step took over ten minutes to complete. I stopped taking steps. I sat on my bed.

"What's wrong with you?" Kat said. "Come out here and talk with us."

I tried, but I got stuck in the doorway. There was a point above the doorway I just had to see, and then see again, and inside of me something screamed *back again back again,* and the grief was very large.

For I had experienced the world free and taken in colors and tasted grilled fish and moon. I had left one illness like a too tight snakeskin, and here I was, thrust back. What's worse than illness is to think you're cured — partake of cure in almost complete belief — and then with no warning to be dashed on a dock, moored.

Here's what they don't tell you about Prozac. The drug, for many obsessives who take it, is known to have wonderfully powerful effects in the first few months when it's new to the body. When I called the Prozac Doctor from Kentucky that evening, he explained to me how the drug, when used to treat OCD as opposed to depression, peaks at about six months and then loses some of its oomph. "Someday we'll develop a more robust pill," Dr. Stanley said. "In the meantime, up your dose."

I upped my dose. No relief. Why not? Please. Over the months I had come to need Prozac in a complicated way, had come to see it as my savior, half hating it, half loving it. I unscrewed the capsules and poured their contents over my fingers. Healing talc, gone. Dead sand. I fingered the empty husks.

"You'll feel better if you come to church with us," Kat said to me that Sunday morning. She peered into my face, which must have been white and drawn. "Are you suffering from some city sickness?"

I shrugged. My eyes hurt from crying. I couldn't read or write; I could only add, subtract, divide, divide again.

"Come to church," Kat said. "We can ask the preacher to pray for you."

But I didn't believe in prayers where my illness was concerned. I had come to think, through my reading and the words of doctors, and especially through my brain's rapid response to a drug, that whatever was wrong with me had a simplistic chemical cause. Such a belief can be devastating to sick people, for on top of their illness they must struggle with the sense that illness lacks any creative possibilities.

I think these beliefs, so common in today's high-tech biomedical era in which the focus is relentlessly reductionistic, rob illness of its potential dignity. Illness can be dignified; we can conceive of pain as a kind of complex answer from an elegant system, an arrow pointing inward, a message from soil or sky.

Not so for me. I wouldn't go to church or temple. I wouldn't talk or ask or wonder, for these are distinctly human activities, and I'd come to view myself as less than human.

An anger rose up in me then, a rage. I woke late one night, hands fisted. It took me an hour to get out of bed, so many numbers I had to do, but I was determined.

And then I was walking outside, pushing past the need to count before every step. The night air was muggy, and insects raised a chorus.

I passed midnight fields, a single shack with lighted windows. Cows slept in a pasture.

I rounded the pasture, walked up a hill. And then, before me, spreading out in moonglow, a lake. I stood by its lip. My mind was buzzing and jerking. I don't know at what point the swans appeared — white swans, they must have been, but in silhouette they looked black. They seemed to materialize straight out of the slumbering water. They rose to the surface of the water as memories rise to the surface of consciousness. Hundreds of black swans suddenly, floating absolutely silent, and as I stood there the counting ceased, my mind became silent, and I watched. The swans drifted until it seemed, for a few moments, that they were inside of me, seven dark, silent birds, fourteen princesses, a single self swimming in a tepid sea.

I don't know how long I stood there, or when, exactly, I left. The swans disappeared eventually. The counting ticking talking of my mind resumed.

Still, even in chattering illness I had been quieted for a bit; doors in me had opened; elegance had entered.

This thought calmed me. I was not completely claimed by illness, nor a prisoner of Prozac, entirely dependent on the medication to function. Part of me was still free, a private space not absolutely permeated by pain. A space I could learn to cultivate.

Over the next few days, I noticed that even in the thicket of obsessions my mind sometimes swam into the world, if only for brief forays. There, while I struggled to take a step, was the sun on a green plate. *Remember that,* I said to myself. And here, while I stood fixated in a doorway, was a beetle with a purplish shell, like eggplants growing in wet soil. *Appreciate this,* I told myself, and I can say I did, those slivers of seconds when I returned to the world. I loved the beetle, ached for the eggplant, paddled in a lake with black swans.

And so a part of me began to learn about living outside the disease, cultivating appreciation for a few free moments. It was nothing I would have wished for myself, nothing to noisily celebrate. But it was something, and I could choose it, even while mourning the paralyzed parts of me, the pill that had failed me.

A long time ago, Freud coined the term "superego." A direct translation from German is "over I." Maybe what Freud meant, or should have meant, was not a punitive voice but the angel in the self who rises above an ego under siege, or a medicated mind, to experience the world from a narrow but occasionally gratifying ledge.

I am thirty-one now, and I know that ledge well. It is a smaller space than I would have wished for myself — I who would like to possess a mind free and flexible. I don't. Even after I raised my dose, the Prozac never worked as well as it once had, and years later I am sometimes sad about that, other times strangely relieved, even though my brain is hounded. I must check my keys, the stove; I must pause many times as I write this and do a ritual count to thirty. It's distracting, to say the least, but still I write this. I can walk and talk and play. I've come to live my life in those brief stretches of silence that arrive throughout the day, working at what I know is an admirable speed, accomplishing all I can in clear pauses, knowing those pauses may be short-lived. I am learning something about the single moment, how rife with potential it is, how truly loud its tick. I have heard clocks and clocks. Time shines, sad and good.

And what of the unclear, mind-cluttered stretches? These, as well, I have bent to. I read books now, even when my brain has real difficulty taking in words. Half a word, or a word blurred by static, is better than nothing at all. There is also a kind of stance I've developed, detaching my mind from my mind, letting the static sizzle on while I walk, talk, read, while the obsessive cycles continue and I, stepping aside, try to link my life to something else. It is a meditative exercise of a high order, and one I'm getting better at. Compensations can be gritty gifts.

Is this adaptation a spiritual thing? When I'm living in moments of clarity, have I transcended disease, or has disease transformed me, taught me how to live in secret niches? I don't know.

A few nights ago, a man at a party, a psychologist, talked about the brain. "The amazing thing," he said, "is that if you cut the corpus callosum of small children, they learn without the aid of medication or reparative surgery how to transfer information from the left to the right hemisphere. And because we know cerebral neurons never rejuvenate, that's evidence," he said, "for a mind that lives beyond the brain, a mind outside of our biologies."

Perhaps. Or perhaps our biologies are broader than we ever thought. Perhaps the brain, because of its wound, has been forced into some kink of creativity we can neither see nor explain. This is what the doctors didn't tell me about illness: that an answer to illness is not necessarily cure, but an ambivalent compensation. Disease, for sure, is disorganization, but cure is not necessarily the synthetic, pill-swallowing righting of the mess. To believe this is to define brain function in rigid terms of "normal" and "abnormal," a devastating definition for many. And to believe this, especially where the psyche is concerned, may also mean dependence on psychotropic drugs, and the risk of grave disappointment if the drugs stop working.

I think of those children, their heads on white sheets, their corpus callosa exposed and cut. I wonder who did that to them, and why. I'm sure there is some compelling medical explanation — wracking seizures that need to be stopped — but still, the image disturbs me. I think more, though, of the children's brains once sewn back inside the bony pockets of skull. There, in the secret dark, between wrenched hemispheres, I imagine tiny tendrils growing, so small and so deep not even the strongest machines can see them. They are real but not real, biological but spiritual. They wind in and out, joining left to right, building webbed wings and rickety bridges, sending out messengers with critical information, like the earliest angels who descended from the sky with news and challenge, wrestling with us in nighttime deserts, straining our thighs, stretching our bodies in pain, no doubt, until our skin took on new shapes.

SUSAN SONTAG

A Century of Cinema

FROM THE NEW YORK TIMES MAGAZINE

CINEMA'S HUNDRED YEARS seem to have the shape of a life cycle: an inevitable birth, the steady accumulation of glories, and the onset in the last decade of an ignominious, irreversible decline. This doesn't mean that there won't be any more new films that one can admire. But such films will not simply be exceptions; that's true of great achievement in any art. They will have to be heroic violations of the norms and practices that now govern moviemaking everywhere in the capitalist and would-be capitalist world — which is to say, everywhere. And ordinary films, films made purely for entertainment (that is, commercial) purposes, will continue to be astonishingly witless; already the vast majority fail resoundingly to appeal to their cynically targeted audiences. While the point of a great film is now, more than ever, to be a one-of-a-kind achievement, the commercial cinema has settled for a policy of bloated, derivative filmmaking, a brazen combinatory or recombinatory art, in the hope of reproducing past successes. Every film that hopes to reach the largest possible audience is designed as some kind of remake. Cinema, once heralded as *the* art of the twentieth century, seems now, as the century closes numerically, to be a decadent art.

Perhaps it is not cinema that has ended, but only cinephilia, the name of the very specific kind of love that cinema inspired. Each art breeds its fanatics. The love that cinema inspired, however, was special. It was born of the sense that cinema was an art unlike any other: quintessentially modern, distinctively accessible, poetic and mysterious and erotic and moral — all at the same time. Cinema had apostles (it was like religion). Cinema was a crusade. Cinema was a world-view. Lovers of poetry or opera or dance don't think there is *only* poetry or opera or dance. But lovers of cinema could think there was only cinema. That the movies encapsulated every-thing — and they did. It was both the book of art and the book of life.

As many people have noted, the start of moviemaking a hundred years ago was, conveniently, a double start. In that first year, 1895, two kinds of films were made, proposing two modes of what cin-ema could be: cinema as the transcription of real, unstaged life (the Lumière brothers) and cinema as invention, artifice, illusion, fantasy (Méliès). But this was never a true opposition. For those first audiences watching the Lumière brothers' *The Arrival of a Train at La Ciotat Station,* the camera's transmission of a banal sight was a fantastic experience. Cinema began in wonder, the wonder that reality can be transcribed with such magical immediacy. All of cinema is an attempt to perpetuate and to reinvent that sense of wonder.

Everything begins with that moment, one hundred years ago, when the train pulled into the station. People took movies into themselves, just as the public cried out with excitement, actually ducked, as the train seemed to move toward *them.* Until the advent of television emptied the movie theaters, it was from a weekly visit to the cinema that you learned (or tried to learn) how to walk, to smoke, to kiss, to fight, to suffer. Movies gave you tips about how to be attractive, such as: it looks good to wear a raincoat even when it isn't raining. But whatever you took home from the movies was only a part of the larger experience of losing yourself in faces, in lives that were *not* yours — which is the more inclusive form of desire embodied in the movie experience. The strongest experi-ence was simply to surrender to, to be transported by, what was on the screen. You wanted to be kidnapped by the movie.

The first prerequisite of being kidnapped was to be overwhelmed by the physical presence of the image. And the conditions of "going to the movies" were essential to that. To see a great film only on TV isn't to have really seen that film. (This is equally true of those made for TV, like Fassbinder's *Berlin Alexanderplatz* and the two *Heimat* films of Edgar Reitz.) It's not only the difference of dimensions: the superiority of the larger-than-you image in the theater to the little image on the box at home. The conditions of paying attention in a domestic space are radically disrespectful of film. Since film no longer has a standard size, home screens *can* be as big as living room or bedroom walls. But you are still in a living room or a bedroom, alone or with familiars. To be kidnapped, you have to be in a movie theater, seated in the dark among anonymous strangers.

No amount of mourning will revive the vanished rituals — erotic, ruminative — of the darkened theater. The reduction of cinema to assaultive images and the unprincipled manipulation of images (faster and faster cutting) to be more attention-grabbing have produced a disincarnated, lightweight cinema that doesn't demand anyone's full attention. Images now appear in any size and on a variety of surfaces: on a screen in a theater, on home screens as small as the palm of your hand or as big as a wall, on disco walls and megascreens hanging above sports arenas and the outsides of tall public buildings. The sheer ubiquity of moving images has steadily undermined the standards people once had both for cinema as art at its most serious and for cinema as popular entertainment.

In the first years there was essentially no difference between cinema as art and cinema as entertainment. And all films of the silent era — from the masterpieces of Feuillade, D. W. Griffith, Djiga Vertov, Pabst, Murnau, King Vidor to the most formula-ridden melodramas and comedies — are on a very high artistic level compared with most of what was to follow. With the coming of sound, the image-making lost much of its brilliance and poetry, and commercial standards tightened. This way of making movies — the Hollywood system — dominated filmmaking for about twenty-five years (roughly from 1930 to 1955). The most original directors, like Erich von Stroheim and Orson Welles, were defeated by the system and eventually went into artistic exile in Europe — where more or less the same quality-defeating system was now in place, with lower budgets; only in France were a large number of superb films produced throughout this period. Then, in the mid-1950s, vanguard ideas took hold again, rooted in the idea of cinema as a craft pioneered by the Italian films of the immediate postwar period. A dazzling number of ambitious, passionate, artisanally crafted films of the highest seriousness got made with new actors and tiny crews, went to film festivals (of which there were more and more), and from there, garlanded with festival prizes, into movie theaters around the world. This golden age actually lasted as long as twenty years.

It was at this specific moment in the hundred-year history of cinema that going to movies, thinking about movies, talking about movies, became a passion among university students and other young people. You fell in love not just with actors but with cinema itself. Cinephilia had first become visible in the 1950s in France: its forum was the legendary film magazine *Cahiers du Cinéma* (followed by similarly fervent magazines in Germany, Italy, Great Britain, Sweden, the United States, Canada). Its temples, as it spread throughout Europe and the Americas, were the many cinemathèques and film clubs specializing in films from the past and directors' retrospectives which sprang up. The 1960s and early 1970s were the feverish age of moviegoing, with the full-time cinephile always hoping to find a seat as close as possible to the big screen, ideally the third row center. "One can't live without Rossellini," declares a character in Bertolucci's *Before the Revolution* (1964) — and means it.

Cinephilia — a source of exultation in the films of Godard and Truffaut and the early Bertolucci and Syberberg; a morose lament in some recent films of Nanni Moretti — was mostly a Western European affair. The great directors of "the other Europe" (Zanussi in Poland, Angelopoulos in Greece, Tarkovsky and Sokurov in Russia, Jancso and Tarr in Hungary) and the great Japanese directors (Ozu, Mizoguchi, Kurosawa, Oshima, Imamura) have tended not to be cinephiles, perhaps because in Budapest or Moscow or Tokyo or Warsaw or Athens there wasn't a chance to get a cinemathèque education. The distinctive thing about cinephile taste was that it embraced both "art" films and popular films. Thus, European cinephilia had a romantic relation to the films of certain directors in Hollywood at the apogee of the studio system: Godard for Howard Hawks, Fassbinder for Douglas Sirk. Of course, this moment — when cinephilia emerged — was also the moment when the Hollywood studio system was breaking up. It seemed that moviemaking had rewon the right to experiment; cinephiles could *afford* to be passionate (or sentimental) about the old Hollywood genre films. A host of new people came into cinema, including a generation of young film critics from *Cahiers du Cinéma;* the towering figure of that generation, indeed of several decades of filmmaking anywhere, was Jean-Luc Godard. A few writers turned out to be wildly talented filmmakers: Alexander Kluge in Germany, Pier Paolo Pasolini in Italy. (The model for the writer who turns to filmmaking actually emerged earlier, in France, with Pagnol in the 1930s and Cocteau in the 1940s; but it was not until the 1960s that this seemed, at least in Europe, normal.) Cinema seemed reborn.

For some fifteen years there were new masterpieces every month, and one allowed oneself to imagine that this would go on forever. How far away that era seems now. To be sure, there was always a conflict between cinema as an industry and cinema as an art, cinema as routine and cinema as experiment. But the conflict was not such as to make impossible the making of wonderful films, sometimes within and sometimes outside of mainstream cinema. Now the balance has tipped decisively in favor of cinema as an industry. The great cinema of the 1960s and 1970s has been thoroughly repudiated. Already in the 1970s Hollywood was plagiarizing and banalizing the innovations in narrative method and editing of successful new European and ever-marginal independent American films. Then came the catastrophic rise in production costs in the 1980s, which secured the worldwide reimposition of industry standards of making and distributing films on a far more coercive, this time truly global scale. The result can be seen in the melancholy fate of some of the greatest directors of the last decades. What place is there today for a maverick like Hans Jürgen Syberberg, who has stopped making films altogether, or for the great Godard, who now makes films about the history of film, on video? Consider some other cases. The internationalizing of financing and therefore of casts was a disaster for Andrei Tarkovsky in the last two films of his stupendous, tragically abbreviated career. And these conditions for making films have proved to be as much an artistic disaster for two of the most valuable directors still working: Krzysztof Zanussi *(The Structure of Crystals, Illumination, Spiral, Contract)* and Theo Angelopoulos *(Reconstruction, Days of '36, The Traveling Players).* And what will happen now to Bela Tarr *(Damnation, Satantango)*? And how will Aleksandr Sokurov *(Save and Protect, Days of Eclipse, The Second Circle, Stone, Whispering Pages)* find the money to go on making films, his sublime films, under the rude conditions of Russian capitalism?

Predictably, the love of cinema has waned. People still like going to the movies, and some people still care about and expect something special, necessary from a film. And wonderful films are still being made: Mike Leigh's *Naked,* Gianni Amelio's *Lamerica,* Fred Keleman's *Fate,* Abbas Kiarostami's *Through the Olive Trees.* But one hardly finds anymore, at least among the young, the distinctive cinephilic love of movies, which is not simply love of but a certain *taste* in films (grounded in a vast appetite for seeing and reseeing as much as possible of cinema's glorious past). Cinephilia itself has come under attack, as something quaint, outmoded, snobbish. For cinephilia implies that films are unique, unrepeatable, magic experiences. Cinephilia tells us that the Hollywood remake of Godard's *Breathless* cannot be as good as the original. Cinephilia has no role in the era of hyperindustrial films. For cinephilia cannot help, by the very range and eclecticism of its passions, but sponsor the idea of the film as, first of all, a poetic object, and cannot help but incite those outside the movie industry, like painters and writers, to want to make films, too. It is precisely this conception of movies that must be defeated. That has been defeated.

If cinephilia is dead, then movies are dead too — no matter how many movies, even very good ones, go on being made. If cinema can be resurrected, it will only be through the birth of a new kind of cine-love.

GAY TALESE

Ali in Havana

FROM ESQUIRE

IT IS A WARM, breezy, palm-flapping winter evening in Havana, and the leading restaurants are crowded with tourists from Europe, Asia, and South America being serenaded by guitarists relentlessly singing "*Guan-tan-a-mera . . . guajira . . . Guan-tan-a-mera*"; and at the Café Cantante there are clamorous salsa dancers, mambo kings, grunting, bare-chested male performers lifting tables with their teeth, and turbaned women swathed in hip-hugging skirts, blowing whistles while gyrating their glistening bodies into an erotic frenzy. In the café's audience as well as in the restaurants, hotels, and other public places throughout the island, cigarettes and cigars are smoked without restraint or restriction. Two prostitutes are smoking and talking privately on the corner of a dimly lit street bordering the manicured lawns of Havana's five-star Hotel Nacional. They are copper-colored women in their early twenties wearing faded miniskirts and halters, and as they chat, they are watching attentively while two men — one white, the other black — huddle over the raised trunk of a parked red Toyota, arguing about the prices of the boxes of black-market Havana cigars that are stacked within.

The white man is a square-jawed Hungarian in his mid-thirties, wearing a beige tropical suit and a wide yellow tie, and he is one of Havana's leading entrepreneurs in the thriving illegal business of selling top-quality hand-rolled Cuban cigars below the local and international market price. The black man behind the car is a well-built, baldish, gray-bearded individual in his mid-fifties from Los Angeles named Howard Bingham; and no matter what price

the Hungarian quotes, Bingham shakes his head and says, "No, no
— that's too much!"

"You're crazy!" cries the Hungarian in slightly accented English,
taking one of the boxes from the trunk and waving it in Howard
Bingham's face. "These are Cohiba Esplendidos! The best in the
world! You will pay one thousand dollars for a box like this in the
States."

"Not me," says Bingham, who wears a Hawaiian shirt with a camera strapped around his neck. He is a professional photographer,
and he is staying at the Hotel Nacional with his friend Muhammad
Ali. "I wouldn't give you more than fifty dollars."

"You really are crazy," says the Hungarian, slicing through the
box's paper seal with his fingernail, opening the lid to reveal a
gleaming row of labeled Esplendidos.

"Fifty dollars," says Bingham.

"A hundred dollars," insists the Hungarian. "And hurry! The
police could be driving around." The Hungarian straightens up
and stares over the car toward the palm-lined lawn and stan-
chioned lights that glow in the distance along the road leading to
the hotel's ornate portico, which is now jammed with people and
vehicles; then he turns and flings a glance back toward the nearby
public street, where he notices that the prostitutes are now blowing
smoke in his direction. He frowns.

"Quick, quick," he says to Bingham, handing him the box. "One
hundred dollars."

Howard Bingham does not smoke. He and Muhammad Ali and
their traveling companions are leaving Havana tomorrow, after
participating in a five-day American humanitarian-aid mission that
brought a planeload of medical supplies to hospitals and clinics
depleted by the United States' embargo, and Bingham would like
to return home with some fine contraband cigars for his friends.
But, on the other hand, one hundred is still too much.

"Fifty dollars," says Bingham determinedly, looking at his watch.
He begins to walk away.

"O.K., O.K.," the Hungarian says petulantly. "Fifty."

Bingham reaches into his pocket for the money, and the Hungarian grabs it and gives him the Esplendidos before driving off
in the Toyota. One of the prostitutes takes a few steps toward Bingham, but the photographer hurries on to the hotel. Fidel Castro is

having a reception tonight for Muhammad Ali, and Bingham has only a half hour to change and be at the portico to catch the chartered bus that will take them to the government's headquarters. He will be bringing one of his photographs to the Cuban leader: an enlarged, framed portrait showing Muhammad Ali and Malcolm X walking together along a Harlem sidewalk in 1963. Malcolm X was thirty-seven at the time, two years away from an assassin's bullet; the twenty-one-year-old Ali was about to win the heavyweight title in a remarkable upset over Sonny Liston in Miami. Bingham's photograph is inscribed, TO PRESIDENT FIDEL CASTRO, FROM MUHAMMAD ALI. Under his signature, the former champion has sketched a little heart.

Although Muhammad Ali is now fifty-four and has been retired from boxing for more than fifteen years, he is still one of the most famous men in the world, being identifiable throughout five continents; and as he walks through the lobby of the Hotel Nacional toward the bus, wearing a gray sharkskin suit and a white cotton shirt buttoned at the neck without a tie, several guests approach him and request his autograph. It takes him about thirty seconds to write "Muhammad Ali," so shaky are his hands from the effects of Parkinson's syndrome; and though he walks without support, his movements are quite slow, and Howard Bingham and Ali's fourth wife, Yolanda, are following nearby.

Bingham met Ali thirty-five years ago in Los Angeles, shortly after the fighter had turned professional and before he discarded his "slave name" (Cassius Marcellus Clay) and joined the Black Muslims. Bingham subsequently became his closest male friend and has photographed every aspect of Ali's life: his rise and fall three times as the heavyweight champion; his three-year expulsion from boxing, beginning in 1967, for refusing to serve in the American military during the Vietnam War ("I ain't got no quarrel with them Vietcong"); his four marriages; his fatherhood of nine children (one adopted, two out of wedlock); his endless public appearances in all parts of the world — Germany, England, Egypt (sailing on the Nile with a son of Elijah Muhammad's), Sweden, Libya, Pakistan (hugging refugees from Afghanistan), Japan, Indonesia, Ghana (wearing a dashiki and posing with President Kwame Nkrumah), Zaire (beating George Foreman), Manila (beating Joe Fra-

zier) . . . and now, on the final night of his 1996 visit to Cuba, he is
en route to a social encounter with an aging contender he has long
admired — one who has survived at the top for nearly forty years
despite the ill will of nine American presidents, the CIA, the Mafia,
and various militant Cuban Americans.

Bingham waits for Ali near the open door of the charter bus
that is blocking the hotel's entrance; but Ali lingers within the
crowd in the lobby, and Yolanda steps aside to let some people get
closer to her husband.

She is a large and pretty woman of thirty-eight, with a radiant
smile and a freckled, fair complexion that reflects her interracial
ancestry. A scarf is loosely draped over her head and shoulders,
her arms are covered by long sleeves, and her well-designed dress
in vivid hues hangs below her knees. She converted to Islam from
Catholicism when she married Ali, a man sixteen years her senior
but one with whom she shared a familial bond dating back to her
girlhood in their native Louisville, where her mother and Ali's
mother were sisterly soul mates who traveled together to attend
his fights. Yolanda had occasionally joined Ali's entourage, becoming acquainted with not only the boxing element but with Ali's
female contemporaries who were his lovers, his wives, the mothers
of his children; and she remained in touch with Ali throughout
the 1970s, while she majored in psychology at Vanderbilt and later
earned her master's degree in business at UCLA. Then — with the
end of Ali's boxing career, his third marriage, and his vibrant
health — Yolanda intimately entered his life as casually and naturally as she now stands waiting to reclaim her place at his side.

She knows that he is enjoying himself. There is a slight twinkle
in his eyes, not much expression on his face, and no words forthcoming from this once most talkative of champions. But the mind
behind his Parkinson's mask is functioning normally, and he is
characteristically committed to what he is doing: he is spelling out
his full name on whatever cards or scraps of paper his admirers
are handing him. "Muhammad Ali." He does not settle for a
time-saving "Ali" or his mere initials. He has never shortchanged
his audience.

And in this audience tonight are people from Latin America,
Canada, Africa, Russia, China, Germany, France. There are two
hundred French travel agents staying at the hotel in conjunction

with the Cuban government's campaign to increase its growing
tourist trade (which last year saw about 745,000 visitors spending
an estimated one billion dollars on the island). There is also on
hand an Italian movie producer and his lady friend from Rome
and a onetime Japanese wrestler, Antonio Inoki, who injured Ali's
legs during a 1976 exhibition in Tokyo (but who warmly embraced
him two nights ago in the hotel's lounge as they sat listening
to Cuban pianist Chucho Valdes playing jazz on a Russian-made
Moskva baby grand); and there is also in the crowd, standing taller
than the rest, the forty-three-year-old, six-foot five-inch Cuban
heavyweight hero Teófilo Stevenson, who was a three-time Olympic
gold medalist, in 1972, 1976, and 1980, and who, on this island
at least, is every bit as renowned as Ali or Castro.

Though part of Stevenson's reputation derives from his erst-
while power and skill in the ring (although he never fought Ali),
it is also attributable to his not having succumbed to the offers of
professional boxing promoters, stubbornly resisting the Yankee
dollar — although Stevenson hardly seems deprived. He dwells
among his countrymen like a towering Cuban peacock, occupying
high positions within the government's athletic programs and
gaining sufficient attention from the island's women to have gar-
nered four wives so far, who are testimony to his eclectic taste.

His first wife was a dance instructor. His second was an industrial
engineer. His third was a medical doctor. His fourth and present
wife is a criminal attorney. Her name is Fraymari, and she is a
girlishly petite olive-skinned woman of twenty-three who, standing
next to her husband in the lobby, rises barely higher than the midsection of his embroidered guayabera — a tightly tailored, short-
sleeved shirt that accentuates his tapered torso, his broad shoulders, and the length of his dark, muscular arms, which once
prevented his opponents from doing any injustice to his winning
Latin looks.

Stevenson always fought from an upright position, and he maintains that posture today. When people talk to him, his eyes look
downward, but his head remains high. The firm jaw of his oval-
shaped head seems to be locked at a right angle to his straight-
spined back. He is a proud man who exhibits all of his height. But
he does listen, especially when the words being directed up at him
are coming from the perky little attorney who is his wife. Fraymari

is now reminding him that it is getting late — everyone should be on the bus; Fidel may be waiting.

Stevenson lowers his eyes toward her and winks. He has gotten the message. He has been Ali's principal escort throughout this visit. He was also Ali's guest in the United States during the fall of 1995; and though he knows only a few words of English, and Ali no Spanish, they are brotherly in their body language.

Stevenson edges himself into the crowd and gently places his right arm around the shoulders of his fellow champion. And then, slowly but firmly, he guides Ali toward the bus.

The road to Fidel Castro's Palace of the Revolution leads through a memory lane of old American automobiles chugging along at about twenty-five miles an hour — springless, pre-embargo Ford coupes and Plymouth sedans, DeSotos and LaSalles, Nashes and Studebakers, and various vehicular collages created out of Cadillac grilles and Oldsmobile axles and Buick fenders patched with pieces of oil-drum metal and powered by engines interlinked with kitchen utensils and pre-Batista lawn mowers and other gadgets that have elevated the craft of tinkering in Cuba to the status of high art.

The relatively newer forms of transportation seen on the road are, of course, non-American products — Polish Fiats, Russian Ladas, German motor scooters, Chinese bicycles, and the glistening, newly imported, air-conditioned Japanese bus from which Muhammad Ali is now gazing through a closed window out toward the street. At times, he raises a hand in response to one of the waving pedestrians or cyclists or motorists who recognize the bus, which has been shown repeatedly on the local TV news conveying Ali and his companions to the medical centers and tourist sites that have been part of the busy itinerary.

On the bus, as always, Ali is sitting alone, spread out across the two front seats in the left aisle directly behind the Cuban driver. Yolanda sits a few feet ahead of him to the right; she is adjacent to the driver and within inches of the windshield. The seats behind her are occupied by Teófilo Stevenson, Fraymari, and the photographer Bingham. Seated behind Ali, and also occupying two seats, is an American screenwriter named Greg Howard, who weighs more than three hundred pounds. Although he has traveled with Ali for only a few months while researching a film on the fighter's life, Greg Howard has firmly established himself as an intimate sidekick, and as such is among the very few on this trip who have heard Ali's voice. Ali speaks so softly that it is impossible to hear him in a crowd, and as a result whatever public comments or sentiments he is expected to, or chooses to, express are verbalized by Yolanda, or Bingham, or Teófilo Stevenson, or even at times by this stout young screenwriter.

"Ali is in his Zen period," Greg Howard has said more than once, in reference to Ali's quiescence. Like Ali, he admires what he has seen so far in Cuba — "There's no racism here" — and as a black man he has long identified with many of Ali's frustrations and confrontations. His student thesis at Princeton analyzed the Newark race riots of 1967, and the Hollywood script he most recently completed focuses on the Negro baseball leagues of the pre–World War II years. He envisions his new work on Ali in the genre of *Gandhi*.

The two-dozen bus seats behind those tacitly reserved for Ali's inner circle are occupied by the secretary-general of the Cuban Red Cross and the American humanitarian personnel who have entrusted him with $500,000 worth of donated medical supplies; and there are also the two Cuban interpreters and a dozen members of the American media, including the CBS-TV commentator Ed Bradley and his producers and camera crew from *60 Minutes*.

Ed Bradley is a gracious but reserved individualist who has appeared on television for a decade with his left earlobe pierced by a small circular ring — which, after some unfavorable comment initially expressed by his colleagues Mike Wallace and Andy Rooney, prompted Bradley's explanation: "It's *my* ear." Bradley also indulges in his identity as a cigar smoker; and as he sits in the midsection of the bus next to his Haitian lady friend, he is taking full advantage of the Communist regime's laissez-faire attitude toward tobacco, puffing away on a Cohiba Robusto, for which he paid full price at the Nacional's tobacco shop — and which now exudes a costly cloud of fragrance that appeals to his friend (who occasionally also smokes cigars) but is not appreciated by the two California women who are seated two rows back and are affiliated with a humanitarian-aid agency.

Indeed, the women have been commenting about the smoking

habits of countless people they have encountered in Havana, being especially disappointed to discover earlier this very day that the pediatric hospital they visited (and to which they committed donations) is under the supervision of three tobacco-loving family physicians. When one of the American women, a blonde from Santa Barbara, reproached one of the cigarette-smoking doctors indirectly for setting such a poor example, she was told in effect that the island's health statistics regarding longevity, infant mortality, and general fitness compared favorably with those in the United States and were probably better than those of Americans residing in the capital city of Washington. On the other hand, the doctor made it clear that he did not believe that smoking was good for one's health — after all, Fidel himself had given it up; but unfortunately, the doctor added, in a classic understatement, "some people have not followed him."

Nothing the doctor said appeased the woman from Santa Barbara. She did not, however, wish to appear confrontational at the hospital's news conference, which was covered by the press; nor during her many bus rides with Ed Bradley did she ever request that he discard his cigar. "Mr. Bradley intimidates me," she confided to her California coworker. But he was of course living within the law on this island that the doctor had called "the cradle of the best tobacco in the world." In Cuba, the most available American periodical on the newsstands is *Cigar Aficionado*.

The bus passes through the Plaza de la Revolución and comes to a halt at a security checkpoint near the large glass doors that open onto the marble-floored foyer of a 1950s modern building that is the center of communism's only stronghold in the Western Hemisphere.

As the bus door swings open, Greg Howard moves forward in his seat and grabs the 235-pound Muhammad Ali by the arms and shoulders and helps him to his feet; and after Ali has made his way down to the metal step, he turns and stretches back into the bus to take hold of the extended hands and forearms of the 300-pound screenwriter and pulls him to a standing position. This routine, repeated at each and every bus stop throughout the week, is never accompanied by either man's acknowledging that he has received any assistance, although Ali is aware that some passengers find the pas de deux quite amusing, and he is not reluctant to use his friend to further comic effect. After the bus had made an earlier stop in front of the sixteenth-century Morro Castle — where Ali had followed Teófilo Stevenson up a 117-step spiral staircase for a rooftop view of Havana Harbor — he spotted the solitary figure of Greg Howard standing below in the courtyard. Knowing that there was no way the narrow staircase could accommodate Howard's wide body, Ali suddenly began to wave his arms, summoning Howard to come up and join him.

Castro's security guards, who know in advance the names of all the bus passengers, guide Ali and the others through the glass doors and then into a pair of waiting elevators for a brief ride that is followed by a short walk through a corridor and finally into a large white-walled reception room, where it is announced that Fidel Castro will soon join them. The room has high ceilings and potted palms in every corner and is sparsely furnished with modern tan leather furniture. Next to a sofa is a table with two telephones, one gray and the other red. Overlooking the sofa is an oil painting of the Viñales valley, which lies west of Havana; and among the primitive art displayed on a circular table in front of the sofa is a grotesque tribal figure similar to the one Ali had examined earlier in the week at a trinket stand while touring with the group in Havana's Old Square. Ali had then whispered into the ear of Howard Bingham, and Bingham had repeated aloud what Ali had said: "Joe Frazier."

Ali now stands in the middle of the room, next to Bingham, who carries under his arm the framed photograph he plans to give Castro. Teófilo Stevenson and Fraymari stand facing them. The diminutive and delicate-boned Fraymari has painted her lips scarlet and has pulled back her hair in a matronly manner, hoping no doubt to appear more mature than her twenty-three years suggest, but standing next to the three much older and heavier and taller men transforms her image closer to that of an anorexic teenager. Ali's wife and Greg Howard are wandering about within the group that is exchanging comments in muted tones, either in English or Spanish, sometimes assisted by the interpreters. Ali's hands are shaking uncontrollably at his sides; but since his companions have witnessed this all week, the only people who are now paying attention are the security guards posted near the door.

Also waiting near the door for Castro is the four-man CBS camera team, and chatting with them and his two producers is Ed Bradley, without his cigar. There are no ashtrays in this room! This is a most uncommon sight in Cuba. Its implications might be political. Perhaps the sensibilities of the blond woman from Santa Barbara were taken into account by the doctors at the hospital and communicated to Castro's underlings, who are now making a conciliatory gesture toward their American benefactress.

Since the security guards have not invited the guests to be seated, everybody remains standing — for ten minutes, for twenty minutes, and then for a full half hour. Teófilo Stevenson shifts his weight from foot to foot and gazes over the heads of the crowd toward the upper level of the portal through which Castro is expected to enter — if he shows up. Stevenson knows from experience that Castro's schedule is unpredictable. There is always a crisis of some sort in Cuba, and it has long been rumored on the island that Castro constantly changes the location of where he sleeps. The identity of his bed partners is, of course, a state secret. Two nights ago, Stevenson and Ali and the rest were kept waiting until midnight for an expected meeting with Castro at the Hotel Biocaribe (to which Bingham had brought his gift photograph). But Castro never appeared. And no explanation was offered.

Now in this reception room, it is already 9 P.M. Ali continues to shake. No one has had dinner. The small talk is getting smaller. A few people would like to smoke. The regime is not assuaging anyone in this crowd with a bartender. It is a cocktail party without cocktails. There are not even canapés or soft drinks. Everyone is becoming increasingly restless — and then suddenly there is a collective sigh. The very familiar man with the beard strides into the room, dressed for guerrilla combat; and in a cheerful, high-pitched voice that soars beyond his whiskers, he announces, *"Buenas noches!"*

In an even higher tone, he repeats, *"Buenas noches,"* this time with a few waves to the group while hastening toward the guest of honor; and then, with his arms extended, the seventy-year-old Fidel Castro immediately obscures the lower half of Ali's expressionless face with a gentle embrace and his flowing gray beard.

"I am glad to see you," Castro says to Ali, via the interpreter who followed him into the room, a comely, fair-skinned woman with a refined English accent. "I am very, very glad to see you," Castro continues, backing up to look into Ali's eyes while holding on to his trembling arms, "and I am thankful for your visit." Castro then releases his grip and awaits a possible reply. Ali says nothing. His expression remains characteristically fixed and benign, and his eyes do not blink despite the flashbulbs of several surrounding photographers. As the silence persists, Castro turns toward his old friend Teófilo Stevenson, feigning a jab. The Cuban boxing champion lowers his eyes and, with widened lips and cheeks, registers a smile. Castro then notices the tiny brunette standing beside Stevenson.

"Stevenson, who is this young woman?" Castro asks aloud in a tone of obvious approval. But before Stevenson can reply, Fraymari steps forward with a hint of lawyerly indignation: "You mean you don't remember me?"

Castro seems stunned. He smiles feebly, trying to conceal his confusion. He turns inquiringly toward his boxing hero, but Stevenson's eyes only roll upward. Stevenson knows that Castro has met Fraymari socially on earlier occasions, but unfortunately the Cuban leader has forgotten, and it is equally unfortunate that Fraymari is now behaving like a prosecutor.

"You held my son in your arms before he was one year old!" she reminds him while Castro continues to ponder. The crowd is attentive; the television cameras are rolling.

"At a volleyball game?" Castro asks tentatively.

"No, no," Stevenson interrupts, before Fraymari can say anything more, "that was my former wife. The doctor."

Castro slowly shakes his head in mock disapproval. Then he abruptly turns away from the couple, but not before reminding Stevenson, "You should get name tags."

Castro redirects his attention to Muhammad Ali. He studies Ali's face.

"Where is your wife?" he asks softly. Ali says nothing. There is more silence and turning of heads in the group until Howard Bingham spots Yolanda standing near the back and waves her to Castro's side.

Before she arrives, Bingham steps forward and presents Castro with the photograph of Ali and Malcolm X in Harlem in 1963. Castro holds it up level with his eyes and studies it silently for several seconds. When this picture was taken, Castro had been in control of Cuba for nearly four years. He was then thirty-seven. In 1959, he defeated the U.S.-backed dictator Fulgencio Batista, overcoming odds greater than Ali's subsequent victory over the supposedly unbeatable Sonny Liston. Batista had actually announced Castro's death back in 1956. Castro, then hiding in a secret outpost, thirty years old and beardless, was a disgruntled Jesuit-trained lawyer who was born into a landowning family and who craved Batista's job. At thirty-two, he had it. Batista was forced to flee to the Dominican Republic.

During this period, Muhammad Ali was only an amateur. His greatest achievement would come in 1960, when he received a gold medal in Rome as a member of the United States Olympic boxing team. But later in the sixties, he and Castro would share the world stage as figures moving against the American establishment — and now, in the twilight of their lives, on this winter's night in Havana, they meet for the first time: Ali silent and Castro isolated on his island.

"Que bien!" Castro says to Howard Bingham before showing the photograph to his interpreter. Then Castro is introduced by Bingham to Ali's wife. After they exchange greetings through the interpreter, he asks her, as if surprised, "You don't speak Spanish?"

"No," she says softly. She begins to caress her husband's left wrist, on which he wears a $250 silver Swiss Army watch she bought him. It is the only jewelry Ali wears.

"But I thought I saw you speaking Spanish on the TV news this week," Castro continues wonderingly before acknowledging that her voice had obviously been dubbed.

"Do you live in New York?"

"No, we live in Michigan."

"Cold," says Castro.

"Very cold," she repeats.

"In Michigan, don't you find many people that speak Spanish?"

"No, not many," she says. "Mostly in California, New York . . ." and, after a pause, "Florida."

Castro nods. It takes him a few seconds to think up another question. Small talk has never been the forte of this man who specializes in nonstop haranguing monologues that can last for hours; and yet here he is, in a room crowded with camera crews and news photographers — a talk-show host with a guest of honor who is speechless. But Fidel Castro plods on, asking Ali's wife if she has a favorite sport.

"I play a little tennis," Yolanda says, and then asks him, "Do you play tennis?"

"Ping-Pong," he replies, quickly adding that during his youth he had been active in the ring. "I spent hours boxing . . ." he begins to reminisce, but before he finishes his sentence, he sees the slowly rising right fist of Muhammad Ali moving toward his chin! Exuberant cheering and handclapping resound through the room, and Castro jumps sideways toward Stevenson, shouting, *"Asesorame!"* — "Help me!"

Stevenson's long arms land upon Ali's shoulders from behind, squeezing him gently; and then, after he releases him, the two ex-champions face each other and begin to act out in slow motion the postures of competing prizefighters — bobbing, weaving, swinging, ducking — all of it done without touching and all of it accompanied by three minutes of ongoing applause and the clicking of cameras, and also some feelings of relief from Ali's friends because, in his own way, he has decided to join them. Ali still says nothing, his face still inscrutable, but he is less remote, less alone, and he does not pull away from Stevenson's embrace as the latter eagerly tells Castro about a boxing exhibition that he and Ali had staged earlier in the week at the Balado gym, in front of hundreds of fans and some of the island's up-and-coming contenders.

Stevenson did not actually explain that it had been merely another photo opportunity, one in which they sparred openhanded in the ring, wearing their street clothes and barely touching each other's bodies and faces; but then Stevenson had climbed out of the ring, leaving Ali to the more taxing test of withstanding two abbreviated rounds against one and then another young bully of grade school age who clearly had not come to participate in a kiddie show. They had come to floor the champ. Their bellicose little bodies and hot-gloved hands and helmeted hell-bent heads were consumed with fury and ambition; and as they charged ahead, swinging wildly and swaggering to the roars of their teenage friends and relatives at ringside, one could imagine their future boastings to their grandchildren: On one fine day back in the winter of '96, I whacked Muhammad Ali! Except, in truth, on this particular day, Ali was still too fast for them. He backpedaled and shifted and swayed, stood on the toes of his black woven-leather pointed shoes, and showed that his body was made for motion — his Parkinson's problems were lost in his shuffle, in the thrusts of his butterfly sting that whistled two feet above the heads of his aspiring assailants, in the dazzling dips of his rope-a-dope that had confounded George Foreman in Zaire, in his ever-memorable style, which in this Cuban gym moistened the eyes of his ever-observant photographer friend and provoked the overweight screenwriter to cry out in a voice that few in this noisy Spanish crowd could understand, "Ali's on a high! Ali's on a high!"

Teófilo Stevenson raises Ali's right arm above the head of Castro, and the news photographers spend several minutes posing the three of them together in flashing light. Castro then sees Fraymari watching alone at some distance. She is not smiling. Castro nods toward her. He summons a photographer to take a picture of Fraymari and himself. But she relaxes only after her husband comes over to join her in the conversation, which Castro immediately directs to the health and growth of their son, who is not yet two years old.

"Will he be as tall as his father?" Castro asks.

"I assume so," Fraymari says, glancing up toward her husband. She also has to look up when talking to Fidel Castro, for the Cuban leader is taller than six feet and his posture is nearly as erect as her husband's. Only the six-foot three-inch Muhammad Ali, who is standing with Bingham on the far side of her husband — and whose skin coloring, oval-shaped head, and burr-style haircut are very similar to her husband's — betrays his height with the slope-shouldered forward slouch he has developed since his illness.

"How much does your son weigh?" Castro continues.

"When he was one year old, he was already twenty-six pounds," Fraymari says. "This is three above normal. He was walking at nine months."

"She still breast-feeds him," Teófilo Stevenson says, seeming pleased.

"Oh, that's very nourishing," agrees Castro.

"Sometimes the kid becomes confused and thinks my chest is his mother's breast," Stevenson says, and he could have added that his son is also confused by Ali's sunglasses. The little boy engraved teeth marks all over the plastic frames while chewing on them during the days he accompanied his parents on Ali's bus tour.

As a CBS boom pole swoops down closer to catch the conversation, Castro reaches out to touch Stevenson's belly and asks, "How much do you weigh?"

"Two hundred thirty-eight pounds, more or less."

"That's thirty-eight more than me," Castro says, but he complains, "I eat very little. Very little. The diet advice I get is never accurate. I eat around fifteen hundred calories — less than thirty grams of protein, less than that."

Castro slaps a hand against his own midsection, which is relatively flat. If he does have a potbelly, it is concealed within his well-tailored uniform. Indeed, for a man of seventy, he seems in fine health. His facial skin is florid and unsagging, his dark eyes dart around the room with ever-alert intensity, and he has a full head of lustrous gray hair not thinning at the crown. The attention he pays to himself might be measured from his manicured fingernails down to his square-toed boots, which are unscuffed and smoothly buffed without the burnish of a lackey's spit shine. But his beard seems to belong to another man and another time. It is excessively long and scraggly. Wispy white hairs mix with the faded black and dangle down the front of his uniform like an old shroud, weatherworn and drying out. It is the beard from the hills. Castro strokes it constantly, as if trying to revive the vitality of its fiber.

Castro now looks at Ali.

"How's your appetite?" he asks, forgetting that Ali is not speaking.

"Where's your wife?" he then asks aloud, and Howard Bingham calls out to her. Yolanda has once more drifted back into the group.

When she arrives, Castro hesitates before speaking to her. It is as if he is not absolutely sure who she is. He has met so many people since arriving, and with the group rotating constantly due to the jostling of the photographers, Castro cannot be certain whether the woman at his side is Muhammad Ali's wife or Ed Bradley's friend or some other woman he has met moments ago who has left him with an unlasting impression. Having already committed a faux pas regarding one of the wives of the two multi-married ex-champions standing nearby, Castro waits for some hint from his interpreter. None is offered. Fortunately, he does not have to worry in this country about the women's vote — or any vote, for that matter — but he does sigh in mild relief when Yolanda reintroduces herself as Ali's wife and does so by name.

"Ah, Yolanda," Castro repeats, "what a beautiful name. That's the name of a queen somewhere."

"In our household," she says.

"And how is your husband's appetite?"

"Good, but he likes sweets."

"We can send you some of our ice cream to Michigan," Castro says. Without waiting for her to comment, he asks, "Michigan is very cold?"

"Oh, yes," she replies, not indicating that they had already discussed Michigan's winter weather.

"How much snow?"

"We didn't get hit with the blizzard," Yolanda says, referring to a storm in January, "but it can get three, four feet —"

Teófilo Stevenson interrupts to say that he had been in Michigan during the previous October.

"Oh," Castro says, raising an eyebrow. He mentions that during the same month he had also been in the United States (attending the United Nations' fiftieth-anniversary tribute). He asks Stevenson the length of his American visit.

"I was there for nineteen days," says Stevenson.

"Nineteen days!" Castro repeats. "Longer than I was."

Castro complains that he was limited to five days and prohibited from traveling beyond New York.

"Well, *comandante*," Stevenson responds offhandedly, in a slightly superior tone, "if you like, I will sometime show you my video."

Stevenson appears to be very comfortable in the presence of the Cuban leader, and perhaps the latter has habitually encouraged this; but at this moment, Castro may well be finding his boxing hero a bit condescending and worthy of a retaliatory jab. He knows how to deliver it.

"When you visited the United States," Castro asks pointedly, "did you bring your wife, the lawyer?"

Stevenson stiffens. He directs his eyes toward his wife. She turns away.

"No," Stevenson answers quietly. "I went alone."

Castro abruptly shifts his attention to the other side of the room, where the CBS camera crew is positioned, and he asks Ed Bradley, "What do you do?"

"We're making a documentary on Ali," Bradley explains, "and we followed him to Cuba to see what he was doing in Cuba and . . ."

Bradley's voice is suddenly overwhelmed by the sounds of laughter and handclapping. Bradley and Castro turn to discover that Muhammad Ali is now reclaiming everyone's attention. He is holding his shaky left fist in the air; but instead of assuming a boxer's pose, as he had done earlier, he is beginning to pull out from the top of his upraised fist, slowly and with dramatic delicacy, the tip of a red silk handkerchief that is pinched between his right index finger and thumb.

After he has pulled out the entire handkerchief, he dangles it in the air for a few seconds, waving it closer and closer to the forehead of the wide-eyed Fidel Castro. Ali seems bewitched. He continues to stare stagnantly at Castro and the others, surrounded by applause that he gives no indication he hears. Then he proceeds to place the handkerchief back into the top of his cupped left hand — pecking with the pinched fingers of his right — and then quickly opens his palms toward his audience and reveals that the handkerchief has disappeared.

"Where is it?" cries Castro, who seems to be genuinely surprised and delighted. He approaches Ali and examines his hands, repeating, "Where is it? Where have you put it?"

Everyone who has traveled on Ali's bus during the week knows where he has hidden it. They have seen him perform the trick repeatedly in front of some of the patients and doctors at the hospitals and clinics as well as before countless tourists who have recognized him in his hotel lobby or during his strolls through the town square. They have also seen him follow up each performance with a demonstration that exposes his method. He keeps hidden in his fist a flesh-colored rubber thumb that contains the handkerchief that he will eventually pull out with the fingers of his other hand; and when he is reinserting the handkerchief, he is actually shoving the material back into the concealed rubber thumb, into which he then inserts his own right thumb. When he opens his hands, the uninformed among his onlookers are seeing his empty palms and missing the fact that the handkerchief is tucked within the rubber thumb that is covering his outstretched right thumb. Sharing with his audience the mystery of his magic always earns him additional applause.

After Ali has performed and explained the trick to Castro, he gives Castro the rubber thumb to examine — and, with more zest than he has shown all evening, Castro says, "Oh, let me try it, I want to try — it's the first time I have seen such a wonderful thing!" And after a few minutes of coaching from Howard Bingham, who long ago learned how to do it from Ali, the Cuban leader performs with sufficient dexterity and panache to satisfy his magical ambitions and to arouse another round of applause from the guests.

Meanwhile, more than ten minutes have passed since Ali began his comic routine. It is already after 9:30 P.M., and the commentator Ed Bradley, whose conversation with Castro had been interrupted, is concerned that the Cuban leader might leave the room without responding to the questions Bradley has prepared for his show. Bradley edges close to Castro's interpreter, saying in a voice that is sure to be heard, "Would you ask him if he followed . . . was able to follow Ali when he was boxing professionally?"

The question is relayed and repeated until Castro, facing the CBS cameras, replies, "Yes, I recall the days when they were discussing the possibilities of a match between the two of them" — he nods toward Stevenson and Ali — "and I remember when he went to Africa."

"In Zaire," Bradley clarifies, referring to Ali's victory in 1974 over George Foreman. And he follows up: "What kind of impact did he have in this country, because he was a revolutionary as well as . . . ?"

"It was great," Castro says. "He was very much admired as a sportsman, as a boxer, as a person. There was always a high opinion of him. But I never guessed one day we would meet here, with this kind gesture of bringing medicine, seeing our children, visiting our polyclinics. I am very glad, I am thrilled, to have the opportunity to meet him personally, to appreciate his kindness. I see he is strong. I see he has a very kind face."

Castro is speaking as if Ali were not in the room, standing a few feet away. Ali maintains his fixed façade even as Stevenson whispers into his ear, asking in English, "Muhammad, Muhammad, why you no speak?" Stevenson then turns to tell the journalist who stands behind him, "Muhammad does speak. He speaks to me." Stevenson says nothing more because Castro is now looking at him while continuing to tell Bradley, "I am very glad that he and Stevenson have met." After a pause, Castro adds, "And I am glad that they never fought."

"He's not so sure," Bradley interjects, smiling in the direction of Stevenson.

"I find in that friendship something beautiful," Castro insists softly.

"There is a tie between the two of them," Bradley says.

"Yes," says Castro. "It is true." He again looks at Ali, then at Stevenson, as if searching for something more profound to say.

"And how's the documentary?" he finally asks Bradley.

"It'll be on *60 Minutes*."

"When?"

"Maybe one month," Bradley says, reminding Castro's interpreter, "This is the program on which the *comandante* has been interviewed by Dan Rather a number of times in the past, when Dan Rather was on *60 Minutes*."

"And who's there now?" Castro wants to know.

"I am," Bradley answers.

"You," Castro repeats, with a quick glance at Bradley's earring. "So you are there — the boss now?"

Bradley responds as a media star without illusions: "I'm a worker."

Trays containing coffee, tea, and orange juice finally arrive, but only in amounts sufficient for Ali and Yolanda, Howard Bingham, Greg Howard, the Stevensons, and Castro — although Castro tells the waiters he wants nothing.

Castro motions for Ali and the others to join him across the room, around the circular table. The camera crews and the rest of the guests follow, standing as near to the principals as they can. But throughout the group there is a discernible restlessness. They have been standing for more than an hour and a half. It is now approaching 10 P.M. There has been no food. And for the vast majority, it is clear that there will also be nothing to drink. Even among the special guests, seated and sipping from chilled glasses or hot cups, there is a waning level of fascination with the evening. Indeed, Muhammad Ali's eyes are closed. He is sleeping.

Yolanda sits next to him on the sofa, pretending not to notice. Castro also ignores it, although he sits directly across the table, with the interpreter and the Stevensons.

"How large is Michigan?" Castro begins a new round of questioning with Yolanda, returning for the third time to a subject they had explored beyond the interest of anyone in the room except Castro himself.

"I don't know how big the state is as far as demographics," Yolanda says. "We live in a very small village [Barrien Springs] with about two thousand people."

"Are you going back to Michigan tomorrow?"

"Yes."

"What time?"

"Two-thirty."

"Via Miami?" Castro asks.

"Yes."

"From Miami, where do you fly?"

"We're flying to Michigan."

"How many hours' flight?"

"We have to change at Cincinnati — about two and a half hours."

"Flying time?" asks Castro.

Muhammad Ali opens his eyes, then closes them.

"Flying time," Yolanda repeats.

"From Miami to Michigan?" Castro continues.

"No," she again explains, but still with patience, "we have to go to Cincinnati. There are no direct flights."

"So you have to take two planes?" Castro asks.

"Yes," she says, adding for clarification, "Miami to Cincinnati — and then Cincinnati to South Bend, Indiana."

"From Cincinnati . . . ?"

"To South Bend," she says. "That's the closest airport."

"So," Fidel goes on, "it is on the outskirts of the city?"

"Yes."

"You have a farm?"

"No," Yolanda says, "just land. We let someone else do the growing."

She mentions that Teófilo Stevenson has traveled through this part of the Midwest. The mention of his name gains Stevenson's attention.

"I was in Chicago," Stevenson tells Castro.

"You were at their home?" Castro asks.

"No," Yolanda corrects Stevenson, "you were in Michigan."

"I was in the countryside," Stevenson says. Unable to resist, he adds, "I have a video of that visit. I'll show it to you sometime."

Castro seems not to hear him. He directs his attention back to Yolanda, asking her where she was born, where she was educated, when she became married, and how many years separate her age from that of her husband, Muhammad Ali.

After Yolanda acknowledges being sixteen years younger than Ali, Castro turns toward Fraymari and with affected sympathy says that she married a man who is twenty years her senior.

"*Comandante!*" Stevenson intercedes, "I am in shape. Sports keep you healthy. Sports add years to your life and life to your years!"

"Oh, what conflict she has," Castro goes on, ignoring Stevenson and catering to Fraymari — and to the CBS cameraman who steps forward for a closer view of Castro's face. "She is a lawyer, and she does not put this husband in jail." Castro is enjoying much more than Fraymari the attention this topic is now getting from the group. Castro had lost his audience and now has it back and seemingly wants to retain it, no matter at what cost to Stevenson's harmony with Fraymari. Yes, Castro continues, Fraymari had the misfortune to select a husband "who can never settle down. . . . Jail would be an appropriate place for him."

"*Comandante,*" Stevenson interrupts in a jocular manner that seems intended to placate both the lawyer who is his spouse and the lawyer who rules the country, "I might as well be locked up!" He implies that should he deviate from marital fidelity, his lawyer wife "will surely put me in a place where she is the only woman who can visit me!"

Everyone around the table and within the circling group laughs. Ali is now awake. The banter between Castro and Stevenson resumes until Yolanda, all but rising in her chair, tells Castro, "We have to pack."

"You're going to have dinner now?" he asks.

"Yes, sir," she says. Ali stands, along with Howard Bingham. Yolanda thanks Castro's interpreter directly, saying, "Be sure to tell him, 'You're always welcome in our home.'" The interpreter quotes Castro as again complaining that when he visits America, he is usually restricted to New York, but he adds, "Things change."

The group watches as Yolanda and Ali pass through, and Castro follows them into the hallway. The elevator arrives, and its door is held open by a security guard. Castro extends his final farewell with handshakes — and only then does he discover that he holds Ali's rubber thumb in his hand. Apologizing, he tries to hand it back to Ali, but Bingham politely protests. "No, no," Bingham says, "Ali wants you to have it."

Castro's interpreter at first fails to understand what Bingham is saying.

"He wants you to keep it," Bingham repeats.

Bingham enters the elevator with Ali and Yolanda. Before the door closes, Castro smiles, waves goodbye, and stares with curiosity at the rubber thumb. Then he puts it in his pocket.

LÊ THI DIEM THÚY

The Gangster We Are All Looking For

FROM THE MASSACHUSETTS REVIEW

VIETNAM IS A black-and-white photograph of my grandparents sitting in bamboo chairs in their front courtyard. They are sitting tall and proud, surrounded by chickens and roosters. Their feet are separated from the dirt by thin sandals. My grandfather's broad forehead is shining. So too are my grandmother's famed sad eyes. The animals are obliviously pecking at the ground. This looks like a wedding portrait, though it is actually a photograph my grandparents had taken late in life, for their children, especially for my mother. When I think of this portrait of my grandparents in the last years of their life, I always envision a beginning. To what or where, I don't know, but always a beginning.

When my mother, a Catholic schoolgirl from the South, decided to marry my father, a Buddhist gangster from the North, her parents disowned her. This is in the photograph, though it is not visible to the eye. If it were, it would be a deep impression across the soft dirt of my grandparents' courtyard. Her father chased her out of the house, beating her with the same broom she had used every day of her life, from the time she could stand up and sweep to the morning of the very day she was chased away.

The year my mother met my father, there were several young men working at her house, running errands for her father, pickling vegetables with her mother. It was understood by everyone that

these men were courting my mother. My mother claims she had
no such understanding.

She treated these men as brothers, sometimes as uncles even,
later exclaiming in self-defense, "I didn't even know about love
then."

Ma says love came to her in a dark movie theater. She doesn't
remember what movie it was or why she'd gone to see it, only that
she'd gone alone and found herself sitting beside him. In the dark,
she couldn't make out his face but noticed he was handsome. She
wondered if he knew she was watching him out of the corner of
her eye. Watching him without embarrassment or shame. Watching him with a strange curiosity, a feeling that made her want to
trace and retrace his silhouette with her fingertips until she'd
memorized every feature and could call his face to her in any dark
place she passed through. Later, in the shadow of the beached
fishing boats on the blackest nights of the year, she would call him
to mind, his face a warm companion for her body on the edge of
the sea.

In the early days of my parents' courtship, my mother told stories.
She confessed elaborate dreams about the end of war: foods she'd
eat (a banquet table, mangoes piled high to the ceiling); songs
she'd make up and sing, clapping her hands over her head and
throwing her hair like a horse's mane; dances she'd do, hopping
from one foot to the other. Unlike the responsible favorite daughter or sister she was to her family, with my father, in the forest, my
mother became reckless, drunk on her youth and the possibility
of love. Ignoring the chores to be done at home, she rolled her
pants up to her knees, stuck her bare feet in puddles, and learned
to smoke a cigarette.

She tied a vermilion ribbon in her hair. She became moody. She
did her chores as though they were favors to her family, forgetting
that she ate the same rice and was dependent on the same supply
of food. It seemed to her the face that stared back at her from
deep inside the family well was the face of a woman she had never
seen before. At night she lay in bed and thought of his hands, the
way his thumb flicked down on the lighter and brought fire to her

cigarette. She began to wonder what the forests were like before the trees were dying. She remembered her father had once described to her the smiling broadness of leaves, jungles thick in the tangle of rich soil.

One evening, she followed my father in circles through the forest, supposedly in search of the clearing that would take them to his aunt's house. They wandered aimlessly into darkness, never finding the clearing or the aunt she knew he never had.

"You're not from here," she said.

"I know."

"So tell me, what's your aunt's name?"

"Xuan."

"Spring?"

"Yes."

She laughed. I can't be here, she thought.

"My father will be looking for me —"

"I'll walk you home. It's not too late."

In the dark, she could feel his hand extending toward her, filling the space between them. They had not touched once the entire evening and now he stood offering his hand to her. She stared at him for a long time. There was a small scar on his chin, curved like her fingernail. It was too dark to see this. She realized she had memorized his face.

My first memory of my father's face is framed by the coiling barbed wire of a prison camp in South Vietnam. My mother's voice crosses through the wire. She is whispering his name and, in this utterance, caressing him. Over and over she calls him to her: "Anh Minh, Anh Minh." His name becomes a tree she presses her body against. The act of calling blows around them like a warm breeze, and when she utters her own name, it is the second half of a verse that began with his. She drops her name like a pebble is dropped into a well. She wants to be engulfed by him. "Anh Minh, em My. Anh Minh. Em, em My."

She is crossing through barbed wire the way some people step through open windows. She arrives warm, the slightest film of sweat on her bare arms. She says, "It's me, it's me." Shy and formal and breathless, my parents are always meeting for the first time. Savoring the sound of a name, marveling at the bone structure.

I trail behind them, the tip of their dragon's tail. I am suspended like a silk banner from the body of a kite. They flick me here and there. I twist and turn in the air, connected to them by this fabric that worms spin.

For a handful of pebbles and my father's sharp profile my mother left home and never returned. Imagine a handful of pebbles. The casual way he tossed them at her as she was walking home from school with her girlfriends. He did this because he liked her and wanted to let her know. Boys are dumb that way, my mother told me. A handful of pebbles, to be thrown in anger, in desperation, in joy. My father threw them in love. Ma says they touched her like warm kisses, these pebbles he had been holding in the sun. Warm kisses on the curve of her back, sliding down the crook of her arm, grazing her ankles and landing around her feet in the hot sand.

What my father told her could have been a story. There was no one in the South to confirm the details of his life. He said he came from a semi-aristocratic Northern family. Unlacing his boot, he pulled out his foot and told her to pay close attention to how his second toe was significantly longer than his other toes. "A sure sign of aristocracy," he claimed. His nose was high, he said, because his mother was French, one of the many mistresses his father kept. He found this out when he was sixteen. That year, he ran away from home and came south.

"There are thieves, gamblers, drunks I've met who remind me of people in my family. It's the way they're dreamers. My family's a garden full of dreamers lying on their backs, staring at the sky, drunk and choking on their dreaming." He said this while leaning against a tree, his arms folded across his bare chest, his eyes staring at the ground, his shoulders golden.

She asked her mother, "What does it mean if your second toe is longer than your other toes?"

"It means . . . your mother will die before your father," her mother said.

"I heard somewhere it's a sign of aristocracy."

"Huh! What do we know about aristocracy?"

My father's toes fascinated my mother. When she looked at his bare feet she saw ten fishing boats, two groups of five. Within each group, the second boat ventured ahead, leading the others. She would climb a tree, stand gripping the branch with her own toes, and stare down at his. She directed him to stand in the mud. There, she imagined what she saw to be ten small boats surrounded by black water, a fleet of junks journeying in the dark.

She would lean back and enjoy this vision, never explaining to him what it was she saw. She left him to wonder about her senses as he stood, cigarette in hand, staring at her trembling ankles, not moving until she told him to.

I was born in the alley behind my grandparents' house. At three in the morning my mother dragged herself out of the bed in the small house she and my father lived in after they married.

He was in prison, so, alone, she began to walk. She cut a crooked line on the beach. Moving in jerky steps, like a ball tossed on the waves, she seemed to be thrown along without direction. She walked to the schoolhouse, sat on the sand, and leaned against the first step. She felt grains of sand pressing against her back. Each grain was a minute pinprick that became increasingly painful to her. She felt as though her back would break out in a wash of blood. She thought, I am going to bleed to death. We are going to die.

In front of the schoolhouse lay a long metal tube. No one knew where it came from. It seemed always to have been there. Children hid in it, crawled through it, spoke to one another at either end of it, marched across it, sat on it, and confided secrets beside it. There had been so little to play with at the school recesses. This long metal tube became everything. A tarp was suspended over it, to shield it from the sun. The tube looked like a blackened log that sat in a room without walls. When the children sat in a line on the tube, their heads bobbing this way and that in conversation, it seemed they were sitting under a canopied raft.

The night I was born, my mother looked at this tube and imagined it to be the badly burnt arm of a dying giant whose body was buried in the sand. She could not decide if he had been buried in the sand and was trying to get out or if he had tried to bury himself in the sand but was unable to pull his arm under in time. In time for what? She had heard a story about a girl in a neighboring town who was killed during a napalm bombing. The bombing happened on an especially hot night when this girl had walked to the beach to cool her feet in the water. They found her floating on the sea. The phosphorus from the napalm made her body glow like a lantern. In her mind, my mother built a canopy for this girl. She started to cry, thinking of the buried giant, the floating girl, these bodies stopped in midstep, on their way somewhere.

She began to walk toward the tube. She had a sudden urge to be inside it. The world felt dangerous to her and she was alone. At the mouth of the tube she bent down; her belly blocked the opening. She tried the other side, the other mouth. Again her belly stopped her. "But I remember," she muttered out loud, "as a girl I sometimes slept in here." This was what she wanted now, to sleep inside the tube.

"Tall noses come from somewhere —"
  "Not from here."
  "Not tall noses."

Eyes insinuate, moving from her nose to mine then back again. Mouths suck air in, form it into the darkest shade of contempt, then spit it at her feet as she walks by. I am riding on her hip. I am the new branch that makes the tree bend, but she walks with her head held high. She knows where she pulled me from. No blue eye.

Ma says war is a bird with a broken wing flying over the countryside, trailing blood and burying crops in sorrow. If something grows in spite of this, it is both a curse and a miracle. When I was born, she cried when I cried, knowing I had breathed war in and she could never shake it out of me. Ma says war makes it dangerous to breathe, though she knows you die if you don't. She says she could have thrown me against the wall, breaking me until I coughed up this war which is killing us all. She could have stomped on it in the dark and danced on it like a madwoman dancing on gravestones. She could have ground it down to powder and spit on it, but didn't I know? War has no beginning and no end. It crosses oceans like a splintered boat filled with people singing a sad song.

Every morning Ahn wakes up in the house next to mine, a yellow duplex she and I call a townhouse because we found out from a real estate ad that a townhouse is a house that has an upstairs and a downstairs. My father calls Ahn the "chicken-egg girl." Each morning Ahn's mother loads a small pushcart with stacks of eggs and Ahn walks all over Linda Vista selling eggs. Her back yard is full of chickens and roosters. Sometimes you can see a rooster fly up and balance itself on the back gate, and it will crow and crow, off and on, all day long until dark comes.

We live in the country of California, the province of San Diego, the village of Linda Vista. We live in old Navy Housing, bungalows that were built in the 1940s and '50s. Since the 1980s these bungalows have housed Vietnamese, Cambodian, and Laotian refugees from the Vietnam War. When we moved in, we had to sign a form promising not to push fish bones down the garbage disposal.

We live in a yellow row house on Westinghouse Street. Our house is one story, made of wood and plaster. We are connected to six two-story houses and another one-story house at the other end. Across from our row of houses, separated by a field of brown dirt, sits another row of yellow houses, same as ours and facing us like a sad twin. Linda Vista is full of houses like ours, painted in peeling shades of olive green, baby blue, and sunbaked yellow.

There's new Navy Housing on Linda Vista Road, the long street that takes you out of here. We see the people there watering their lawns, the children riding pink tricycles up and down the cul-de-sacs. We see them in Victory Supermarket, buying groceries with cash. In Kelley Park they have picnics and shoot each other with water guns. At school their kids are Most Popular, Most Beautiful, Most Likely to Succeed. Though there are more Vietnamese, Cambodian, and Laotian kids at the school, we are not Most of anything in the yearbook. They call us Yang because one year a bunch of Laotian kids with the last name Yang came to our school. The Navy Housing kids started calling all the refugee kids Yang.

Yang. Yang. Yang.

Ma says living next to Ahn's family reminds her of Vietnam because the blue tarp suspended above Ahn's back yard is the bright blue of the South China Sea. Ma says isn't it funny how sky and sea follow you from place to place as if they too were traveling and not just the boat that travels across or between them. Ma says even Ahn reminds her of Vietnam, the way she sets out for market each morning.

Ba becomes a gardener. Overnight. He buys a truck full of equipment and a box of business cards from Uncle Twelve, who is moving to Texas to become a fisherman. The business cards read "Tom's Professional Gardening Service" and have a small, green embossed picture of a man pushing a lawn mower. The man's back is to the viewer, so no one who doesn't already know can tell it's not Ba. He says I can be his secretary because I speak the best English. If you call us on the business phone, you will hear me say: "Hello, you have reached Tom's Professional Gardening Service. We are not here right now, but if you leave us a message, we will get back to you as soon as possible. Thank you."

It is hot and dusty where we live. Some people think it's dirty, but they don't know much about us. They haven't seen our gardens full of lemongrass, mint, cilantro, and basil. They've only seen the pigeons pecking at day-old rice and the skinny cats and dogs sitting in the skinny shade of skinny trees as they drive by. Have they seen the berries we pick which turn our lips and fingertips red? How about the small staircase Ba built from our bedroom window to the back yard so I would have a short cut to the clothesline? How about the Great Wall of China which snakes like a river from the top of the steep Crandall Street hill to the slightly curving bottom? Who has seen this?

It was so different at the Green Apartment. We had to close the gate behind us every time we came in. It clanged heavily, and I imagined a host of eyes, upstairs and downstairs, staring at me from behind slightly parted curtains. There were four palm trees planted at the four far corners of the courtyard and a central staircase that was narrow at the top and fanned out at the bottom. The steps were covered in fake grass, like the set of an old Hollywood movie, the kind that stars an aging beauty who wakes up to find something is terribly wrong.

We moved out of the Green Apartment after we turned on the TV one night and heard that our manager and his brother had hacked a woman to pieces and dumped her body into the Pacific Ocean in ten-gallon garbage bags that washed onto the shore. Ma said she didn't want to live in a place haunted by a murdered lady. So we moved to Linda Vista, where she said there were a lot of Vietnamese people like us, people whose only sin was a little bit of gambling and sucking on fish bones and laughing hard and arguing loudly.

Ma shaved all her hair off in Linda Vista because she got mad at Ba for gambling her money away and getting drunk every week watching *Monday Night Football*. Ba gave her a blue baseball cap to wear until her hair grew back, and she wore it backward, like a real bad-ass.

After that, some people in Linda Vista said that Ma was crazy and Ba was crazy for staying with her. But what do some people know?

When the photograph came, Ma and Ba got into a fight. Ba threw the fish tank out the front door and Ma broke all the dishes. They said they never should've been together.

Ma's sister had sent her the photograph from Vietnam. It came in a stiff envelope. There was nothing inside but the photograph, as if anything more would be pointless. Ma started to cry. "Child," she sobbed, over and over again. She wasn't talking about me. She was talking about herself.

Ba said, "Don't cry. Your parents have forgiven you."

Ma kept crying anyway and told him not to touch her with his gangster hands. Ba clenched his hands into tight fists and punched the walls.

"What hands?! What hands?!" he yelled. "Let me see the gangster! Let me see his hands!" I see his hands punch hands punch hands punch blood.

Ma is in the kitchen. She has torn the screen off the window. She is punctuating the pavement with dishes, plates, cups, rice bowls. She sends them out like birds gliding through the sky with nowhere in particular to go. Until they crash. Then she exhales "Huh!" in satisfaction.

I am in the hallway gulping air. I breathe in the breaking and the bleeding. When Ba plunges his hands into the fish tank, I detect the subtle tint of blood in water. When he throws the fish tank out the front door, yelling, "Let me see the gangster!" I am drinking up spilled water and swallowing whole the beautiful colored tropical fish before they hit the ground, caking themselves in brown dirt until just the whites of their eyes remain, blinking at the sun.

All the hands are in my throat, cutting themselves on broken dishes, and the fish swim in circles; they can't see for all the blood.

Ba jumps in his truck and drives away.

When I grow up I am going to be the gangster we are all looking for.

The neighborhood kids are standing outside our house, staring in through the windows and the open door. Even Ahn, our chicken-egg seller. I'm sure their gossiping mothers sent them to spy on us. I run out front and dance like a crazy lady, dance like a fish, wiggle my head and throw my body so everything eyes nose tongue comes undone. At first they laugh but then they stop, not knowing what to think. Then I stop and stare each one of them down.

"What're you looking at?" I ask.

"Lookin' at you," one boy says, half giggling.

"Well," I say, with my hand on my hip and my head cocked to one side, "I'm looking at you too," and I give him my evil one-eye look, focusing all my energy into one eye. I stare at him hard like my eye is a bullet and he can be dead.

I turn my back on them and walk into the house.

I find Ma sitting in the windowsill. The curve of her back is inside the bedroom while the rest of her body is outside, on the first step Ba built going from the bedroom to the garden. Without turning to look at me, she says, "Let me lift you into the attic."

"Why?"

"We have to move your grandparents in."

I don't really know what she is talking about, but I say O.K. anyway.

We have never needed the attic for anything. In fact, we have never gone up there. When we moved my grandparents in, Ma simply lifted me up and I pushed the attic door open with one hand, while with the other I slipped in the stiff envelope containing the photograph of my grandparents. I pushed it the length of my arm and down to my fingertips. I pushed it so far it was beyond reach, but Ma said it was enough, they had come to live with us, and sometimes you don't need to see or touch people to know they're there.

Ba came home drunk that night and asked to borrow my blanket. I heard him climbing the tree in the back yard. It took him a long time. He kept missing the wooden blocks that run up and down the tree like a ladder. Ba put them in when he built the steps going from the bedroom window into the garden. If you stand on the very top block, your whole body is hidden by tree branches. Ba put those blocks in for me, so I could win at hide-and-go-seek.

When Ba finally made it onto the roof, he lay down over my room and I could hear him rolling across my ceiling. Rolling and crying. I was scared he would roll off the edge and kill himself, so I went to wake Ma.

She was already awake. She said it would be a good thing if he rolled off. But later I heard someone climb the tree, and all night two bodies rolled across my ceiling. Slowly and firmly they pressed against my sleep, the Catholic schoolgirl and the Buddhist gangster, two dogs chasing each other's tails. They have been running like this for so long, they have become one dog one tail.

Without any hair and looking like a man, my mother is still my mother, though sometimes I can't see her even when I look and look and look so long all the colors of the world begin to swim and bob around me. Her hands always bring me up, her big peasant hands with the flat, wide nails, wide like her nose and just as expressive. I will know her by her hands and her walk which is at once slow and urgent, the walk of a woman going to the market with her goods securely bound to her side. Even walking empty-handed, my mother suggests invisible bundles whose contents no one but she can unravel. And if I never see her again, I will know my mother by the smell of sea salt and the prints of my own bare feet crossing sand, running to and away from, to and away from, family.

When the eviction notice came, we didn't believe it so we threw it away. It said we had a month to get out. The houses on our block had a new owner who wanted to tear everything down and build better housing for the community. It said we were priority tenants for the new complex, but we couldn't afford to pay the new rent so it didn't matter. The notice also said that if we didn't get out in time, all our possessions would be confiscated in accordance with some section of a law book or manual we were supposed to have known about but had never seen. We couldn't believe the eviction notice so we threw it away.

The fence is tall, silver, and see-through. Chainlink, it rattles when you shake it and wobbles when you lean against it. It circles the block like a bad dream. It is not funny like a line of laundry whose flying shirts and empty pants suggest human birds and vanishing acts. This fence presses sharply against your brain. We three stand still as posts. Looking at it, then at each other — this side and that — out of the corners of our eyes. What are we thinking?

At night we come back with three uncles. Ba cuts a hole in the fence and we step through. Quiet, we break into our own house through the back window. Quiet, we steal back everything that is ours. We fill ten-gallon garbage bags with clothes, pots and pans, flip-flops, the porcelain figure of Mary, and our wooden Buddha. In the arc of four flashlights we find our favorite hairbrushes behind bedposts. When we are done, we are clambering and breathless. We can hear police cars coming to get us, though it's quiet.

We tumble out the window like people tumbling across continents. We are time traveling, weighed down by heavy furniture and bags of precious junk. We find ourselves leaning against Ba's yellow truck. Ma calls his name, her voice reaching like a hand feeling for a tree trunk in darkness.

In the car, Ma starts to cry. "What about the sea?" she asks. "What about the garden?" Ba says we can come back in the morning and dig up the stalks of lemongrass and fold the sea into a blue square. Ma is sobbing. She is beating the dashboard with her fists. "I want to know," she says, "I want to know, I want to know . . . who is doing this to us?" Hiccupping, she says, "I want to know why, why there's always a fence. Why there's always someone on the outside wanting someone . . . something on the inside and between them . . . this . . . sharp fence. Why are we always leaving like this?"

Everyone is quiet when Ma screams.

"Take me back!" she says. "I can't go with you. I've forgotten my

mother and father. I can't believe . . . Anh Minh, we've left them
to die. Take me back."

Ma wants Ba to stop the car, but Ba doesn't know why. The three
uncles, sitting in a line in the back of the truck, think Ma is crazy.
They yell in through the window, "My, are you going to walk back
to Vietnam?"

"Yeah, are you going to walk home to your parents' house?"

In the silence another laughs.

Ba puts his foot on the gas pedal. Our car jerks forward, then
plunges down the Crandall Street hill. Ma says, "I need air, water
. . ." I roll the window down. She puts her head in her hands. She
keeps crying, "Child." Outside, I see the Great Wall of China. In
the glare of the streetlamps, it is just a long strip of cardboard.

In the morning, the world is flat. Westinghouse Street is lying down
like a jagged brushstroke of sunburnt yellow. There is a big sign
inside the fence that reads

COMING SOON:

CONDOMINIUMS   TOWNHOUSES   FAMILY HOMES

Beside these words is a watercolor drawing of a large, pink complex.

We stand on the edge of the chainlink fence, sniffing the air for
the scent of lemongrass, scanning this flat world for our blue sea.
A wrecking ball dances madly through our house. Everything has
burst wide open and sunk down low. Then I hear her calling them.
She is whispering, "Ma/Ba, Ma/Ba." The whole world is two butterfly wings rubbing against my ear.

Listen . . . they are sitting in the attic, sitting like royalty. Shining
in the dark, buried by a wrecking ball. Paper fragments floating
across the surface of the sea.

Not a trace of blood anywhere except here, in my throat, where
I am telling you all this.

JOY WILLIAMS

The Case Against Babies

FROM GRANTA

BABIES, BABIES, BABIES. There's a plague of babies. Too many rabbits or elephants or mustangs or swans brings out the myxomatosis, the culling guns, the sterility drugs, the scientific brigade of egg smashers. Other species can "strain their environments" or "overrun their range" or clash with their human "neighbors," but human babies are always welcome at life's banquet. Welcome, Welcome, Welcome — Live Long and Consume! You can't draw the line when it comes to babies because . . . where are you going to draw the line? *Consider having none or one and be sure to stop after two,* the organization Zero Population Growth suggests politely. Can barely hear them what with all the babies squalling. Hundreds of them popping out every minute. Ninety-seven million of them each year. While legions of other biological life forms go extinct (or, in the creepy phrase of ecologists, "wink out"), human life bustles self-importantly on. Those babies just keep coming! They've gone way beyond being "God's gift"; they've become entitlements. Everyone's having babies, even women who can't have babies, *particularly* women who can't have babies — they're the ones who sweep fashionably along the corridors of consumerism with their double-wide strollers, stuffed with twins and triplets. (Women push those things with the effrontery of someone piloting a bulldozer, which strollers uncannily bring to mind.) When you see twins or triplets, do you think *awahhh* or *owhoo* or *that's sort of cool, that's unusual,* or do you think *that woman dropped a wad on in vitro fertilization, twenty-five, thirty thousand dollars at least . . . ?*

The human race hardly needs to be more fertile, but fertility clinics are booming. The new millionaires are the hotshot fertility doctors who serve anxious gottahavababy women, techno-shamans who have become the most important aspect of the baby process, giving women what they want: BABIES. (It used to be a mystery what women wanted, but no more . . . Nietzsche was right . . .) Ironically — though it is far from being the only irony in this baby craze — women think of themselves as being *successful, personally fulfilled* when they have a baby, even if it takes a battery of men in white smocks and lots of hormones and drugs and needles and dishes and mixing and inserting and implanting to make it so. Having a baby means *individual completion* for a woman. What do boys have to do to be men? Sleep with a woman. Kill something. Yes, killing something, some luckless deer, duck, bear, pretty much anything large-ish in the animal kingdom, or even another man, appropriate in times of war, has ushered many a lad into manhood. But what's a woman to do? She gets to want to have a baby.

While much effort has been expended in Third World countries educating women into a range of options that do not limit their role merely to bearing children, well-off, educated, and indulged American women are clamoring for babies, babies, BABIES to complete their status. They've had it all, and now they want a baby. And women over thirty-five want them NOW. They're the ones who opt for the aggressive fertility route, they're impatient, they're sick of being laissez-faire about this. Sex seems such a laborious way to go about it. At this point they don't want to endure all that intercourse over and over and maybe get no baby. What a waste of time! And time's awasting. *A life with no child would be a life perfecting hedonism,* a forty-something infertile woman said, now the proud owner of pricey twins. Even women who have the grace to submit to fate can sound wistful. *It's not so much that I wish that I had children now,* a travel writer said, *but that I wish I had had them. I hate to fail at anything.* Women are supposed to wish and want and not fail. (Lesbians want to have babies too, and when lesbians have babies, watch out! They lay names on them like Wolf.)

The eighties were a decade when it was kind of unusual to have a baby. Oh, the lower classes still had them with more or less gusto, but professionals did not. Having a baby was indeed so quaintly rebellious and remarkable that a publishing niche was developed for men writing about babies, *their* baby, their baby's first year in which every single day was recorded (he slept through the night . . . he didn't sleep through the night . . .). The writers would marvel over the size of their infant's scrotum; give advice on how to tip the obstetrician (not a case of booze; a clock from Tiffany's is nicer); and bemusedly admit that their baby exhibited intelligent behavior like rolling over, laughing, and showing fascination with the TV screen far earlier than normal children. Aside from the talk about the poopie and the rashes and the cat's psychological decline, these books frequently contained a passage, an overheard bit of Mommy-to-Baby monologue along these lines: *I love you so much I don't ever want you to have teeth or stand up or walk or go on dates or get married. I want you to stay right here with me and be my baby* . . . Babies are one thing. Human beings are another. We have way too many human beings. Almost everyone knows this.

Adoption was an eighties thing. People flying to Chile, all over the globe, God knows where, returning triumphantly with their BABY. It was difficult, adventurous, expensive, and generous. It was trendy then. People were into adopting bunches of babies in all different flavors and colors: Korean, Chinese, part Indian (part Indian was very popular), Guatemalan (Guatemalan babies are way cute). Adoption was a fad, just like the Cabbage Patch dolls, which fed the fad to tens of thousands of pre-pubescent girl consumers.

Now it is *absolutely* necessary to digress for a moment and provide an account of this marketing phenomenon. These fatuous-faced soft-sculpture dolls were immensely popular in the eighties. The gimmick was that these dolls were "born"; you couldn't just buy the damn things — if you wanted one, you had to "adopt" it. Today they are still being born and adopted, although at a slower rate, in Babyland General Hospital, a former medical clinic right on the fast-food and car-dealership strip in the otherwise unexceptional north Georgia town of Cleveland. There are several rooms at Babyland General. One of them is devoted to the premies (all snug in their little gowns, each in its own spiffy incubator) and another is devoted to the cabbage patch itself, a suggestive mound with a fake tree on it from which several times a day comes the announcement CABBAGE IN LABOR! A few demented moments later, a woman in full nurse regalia appears from a door in the tree holding a brand-new Cabbage Patch Kid by the feet and giving it a little whack on the bottom. All around her in the fertile patch are happy little soft heads among the cabbages. Each one of these things costs $175, and you have to sign papers promising to care for it and treasure it forever. There are some cheesy dolls in boxes that you wouldn't have to adopt, but children don't want those — they want to sign on the line, want the documentation, the papers. The dolls are all supposed to be different, but they certainly look identical. They've got tiny ears, big eyes, a pinched rictus of a mouth, and lumpy little arms and legs. The colors of the cloth vary for racial verisimilitude, but their expressions are the same. They're glad to be here and they expect everything.

But these are just dolls, of course. The *real* adopted babies who rode the wave of fashion into many hiply caring homes are children now, an entirely different kettle of fish, and though they may be providing (just as they were supposed to) great joy, they are not darling babies anymore. A baby is not really a child; a baby is a BABY, a cuddleball, representative of virility, wombrismo, and humankind's unquenchable wish to outfox Death.

Adoptive parents must feel a little out of it these days, so dreadfully dated in the nineties. Adoption — how foolishly sweet. It's so Benetton, so kind of naive. With adopted babies, you just don't know, it's too much of a crapshoot. Oh, they *told* you that the father was an English major at Yale and that the mother was a brilliant mathematician and harpsichordist who was just not quite ready to juggle career and child, but what are you going to think when the baby turns into a kid who rather than showing any talent whatsoever is trying to drown the dog and set national parks on fire? Adoptive parents do their best, of course, at least as far as their liberal genes allow; they look into the baby's *background,* they don't want just any old baby (even going to the dog and cat pound you'd want to pick and choose, right?); they want a pleasant, healthy one, someone who will appreciate the benefits of a nice environment and respond to a nurturing and attentive home. They steer away (I mean, one has to be realistic, one can't save the world) from the crack and smack babies, the physically and mentally handicapped babies, the HIV and fetal-alcoholic-syndrome babies.

Genes matter more and more, and adoption is just too . . . where's the connection? Not a single DNA strand to call your own. Adoption signifies you didn't do everything you could; you were too cheap or shy or lacked the imagination to go the energetic fertility route, which, when successful, would come with the assurance that some part of the Baby or Babies would be a continuation of you, or at the very least your companion, loved one, partner, whatever.

I once prevented a waitress from taking away my martini glass, which had a tiny bit of martini remaining in it, and she snarled, *Oh, the precious liquid,* before slamming it back down on the table. It's true that I probably imagined that there was more martini in the glass than there actually was (what on earth could have happened to it all?), but the precious-liquid remark brings unpleasantly to mind the reverent regard in which so many people hold themselves. Those eggs, that sperm, oh precious, precious stuff! There was a terrible fright among humankind recently when some scientists suggested that an abundance of synthetic chemicals was causing lower sperm counts in human males — awful, awful, awful — but this proves not to be the case; sperm counts are holding steady and are even on the rise in New York. Los Angeles males don't fare as well (do they drink more water than beer?), nor do the Chinese who, to add insult to insult, are further found to have smaller testicles, a finding that will undoubtedly result in even more wildlife mutilation in the quest for aphrodisiacs. Synthetic chemicals *do* "adversely affect" the reproductive capabilities of nonhuman animals (fish, birds), but this is considered relatively unimportant. It's human sperm that's held in high regard, and in this overpopulated age it's become more valuable — *good* sperm, that is, from intelligent, athletic men who don't smoke, drink, do drugs, have AIDS or a history of homicide — because this overpopulated age is also the donor age. Donor sperm, donor womb, donor eggs. Think of all the eggs that are lost to menstruation every month. The mind boggles. Those precious, precious eggs, lost. (Many egg donors say they got into the business because they didn't like the idea of their eggs "going to waste.") They can be *harvested* instead and frozen for a rainy day, or sold nice and fresh. One woman interviewed in the *New York Times* early this year has made it something of a career. *I'm not going to just sit home and bake cookies for my kids, I can accomplish things,* she says. No dreary nine-to-five desk job for her. She was a surrogate mother for one couple, dishing up a single baby; then she donated some eggs to another couple who had a baby; now she's pregnant with twins for yet another couple. *I feel like a good soldier, as if God said to me, "Hey girl, I've done a lot for you, and now I want you to do something for Me,"* this entrepreneurial breeder says. (It's sort of cute to hear God invoked, sort of for luck, or out of a lingering folksy superstition.) Egg donors are regular Jenny Appleseeds, spreading joy, doing the Lord's work, and earning a few bucks all at once, as well as attaining an odd sense of empowerment (I've got a bunch of kids out there, damned if I know who they all are . . .).

One of the most successful calendars of 1996 was Anne Geddes's BABIES. Each month shows the darling little things on cabbage leaves, cupped in a tulip, as little bees in a honeycomb, and so on — solemn, bright-eyed babies. They look a little bewildered, though, and why shouldn't they? How did they get here? They were probably mixed up in a dish. Donor eggs (vacuumed up carefully through long needles); Daddy's sperm (maybe . . . or maybe just some high-powered New York dude's); gestational carrier; the "real" mommy waiting anxiously, restlessly on the sidelines (want to get those babies home, start buying them stuff!). Baby's lineage can be a little complicated in this one big worldwebby family. With the help of drugs like Clomid and Pergonal there are an awful lot of eggs out there these days — all being harvested by those rich and clever, clever doctors in a "simple procedure" and nailed with bull's-eye accuracy by a spermatozoon. One then gets to "choose" among the resulting cell clumps (or the doctor gets to choose, he's the one who knows about these things), and a number of them (for optimum success) are inserted into the womb, sometimes the mother's womb and sometimes not. These fertilized eggs, unsurprisingly, often result in multiple possibilities, which can be decreased by "selective reduction." They're not calendar babies yet, they're embryos, and it is at this point, the multiple-possibility point, that the mother-to-be often gets a little overly ecstatic, even greedy, thinking ahead perhaps to the day when they're not babies any longer, the day when they'll be able to amuse themselves by themselves like a litter of kittens or something — if there's a bunch of them *all at once* there'll be no need to go through that harrowing process of finding appropriate playmates for them. She starts to think, *Nannies probably don't charge that much more for three than for two* or *Heaven knows we've got enough money or we wouldn't have gotten into all this in the first place.* And many women at the multiple-possibility point, after having gone through pretty much all the meddling and hubris that biomedical technology has come up with, say demurely, *I don't want to play God* (I DON'T WANT TO PLAY GOD?) or *It would be grotesque to snuff one out to improve the odds for the others* or *Whatever will be will be.*

So triplets happen, and even quads and quints (network television is still interested in quints). And as soon as the multiples, or even the less prestigious single baby, are old enough to toddle into daycare, they're responsibly taught the importance of their one and only Earth, taught the three R's — Reduce, Reuse, Recycle. Too many people (which is frequently considered undesirable — gimme my space!) is caused by too many people (it's only logical), but it's mean to blame the babies, you can't blame the babies, they're innocent. Those poor bean counters at the United Nations Population Fund say that at current growth rates, the world will double its population in forty years. Overpopulation poses the greatest threat to all life on earth, but most organizations concerned with this problem don't like to limit their suggestions to the most obvious one — DON'T HAVE A BABY! — because it sounds so negative. Instead, they provide additional, more positive tips for easing the pressures on our reeling environment, such as car-pooling or tree-planting. (A portion of the proceeds from that adorable best-selling BABIES calendar goes to the Arbor Day Foundation for the planting of trees.)

Some would have it that not having a baby is *disallowing* a human life, horribly inappropriate in this world of rights. Everyone has rights; the unborn have rights; it follows that the *unconceived* have rights. (Think of all those babies pissed off at the fact that they haven't even been thought of yet.) Women have the *right* to have babies (we've fought so hard for this), and women who can't have babies have an even bigger right to have them. These rights should be independent of marital or economic status, or age. (Fifty- and sixty-something moms tend to name their babies after the gynecologist.) The reproduction industry wants fertility treatments to be available to *anyone* and says that it wouldn't all be so expensive if those recalcitrant insurance companies and government agencies like Medicare and Medicaid weren't so cost-conscious and discriminatory and would just cough up the money. It's not as though you have to take out a *permit* to have a baby, be *licensed* or anything. What about the rights of a poor, elderly, feminist cancer patient who is handicapped in some way (her car has one of those stickers . . .) who wants to assert her right to independent motherhood and feels entitled to both artificial insemination into a gestational "hostess" and the right to sex selection as a basis for abortion should the fetus turn out to be male when she wants a female? Huh? What about her? Or what about the fifteen-year-old of the near future who kind of wants to have her baby even though it means she'll be stuck with a kid all through high school and won't be able to go out with her friends anymore, who discovers through the wonders of amniocentesis and DNA analysis that the baby is going to turn out fat, and the fifteen-year-old just can't deal with fat and shouldn't have to . . . ? Out goes the baby with the bathwater.

But these scenarios are involved merely with messy political or ethical issues, the problematical, somewhat gross byproducts of technological and marketing advances. Let the philosophers and professional ethicists drone on and let the baby business boom. Let the courts figure it out. Each day brings another, more pressing problem. Implanted with their weak-cervixed daughter's eggs and their son-in-law's sperm, women become pregnant with their own grandchildren; frozen embryos are inadvertently thawed; eggs are pirated; eggs are harvested from aborted fetuses; divorced couples battle over the fate of cryo-preserved material. "We have to have better regulation of the genetic product — eggs, sperm, and embryos — so we can legally determine who owns what," a professor of law and medicine at a California university says plaintively. (Physicians tend to oppose more regulation, however, claiming that it would "impede research.")

While high-tech nations are refining their options eugenically and quibbling litigiously, the inhabitants of low-tech countries are just having babies. The fastest growth in human numbers in all history is going to take place in a single generation, an increase of almost five billion people (all of whom started out as babies). Ninety-seven percent of the surge is going to take place in developing countries, with Africa alone accounting for 35 percent of it (the poorer the country, the higher the birth rate, that's just the way it is). These babies are begotten in more "traditional," doubtless less desperate ways, and although they are not considered as fashion statements, they're probably loved just as much as upper-class Western babies (or that singular one-per-family Chinese boy baby) and are even considered productive assets when they get a little older and can labor for the common good of their large families by exploiting more and more, scarcer and scarcer resources.

The argument that Western countries with their wealth and relatively low birth rates do not fuel the population crisis is, of course, fallacious. France, as national policy, urges its citizens to procreate, giving lots of subsidies and perks to those French who make more French. The U.S. population is growing faster than that of eighteen other industrialized nations, and in terms of energy consumption, when an American couple stops spawning at two babies, it's the same as an average East Indian couple stopping at sixty-six, or an Ethiopian couple drawing the line at one thousand.

Yet we burble along, procreating, and in the process suffocating thousands of other species with our selfishness. We're in a baby glut, yet it's as if we've just discovered babies, or invented them. Reproduction is sexy. Assisted reproduction is cool. The announcement that a movie star is going to have a baby is met with breathless wonder. A BABY! Old men on their third marriage regard their new babies with "awe" and crow about the "ultimate experience" of parenting. Bruce Springsteen found "salvation" with the birth of his son. When in doubt, have a baby. When you've tried it all, champagne, cocaine, try a baby. Pop icons who trudged through a decade of adulation and high living confess upon motherhood, This Baby Saved My Life. Bill Gates, zillionaire founder of Microsoft, is going to have (this is so wonderful) a BABY. News commentators are already speculating: Will fatherhood take away his edge, his drive; will it diminish his will to succeed, to succeed, to succeed? National Public Radio recently interviewed other high-powered CEO dads as to that ghastly possibility.

It's as though, all together, in the waning years of this dying century, we collectively opened the Door of our Home and instead of seeing a friend standing there in some sweet spring twilight, someone we had invited over for drinks and dinner and a lovely civilized chat, there was Death, with those creepy little black seeds of his for planting in the garden. And along with Death we got a glimpse of ecological collapse and the coming anarchy of an overpeopled planet. And we all, in denial of this unwelcome vision, decided to slam the door and retreat to our toys and make babies — those heirs, those hopes, those products of our species' selfishness, sentimentality, and global death wish.

Biographical Notes
Notable Essays of 1996

Biographical Notes

HILTON ALS writes most frequently for *The New Yorker.* His first book, *The Women,* was published in 1996.

JO ANN BEARD received a master of arts degree in nonfiction writing from the University of Iowa. Her collection of essays, *The Boys of My Youth,* will be published by Little, Brown in 1998. She was born and raised in the Midwest and now lives in Ithaca, New York.

ROY BLOUNT, JR., a contributing editor of *The Atlantic* and a columnist for *The Oxford American,* is the author of twelve books, including *Crackers, One Fell Soup, First Hubby,* and *Roy Blount's Book of Southern Humor.* His essays, articles, short fiction, and verse have appeared in 114 different periodicals (not counting reprints) and 111 books, and he has performed his one-man show at the American Place Theater and elsewhere. He is writing a memoir tentatively entitled *Be Sweet: A Humorist Comes Clean.*

BERNARD COOPER'S most recent book is *Truth Serum,* a collection of memoirs. He received the 1991 PEN/Hemingway Award for *Maps to Anywhere* and a 1995 O. Henry Prize. His work has appeared in *Harper's Magazine* and *The Paris Review,* as well as in *The Best American Essays* of 1988 and 1995. He teaches in the writing program at Antioch, Los Angeles.

LOUIS DE BERNIÈRES was born in London in 1954. He graduated from the Victoria University of Manchester, took a postgraduate certificate in education at Leicester Polytechnic, and passed his M.A., with distinction, at the University of London. He has held various jobs: landscape gardener, mechanic, officer cadet at Sandhurst, and schoolteacher in both Colombia and England. In 1993 he was selected as one of the twenty Best Young British Novelists, and the following year his fourth novel, *Captain Corelli's Mandolin,* was shortlisted for the *Sunday Express* Book of the Year. This novel has now been translated into eleven languages. In 1995 de Bernières received the prestigious Lannan Literary Award for fiction. He lives in London.

DEBRA DICKERSON is a contributing editor of *U.S. News & World Report.* Her articles have appeared in *The New Republic, Slate, Good Housekeeping, Washington Post Book World, Allure, The Christian Science Monitor Report, The Nation, Underwire, Boston Review,* and *Reconstruction.* She is a graduate of the Harvard Law School and is at work on a memoir about social and political conflict within the black community.

RICHARD FORD is the author of five novels and two collections of stories, the most recent *Women with Men,* and numerous essays. He lives in Montana and in New Orleans.

FRANK GANNON is the author of *Yo, Poe, Vanna Karenina,* and *All About Man.* He is a frequent contributor to *Harper's Magazine, The New Yorker,* and other magazines. His work has appeared in many anthologies, including *Russell Baker's Book of American Humor.* He was born and grew up in New Jersey and is currently working on a novel.

DAGOBERTO GILB is the author of *The Magic of Blood,* a story collection that won the 1994 PEN/Hemingway Award, the Texas Institute of Letters Best Book of Fiction Award, and was a PEN/Faulkner finalist; and the novel *The Last Known Residence of Mickey Acuna.* Over the past two years, his essays have been heard on the National Public Radio program *Fresh Air.* A native of Los Angeles, he lives in El Paso, Texas.

VERLYN KLINKENBORG is the author of *Making Hay* and *The Last Fine Time.* His work has appeared in many magazines, including *The New Yorker, Harper's Magazine, Esquire, National Geographic, The New Republic, Smithsonian,* and *Audubon.* He has taught literature and creative writing at Fordham University, St. Olaf College, Bennington College, and Harvard University, and he is a recipient of a Lila Wallace–Reader's Digest Writers' Award and a National Endowment for the Arts fellowship. He lives in rural Massachusetts.

NATALIE KUSZ is the author of an autobiographical book, *Road Song,* a part of which was selected for *The Best American Essays 1990.* She has been the recipient of a Whiting Writers' Award and a General Electric

Award for younger writers. She currently teaches writing at Harvard University.

NATON LESLIE'S poetry and essays appear regularly in literary magazines throughout the country, including *The North American Review, Puerto del Sol, Cimarron Review, The Ohio Review,* and *The Kansas Quarterly.* He has received a grant from the National Endowment for the Arts and is associate professor of English at Siena College in Loudonville, New York. The essay in this volume is from a newly completed book manuscript, titled *Places Cursed by John Brown and Other Essays on History.*

THOMAS MCGUANE is the author of nine novels, a book of essays, and several films. His work has appeared, among other places, in *Harper's Magazine, The New Yorker,* and *The Atlantic Monthly.* Born in Michigan, he has lived the last thirty years in Montana with his wife and four children.

CULLEN MURPHY is the managing editor of *The Atlantic Monthly,* to which he is also a regular contributor of essays and longer reporting. He also writes the syndicated comic strip *Prince Valiant,* which appears in some 350 newspapers worldwide, and which is drawn by his father, the illustrator John Cullen Murphy. And he is a contributing editor of *Slate,* for which he writes the column "The Good Word," about language. He is the author, with William L. Rathje, of *Rubbish! The Archaeology of Garbage* (1992) and *Just Curious* (1995), a collection of essays. He is working on a book about women and the Bible.

CYNTHIA OZICK is the author of three collections of essays — *Art & Ardor, Metaphor & Memory,* and *Fame & Folly* — three collections of short stories, and five novels, the most recent being *The Puttermesser Papers.* She is the recipient of numerous awards, including four O. Henry first prizes, a Guggenheim fellowship, and the Rea Award for the Short Story. She is a member of the American Academy of Arts and Letters.

LUKIE CHAPMAN REILLY grew up in New York City and has worked for *Charm* and *Mademoiselle* magazines. She studied art for a year in Paris before returning to New York to work as a dress designer. She later studied at the National Academy of Fine Art and won the James A. Sudem Award for watercolor. Her paintings have been exhibited in juried shows around the country and in a gallery she operated in Charleston, South Carolina. In 1994, approaching her sixtieth birthday, she gave up the gallery, bought a computer, and began to write, mostly about her family. She is the divorced mother of two grown children and now lives in North Chatham, Massachusetts.

Luc Sante is the author of *Low Life: Lures and Snares of Old New York;*
Evidence; and *The Factory of Facts,* from which the essay herein was
adapted and which will be published early in 1998. His research for
the book was assisted by a fellowship from the Guggenheim Foundation. Sante has also received a Whiting Writers' Award and an award in
literature from the American Academy of Arts and Letters. His reviews
of books, movies, art, and photography have appeared in many publications.

Paul Sheehan's journalism has appeared in *The Atlantic Monthly,* the
New York Times, and *The New Yorker,* but most of his work has been for
the *Sydney Morning Herald* in his native Australia. He was a Nieman
Fellow at Harvard University, graduated from the Graduate School of
Journalism at Columbia University, and spent ten years in New York
and Washington as a foreign correspondent. He now lives in Sydney.

Charles Simic's first volume of poetry was published in 1967, and
fifteen others have followed. His most recent book of poems is *A Wedding in Hell.* His essay collections include *The Unemployed Fortune Teller*
and the forthcoming *Orphan Factory,* in which "Dinner at Uncle Boris's"
will also appear. Mr. Simic won a Pulitzer Prize in poetry in 1990.

Lauren Slater is the author of a therapist's memoir of madness, *Welcome to My Country,* part of which was selected for *The Best American Essays
1994.* She holds a doctorate in psychology from Boston University and
a master's degree in psychology from Harvard University. She also did
postgraduate work in the writing program at Brown University. She was
the first-place winner of the 1993 New Letters Literary Awards and the
1993 Belletrist Review Fiction Competition. Her writing has appeared
in numerous journals. "Black Swans" will be included in a new book,
Half-Life, to be published by Random House in 1998.

Susan Sontag is the author of three novels, *The Benefactor, Death Kit,*
and *The Volcano Lover;* a collection of stories, *I, Etcetera;* a play, *Alice in
Bed;* and five books of essays, including *On Photography, Illness as Metaphor,* and *Under the Sign of Saturn* — all published by Farrar, Straus and
Giroux. She has also written and directed four feature-length films and
directed plays in the United States and Europe, her most recent theater
work being a staging of Beckett's *Waiting for Godot* in besieged Sarajevo.
Her new novel, *In America,* will be published next year by Farrar, Straus
and Giroux.

Gay Talese is the author of the 1992 bestseller *Unto the Sons,* a historical memoir that spanned two world wars and possessed what Norman
Mailer called "the sweep and detail of a grand nineteenth-century

novel." Mr. Talese's earlier bestsellers deal with the history and influence of the *New York Times (The Kingdom and the Power);* the inside story
of a Mafia family *(Honor Thy Father);* the changing moral values of
America between World War II and the era before AIDS *(Thy Neighbor's
Wife).* His other nonfiction books include *The Bridge; New York: A Ser-
endipiter's Journey;* and *Fame and Obscurity,* which Tom Wolfe credited
with the creation of an inventive form of nonfiction writing called the
New Journalism. Mr. Talese is working on a sequel to *Unto the Sons.*

LÊ THI DIEM THÚY is a writer and solo performance artist. Born in
Vietnam and raised in southern California, she currently resides in
western Massachusetts. She is the recipient of a 1997 Bridge Residency
at the Headlands Center for the Arts. Her prose and poetry have
appeared in *The Massachusetts Review, Harper's Magazine,* and *Muae.* Her
solo performance works *Red Fiery Summer* and *the bodies between us* have
been presented at, among other venues, the Whitney Museum of American Art at Philip Morris, the International Women Playwrights' Festival
in Galway, Ireland, and the New World Theater at the University of
Massachusetts, Amherst. She is working on a book, *The Gangster We Are
All Looking For,* forthcoming from Knopf.

JOY WILLIAMS is the author of three novels and two collections of short
stories as well as a history and guide to the Florida Keys. Her stories
and essays frequently appear in prize anthologies and teaching texts.
She is a recipient of the Strauss Living Award from the American
Academy of Arts and Letters. She lives in Key West.

Notable Essays of 1996

SELECTED BY ROBERT ATWAN